# Born
# Survivors

Eva, Mark and Hana

# Born
# Survivors

*Three Young Mothers and Their
Extraordinary Story of
Courage, Defiance, and Hope*

———————

# WENDY HOLDEN

HARPER  PERENNIAL

NEW YORK • LONDON • TORONTO • SYDNEY • NEW DELHI • AUCKLAND

HARPER ● PERENNIAL

Originally published in Great Britain in 2015 by Sphere, an imprint of Little, Brown Book Group.

FIRST HARPER PERENNIAL EDITION PUBLISHED 2016.

Library of Congress Cataloging-in-Publication Data has been applied for.

ISBN 978-0-06-237026-6 (pbk.)

18   19   20      OFF/RRD      10   9   8   7   6

*'Sometimes even to live is an act of courage.'*

Seneca

This book is dedicated to the courage and tenacity
of three mothers and to their babies,
born into a world that didn't want them to exist

Three women pregnant by their husbands.

Three couples praying for a brighter future.

Three babies, born within weeks of each other in unimaginable circumstances.

By the time they arrived, each weighing less than three pounds, their fathers

had been murdered by the Nazis and their mothers were 'walking skeletons',

living moment to moment in the same concentration camp.

Somehow, all three women managed to survive.

Against the odds, their babies did too.

Seventy years on, these siblings of the heart have come together

for the first time to tell the remarkable stories

of the mothers who defied death to give them life.

All of them, born survivors.

# Contents

BALTIC
SEA

Kolberg

Danzig

EAST
PRUSSIA

POLAND

Warsaw

Chelmno

Łódź

Pabianice

Gorlitz

Breslau

Hradec
Králové

Třebechovoce
pod Oredem

Auschwitz

Krakow

CZECHOSLOVAKIA

Brno

Zlaté Moravce

Vienna

Bratislava

Sered'

HUNGARY

0   20   40   60   80   100

Scale of miles

The stories of these survivors have been carefully pieced together from their memories as recorded in letters and accounts they shared privately with their families, and from statements they gave to researchers and historians over the years. They have been reinforced with painstaking investigation and by the testimonies of others – alive and dead.

Wherever possible those memories have been corroborated by independent witnesses, archive material and historical records. Where exact details or conversations were beyond direct recollection or have been repeated to others over the years with only slight variation, they have been summarised based on the information available, and may not be precisely as others remembered them.

# Foreword

We are indebted to Wendy Holden for her total empathy with our respective mothers and her inexhaustible energy in retracing the harrowing steps through their wartime experiences. In the process, she has given us not only hitherto unknown information but drawn we three 'babies' closer together as 'siblings', and we will be forever grateful.

We are also grateful to have Wendy research and acknowledge the selfless conduct of the Czech citizens of Horní Bříza who did their utmost to provide food and clothing to our mothers and the prisoners of two other camps in the 'death train' on the way to Mauthausen concentration camp. And we continue to admire the tenacity, diligence and skill with which Wendy has tracked and described the efforts of the members of the 11th Armored Division of the Third US Army who were instrumental in liberating Mauthausen and in giving our mothers – and us – a new lease of life.

All of our mothers would have been honoured that their stories have finally been told in full after all these years, devoting to each one-third of this amazing book, which is fortuitously timed to mark our seventieth birthdays and the seventieth anniversary of the end of the war.

We thank you, Wendy – our new honorary sister – on behalf of we who were born into a regime that planned to murder us but who are now destined to become some of the last survivors of the Holocaust.

*Hana Berger Moran, Mark Olsky and Eva Clarke, 2015*

# 1

# Priska

Priska Löwenbeinová's identity card

'Sind Sie schwanger, fesche Frau?' (*Are you pregnant, pretty woman?*) *The question directed at Priska Löwenbeinová was accompanied by a smile as her SS inquisitor stood, legs apart, looking her up and down with forensic fascination.*

Dr Josef Mengele had halted in front of the twenty-eight-year-old Slovak teacher as she stood naked and shivering with embarrassment on an open parade ground within hours of arriving at Auschwitz II-Birkenau. It was October, 1944.

Priska, at just under five feet tall, looked younger than her years. She was flanked by approximately five hundred other naked women, few of whom knew each other. All Jewish, they were as stupefied as she was after being transported to the concentration camp in Nazi-occupied Poland from homes or ghettos across Europe, packed sixty at a time into sealed freight wagons of trains up to fifty-five cars long.

From the moment they emerged gasping for air onto the notorious railway Rampe in the heart of the Nazis' most efficient extermination complex, known collectively as Auschwitz, they'd been assailed on all sides by shouts of 'Raus!' (Get out!) or 'Schnell, Judenschwein!' (Quick, Jewish swine!)

In confusion and commotion, the tide of humanity was shepherded by expressionless prisoner-functionaries in filthy striped uniforms who jostled them across rough ground as SS officers stood in immaculate uniforms, their attack dogs straining on their leashes. There was no time to look for loved ones as men were swiftly separated from women, and children pushed into a line with the sick and elderly.

Anyone too weak to stand or whose limbs were stiff from being squashed into an airless wagon for days was prodded with rifles or beaten with whips. Heartbreaking cries of 'My children! My babies!' hung ominously in the dank air.

Up ahead of the long columns of dispossessed sat two low redbrick buildings, each with an immense chimney spewing oily black smoke into a leaden sky. The grey atmosphere was thick with a putrid, cloying smell that assaulted the nostrils and caught at the back of the throat.

Severed from friends and families, scores of young women from their teens to their fifties were funnelled into a narrow corridor of electrified fencing like that which surrounded the vast camp. Shocked into silence, they stumbled over each other as they were driven past the chimneys and along the lip of several deep ponds until they reached a large single-storey reception building – the Sauna or bath house – hidden among birch trees.

There they were unceremoniously inducted into the life of a concentration camp 'Häftling' (inmate), a process that began with them being forced to relinquish any last possessions and divest themselves of all their clothing. Without a common tongue, they protested in a clamour of languages but were beaten or intimidated into compliance by SS guards with rifles.

Driven naked down a wide passageway to a large chamber, almost all of these mothers, daughters, wives and sisters were then roughly clipped of virtually every hair on their bodies by male and female prisoners as German guards leered.

Barely recognisable to each other after the electric razors had done their work, they were marched five abreast outside to the roll-call area where they waited barefoot in cold, wet clay for over an hour before facing their second 'Selektion' by the man who would later become known as 'The Angel of Death'.

Dr Mengele, impeccably dressed in his tight-fitting grey-green uniform with its shiny chevrons and silver skulls on the collar, held in his hands a pair of pale-kid leather gauntlets with oversized cuffs. His brown hair slicked into position with pomade, he casually flipped his gloves left and right as he strolled up and down the lines to inspect each new prisoner and – more specifically – to ask if they were expecting a child.

When it was her turn, Priska Löwenbeinová had only a few seconds to decide how to respond to the smiling officer with the gap between his front teeth. She didn't hesitate. Shaking her head quickly, the accomplished linguist replied to his question in German: 'Nein.'

By then two months pregnant with her longed-for child by her husband Tibor (who she hoped was somewhere else in the camp), she had no idea if telling the truth might save her or con~~~ and her child to an unknown fate. But she knew she *presence of danger. With one arm shielding her breasts while her other covered what was left of her pubic hair, she prayed Mengele would accept her blunt denial. The SS officer with the suave looks paused for a second to stare into the face of the young 'fesche Frau' before moving on.*

*Three women further along, he roughly squeezed the breast of a woman who recoiled. When a few drops of breast milk betrayed that she was at least sixteen weeks' pregnant, she was – at a leftward flick of his gauntlet – yanked from the line and shoved into a corner of the parade ground to join a shivering cluster of expectant mothers.*

*None of those wide-eyed women knew then that one direction meant life while the other could mean something very different. The fate of those who were chosen that day by Mengele remains unknown.*

Josef Mengele represented the greatest risk to Priska's young life thus far but still she had no concept of what she was soon to face. In the coming months hunger was to become her dreaded enemy, while starvation seemed the likeliest end to her suffering.

Hunger's cousin – thirst – would torment her just as cruelly during her time in the camps, along with exhaustion, fear and disease. But it was her pregnant body's gnawing, aching demands for nourishment that very nearly broke her.

Perversely, the one memory that helped Priska through some of her most ravenous pangs was of pressing her nose to the glass of a patisserie on her way to school before treating herself to a sugar-dusted confection such as a cinnamon *babka* with streusel topping. The recollection of breaking apart those flaky pastries as crumbs cascaded down her blouse in the cake shop in Zlaté Moravce summed up her idyllic childhood in what is now the southwestern corner of the Slovak Republic.

One hundred kilometres or so from Bratislava, the region where Priska grew up was known for gold panning, and the name of one of its rivers, the Zlatnanka, derives from the Slovak word for gold.

The town of 'Golden Moravce' was almost as prosperous as its title suggested, with an imposing church, schools and streets of shops as well as coffee houses, restaurants and a hotel.

Priska's parents, Emanuel and Paula Rona, ran one of the most respectable kosher cafés in town, a venue around which much of local life revolved. In a prime location on the central square, the coffee shop also had a pretty courtyard. Emanuel Rona had spotted the business for rent in a newspaper in 1924 when he was in his late thirties. Seeking to make his fortune, he took the bold decision to relocate his wife and children two hundred and fifty kilometres from their remote town of Stropkov in the eastern hills near the Polish border.

Priska, born on Sunday 6 August 1916, was eight years old when they moved, but she returned to Stropkov with her family whenever they could to visit her maternal grandfather David Friedman, a widower who owned a tavern and was a well-known writer of polemical pamphlets.

In Zlaté Moravce the family café was, Priska would later say, beautiful and always kept spotlessly clean by her hard-working parents and a flock of devoted female staff. It boasted a private function room her mother proudly called a *chambre séparée*, in which eight musicians in dark suits would play for the customers whenever she pulled back a curtain. 'We had great music and wonderful dancers. The cafeteria life was important then. I so terribly loved my youth.'

Her mother, who was four years younger and 'a head taller' than her father, was strikingly good-looking and quietly ambitious for her family. Having taken on the traditional Slovak female suffix of *-ová* after her marriage, Paula Ronová proved to be an excellent wife, mother and cook and was 'an extremely decent woman' who talked little but thought much. 'My mother was also my best friend.'

Her father, on the other hand, was a strict disciplinarian who conversed with her mother in German or Yiddish whenever he didn't want his children to understand. Priska, who picked up languages easily from an early age, secretly understood every word. Although not zealously observant of the faith he'd been born into, Emanuel Rona appreciated the importance of maintaining appearances and took his family to the synagogue for all the major Jewish holidays.

'It was terribly important when I was young to behave decently because of the coffee shop,' said Priska. 'We had to be a good family, good friends and good owners, or clients wouldn't have come to the café.'

One of five children, Priska – named Piroska at birth – was fourth in line. Andrej, known as 'Bandi', was the eldest. Her sister Elizabeth, known as 'Boežka', came next, then Anička, known to all as 'Little Anna'. Four years after Priska came Eugen, known to all as Janíčko or 'Janko', the youngest child. A sixth child had died as an infant in between.

In Zláté Moravce, the family lived behind the café in an apartment spacious enough for the children to enjoy separate bedrooms. They had a large garden sloping down to a stream that flowed the full width of it. An athletic, outgoing child, Priska frequently swam there with friends who also played tennis in their garden. Healthy and happy, with lustrous dark hair, Priska like her sisters was popular with the local children, who affectionately abbreviated her name to 'Piri', or sometimes 'Pira'.

'It didn't matter to me if they were Jews or Gentiles. I was friends with everyone the same. There was no difference.'

She and her siblings grew up surrounded by 'good women' who helped with the household chores and acted like surrogate mothers. The family ate well, with kosher meat presented 'elegantly' at almost every meal. Succulent roast dinners were often followed by desserts from the café. Priska had a sweet tooth and her favourite was the Viennese *Sachertorte*, a rich chocolate cake made with meringue and apricot jam.

Although they didn't study religion at school, the children were raised to attend prayers every Friday evening and to wash their hands thoroughly before sitting down to an elegant *Shabbat* or Sabbath table with special candles and the finest linens.

Priska was one of only six girls in her class of more than thirty. Her sister Boežka was, she said, a 'true intellectual' who picked up languages effortlessly, seemingly absorbing them. Books held little interest for Boežka, however, as she was far more interested in artistic matters – especially needlework, at which she shone.

Priska may have had to work harder at her studies than her sister, but she was diligent and education soon became her passion. In her quest for a deeper understanding of the world, she also differed from her prettier sister Anna who preferred dressing up or playing with dolls. 'I liked that I had knowledge,' Priska admitted. She became fascinated by Christianity from an early age and often sneaked into the Catholic cemetery in Zlaté Moravce on her way home from school. She especially admired its imposing tombs and mausoleums and was always intrigued by a new 'arrival', making up imaginary stories about them and what their lives had been like.

Her mother Paula encouraged her daughter's thirst for education and was proud when she became the first Rona child to attend the local high school – the Gymnázium Janka Kráľa. It was an attractive three-storey white stucco building opened in 1906 opposite the cemetery and town hall. One of five hundred pupils aged between ten and eighteen, Priska studied English and Latin there as well as the obligatory German and French. Her siblings only attended the middle school, apart from her brother Bandi who went to accountancy school.

Competitive by nature, Priska won numerous academic awards and her professors were delighted with her progress. Their star pupil also enjoyed the attention of the boys in her class, who begged her to help them with their English and would congregate devotedly in her garden while she gave lessons. 'I have nothing but wonderful memories of Zlaté Moravce.'

Priska's best friend at school was a girl named Gizelle Ondrejkovičová, known to everyone as 'Gizka'. She was not only beautiful but popular. The daughter of the district police chief, a Gentile, she wasn't nearly as studious as Priska, so her father called on Priska's parents one day to make them an offer. 'If Priska makes sure that Gizka completes her studies, then I will allow you to keep your café open as late as you like.' Nor would there be any extra taxes to pay.

And so it was that the fourth Rona child suddenly became vitally important to the modest family business. As long as Priska remained an unofficial tutor to her classmate she would guarantee that their café – above all others in town – would thrive. It was a responsibility she took very seriously and, although it left her little time to enjoy a social life, she adored Gizka and was happy to help. The two friends sat side by side in the same class and eventually graduated together.

After high school, Priska took up teaching and seemed all set for a career as a professor of languages. A keen singer, she joined a teachers' choir that toured the country performing traditional nationalist songs, one of which proclaimed proudly, 'I am a Slovak and a Slovak I will remain' – a tune she would happily break into throughout her life.

In Zlaté Moravce, she remained highly regarded and enjoyed being greeted first by whoever she met in the street – a traditional Slovak sign of respect. She was also wooed by a Gentile professor who called for her every Saturday night to take her for coffee or dancing, or for dinner at the local hotel.

There was little reason for Priska or her family to worry that anything might alter their comfortable way of life. Although Jews had long been persecuted across Europe, and had suffered especially at the hands of the Russians during the pogroms that dated back to the early nineteenth century, they'd settled easily into the newly sculpted nations of Europe after the First World War and the collapse of the German, Austro-Hungarian and Russian Empires. In Czechoslovakia they had risen to prominence and assimilated well into society. Jews not only played a key role in manufacturing and economic life but contributed to every field of culture, science and the arts. New schools and synagogues were built and Jews were at the centre of café life. The Rona family experienced little anti-Semitism within their own community.

A severe economic depression after the First World War began to change the mood across the border in Germany, however. Adolf Hitler, who since 1921 had been the leader of the Nationalist Socialist German Workers, known as the 'Nazi' Party, accused Jews of controlling the nation's wealth and blamed them for its many woes. After federal elections in 1933, when the Nazis received 17.2 million votes, Hitler was invited into a coalition government and appointed Chancellor. His rise to power marked the end of the democratic Weimar Republic and the beginning of what became widely known as the *Dritte Reich* – the Third Empire.

Hitler's radical speeches denounced capitalism and condemned those who'd allied themselves with Bolsheviks, Communists, Marxists and the Russian Red Army to participate in revolution. Having written in his 1925 autobiographical manifesto *Mein Kampf* that 'the personification of the Devil as the symbol of all evil assumes the living shape of the Jew', he promised to eliminate Jews and other 'undesirables' from Germany in what he described as a 'thorough solution'.

Proclaiming his 'new order' to counter what many Germans saw as the injustices forced on them after the war, he encouraged brown-shirted stormtroopers to harass Jews and blockade or boycott their businesses. Cheered on by his indoctrinated Hitler Youth, his battle cry of '*Sieg Heil!*' (Hail Victory!) blared across the airwaves from Berlin. Within a relatively short time, Hitler appeared to be delivering on his promises and brought about such economic recovery that his support only grew. Bolstered by his success, his government began to implement a series of laws to exclude Jews from political, economic and social life. 'Degenerate' Jewish books were burned, non-Aryans were expelled from universities, and prominent Jews abroad – including Albert Einstein – were exiled.

As German anti-Semitism escalated, synagogues were desecrated or burned to the ground, sometimes with Jews trapped inside. The pavements of towns and cities glistened with broken glass and the windows of Jewish businesses were daubed with the Star of David or offensive slogans. Gentiles, who were dubbed 'Aryans' by the Nazis were encouraged to inform on Jews and in an atmosphere of betrayal and mistrust, those who'd lived happily alongside each other for years and whose children had grown up together often found themselves being spat at in the street, beaten or arrested. There were willing spies everywhere, eager to denounce their neighbours in the hope of getting their hands on their property. Hundreds of homes were looted systematically by those who burst in and took whatever they wanted.

Native Germans were encouraged to inspect and then help themselves to the most desirable Jewish apartments, forcing entire families to leave their homes at short notice. It was said that the new tenants moved in before 'the bread from the oven was even cold'. Those evicted were only permitted to move into smaller quarters in the poorest districts, effectively banning them from the life they'd always known.

The physically disabled and mentally ill – Aryans and Jews alike – were declared 'unworthy of life' and many were sent away to camps or summarily executed. The rest of the populace had little choice but to conform to the imposition of Hitler's Nuremberg Laws, mercilessly enforced and calculated to further alienate Jews and others. Under what the Nazis defined as 'scientific racism' to maintain the purity of German blood, these regulations singled out the 'racially acceptable' and restricted the basic civic rights of 'Jews, gypsies, negroes and their bastard offspring'. The Law for the Protection of German Blood and German Honour annulled all mixed marriages and the death penalty was applied to any Jew found to have had sexual relations with a German, in order to avoid 'racial pollution'.

Jews were stripped of their citizenship and anyone considered 'asocial' or 'harmful' – a nebulous category that encompassed Communists, political activists, alcoholics, prostitutes, beggars and the homeless, plus Jehovah's Witnesses, who refused to accept

Hitler's authority – was arrested and imprisoned in early *Konzen-trationslager* or 'KZ', usually situated in former army barracks.

Aryans were prohibited from employing Jews. Through incremental changes, Jews were also barred from their own professions as lawyers, doctors or journalists and Jewish children could no longer be educated beyond the age of fourteen. Over time, Jews were banned from state hospitals and not allowed to travel further than thirty kilometres from their homes. Public parks, playgrounds, rivers, swimming pools, beaches and libraries were placed out of bounds. The names of all Jewish soldiers were scratched off First World War memorials, although so many had fought for the Kaiser in the conflict.

Ration cards and food stamps were issued but Jews were allocated half of the Aryan allowance. They were also permitted to shop only in designated places between 3 and 5 p.m., by which time most fresh goods had been sold. They were forbidden to enter cinemas and theatres and to travel in the front carriages of trams, only being allowed in the back where it was often crowded and hot. All radios belonging to Jews had to be surrendered at the police station and curfews between 8 p.m. and 6 a.m. were strictly enforced.

Fearful of the new policies, thousands fled to France, Holland and Belgium seeking asylum. The nation that had been named Czechoslovakia since 1918 became another popular refuge. It not only enjoyed strong frontiers but powerful allies – including France, Britain and Russia – and Priska's family would have been among the majority who felt safe there.

Then in March 1938, as Europe trembled, Hitler annexed Austria in what was known as the Anschluss. Declaring German self-determination he demanded Lebensraum or greater 'living space' for his people. Later that year, residency permits for all foreigners living within the Reich were revoked. Then the Polish government unexpectedly declared that it would invalidate the passports of its citizens unless they returned to Poland to have them renewed. To facilitate this, the Nazis ordered that some 12,000

Polish-born Jews be rounded up and expelled. The Poles refused to accept them, leaving them in an unenviable limbo at the border.

Keen to negotiate peace so soon after a world war, the British Prime Minister Neville Chamberlain led international talks that concluded with the Munich Agreement in September of that year. Without Russian or Czech involvement, the major European powers effectively gave Hitler permission to occupy the regions in the north, south and west of Czechoslovakia collectively known as the Sudetenland, and chiefly inhabited by German-speakers. In what many Czechs dubbed 'The Munich Betrayal', their country was left without strategic borders.

In November 1938, the vengeful teenage son of a family of Polish Jews who'd been forced from their home assassinated a German official in Paris. Exacting revenge, the Nazi high command ordered Reichspogromnacht, better known as Kristallnacht – 'Crystal Night' or 'The Night of Broken Glass'. In a single night thousands of Jewish homes, synagogues and businesses in Germany were targeted, at least ninety people murdered, and 30,000 arrested. In the ensuing months, Hitler's supporters continued to instigate anti-Semitic riots but in March 1939 the Führer invited Monsignor Jozef Tiso (the deposed Catholic leader of the Slovak people) to Berlin. Soon afterwards, Emil Hácha (the Catholic president of Czechoslovakia) also arrived. Both were given an ultimatum. They could either voluntarily place their people under Germany's 'protection' – they were also under threat from Hungary's claims to their border territories – or be forcibly invaded by the Nazis.

Tiso and his collaborationist government agreed to Hitler's demands almost immediately, and Tiso was installed as president of the newly minted and nominally independent Slovak State without further Nazi intervention, after collapsing from a suspected heart attack, President Hácha, sixty-six, agreed to the German terms the following day. There was, however, widespread resistance from his people; so, on 15 March 1939, German troops marched in and the Czech nation was declared the Protectorate of Bohemia and

Moravia. Hitler invaded Poland six months later. Then the Soviets invaded from the east a few weeks later, revealing their secret pact with the Germans. Britain and France declared war. Life for the people of Europe would never be the same.

Jews in the new Nazi 'client states' became outcasts overnight. *Juden nicht zugänglich* (No Jews allowed) was a common sign on many public buildings. Sometimes the signs read, *No dogs or Jews allowed*. When people learned of atrocities committed against those of their faith in Germany, Austria and Poland, they stormed the foreign embassies begging for visas, only to be turned away. Faced with a future that seemed inescapable, some committed suicide.

Priska and her family had no choice but to comply with the new regime and each new decree it implemented. It was the little things that hurt the most. The professor no longer called to take her dancing; the people who'd once greeted her first in the street stopped saying hello altogether or looked the other way when she passed. 'There were so many unpleasantries but one had to accept it automatically if you wanted to live.' Other friends, such as Gizka and another classmate whose family were farmers and continued to provide the Rona family with fresh milk, remained fiercely loyal. Some went out of their way to publicly greet their Jewish acquaintances and offer them every assistance.

With rumours of Jews being 'resettled' elsewhere against their will, people began to hoard food and other goods. They buried their valuables or asked friends to hide them, even though to be caught doing so carried a sentence of death. Those Jews who could, fled to the British-controlled Mandatory Palestine where there were hopes of establishing a future Zionist state. Priska's brother Bandi was amongst them and he went alone in 1939, claiming to have seen the 'writing on the wall'. Without even telling her, an early boyfriend of Priska's emigrated to Belgium and then on to Chile. He was wealthy and young and the couple had recently become engaged in preparation for an arranged marriage, but he simply disappeared.

The rest of Priska's family did whatever they could to get by. Her sister Anička had married aged nineteen in 1932 in the hope of avoiding a life of servitude in the family café. She and her husband had a son, Otto, but the marriage didn't last. After her divorce, Anna changed her name to the more Aryan-sounding Helena Hrubá and found a job working in someone else's coffee shop. Priska's brother Janko, who'd trained as an electrical engineer, was drafted into a Jewish labour battalion to become a '*Robotnik Zid*' or 'work Jew', wearing a distinctive blue uniform and given the dirtiest jobs. Boežka, a spinster in her thirties, stayed home sewing clothes for family and friends.

Priska, who was always proud of her Jewish nose – or 'nice proboscis' as she jokingly called it – was delighted to have Boežka's creations to wear, which made her feel less of a social pariah. 'I have never been a beauty but I took care to look good,' she said. 'I was always treated well by the people of my town, who liked that I was the honoured daughter of the coffee house.'

That honour was soon denied her. In 1940, her parents were banned from running the café they had carefully built up over sixteen years. With limited education and few other talents, they had nothing to fall back on. 'They lost everything,' Priska said. 'They were good people.' An Aryan or *Treuhänder* (trustee) who was put in charge of their business was unexpectedly kind to Priska and appreciated that she spoke English, French, Hungarian and German. 'It was important and valued that I could speak those languages,' she said.

Having been prevented from working, Priska and what was left of her immediate family decided to move to Bratislava, the new capital of the Slovak State on the banks of the River Danube. Priska's grandfather David Friedman, robbed of his family inn, fled his hometown of Stropkov and joined them. They had managed to hold on to a little money and hoped it might be easier for Jews to pass unnoticed in a large city, and they were right. At the time of the Nazi invasion an estimated 15,000 Jews lived in Bratislava, comprising twelve per cent of the population, and they had assimilated well and encountered little anti-Semitism.

Although everything had changed under Nazi rule, Priska's family found an apartment on Špitálska Street and, by working privately as a teacher, she was able to once again enjoy the café life she'd known since childhood. She especially favoured the Astorka coffee shop where she rubbed shoulders with the intelligentsia, with whom she could chat in numerous languages. It was in Astorka one day in October 1940 that she spotted a slender man with a moustache sitting at an adjacent table. He was chatting to some friends of hers.

'He was talking very deeply and animatedly to my friend Mimi, who was a pharmacist. Suddenly she got up and came to tell me that he found me attractive.' Priska's bold admirer walked over and introduced himself. Tibor Löwenbein was a Jewish journalist of Polish extraction, fluent in German and French, who came from the town of Púchov in northwestern Slovakia. She always maintained that he was a little tipsy when they met so she told him she didn't like men who drank. Keen to impress her, Tibor promised never to touch alcohol again. He was true to his word.

He did however smoke a pipe and had a collection of forty, none of which Priska was allowed to touch. A meticulous dresser, her handsome suitor also owned forty shirts. As an aspiring author, Tibor was often to be found scribbling in little notebooks he carried. And he collected stamps – although Priska always said with a wry smile that after he met her, she became his only hobby.

Tibor was the only child of Heinrich Löwenbein and his wife Elizabeth, known as 'Berta'. Tibor's father owned a small farm. Wanting more than a farmer's life, Tibor moved to Bratislava and became a writer for the *Allgemeine Jüdische Zeitung* newspaper, covering sport and local politics. He also wrote a slim book entitled *Slovensko-Židovské hnutie a jeho poslanie* (The Slovak-Jewish Movement and its Mission), about being fully assimilated into Slovak life as a Jew.

Priska's husband, the journalist and author Tibor Löwenbein

When the Nuremberg Laws prevented him from remaining at the newspaper, the kindly Greek owner of the Dunajská Bank in Bratislava offered him a job as a clerk. Slender and well-groomed, with a pleasant way about him, Tibor had fairish hair and a pale complexion. He didn't look especially Jewish – which, Priska said, mattered then. He was so well regarded at the bank that he was sent to Prague and Brno on business, something that should have been impossible under Jewish travel restrictions. But his employer had important connections and Tibor seemed to be able to get away with almost anything. Being a journalist, he seemed to know everyone and people were always polite to him, a courtesy extended to the striking young lady on his arm.

Every morning on his way to work Tibor would walk Priska to the Astorka café where she enjoyed her morning coffee and cake. As he left he would stop and salute her, which always made her laugh. In the evenings after work they'd stroll along the banks of the

Danube, a popular spot for courting couples. There they would listen to the music being played on the street and watch the moonlight rippling on the water as barges, riverboats and ferries chugged slowly past.

For the first six months of their courtship Tibor wrote to Priska every day. He dubbed her his '*Pirečka Zlaticko*' (Golden One) and she called him 'Tibko', or more commonly 'Tiborko'. Smitten, she kept every one of his notes, some of which were brief but all were warm. Almost all of them survived the war. In one letter dated 10 March 1941, Priska wrote:

My Tibko, I am so happy when I receive your letters, especially the long ones ... Am in a hurry to let you know my great news! Namely, that I will have free time starting Thursday – so we will see each other four days in a row. What a luxury in this time of squeezed availability ... You wished to know what I think of your letters. They are wonderful. I am amazed that you, who are so serious and nowadays pessimistic and seeing the current situation so dark, write such wonderful lines as you do ... I think about you so much and know that you find solace in your books. I am a little jealous of their presence in your life while I am away – though I promise that it is temporary – please say hello to your books, which keep you valuable company without me. I am sending you a million kisses – Your Pira.

And in his reply, dated 12 March, Tibor wrote,

My Golden Pirečka, I was extremely happy to read your letter. What happiness. In the dreary reality of everyday your words were like a ray of sunshine piercing the dark clouds. I am trying to express my thanks and joy ... Probably am not able to do justice ...! As I am expecting to see you tomorrow at 4.30 p.m., at my place, and as I think about this joyous

occasion, I am also faced with thoughts of how destiny plays
with us. This thought came to me as I realised that on our five
months' anniversary we cannot be together. Thus I will need
to leave the words I wish to share with you for the afternoon
when I will finally see you . . . I cannot wait to hold you in my
arms . . . see you tomorrow my darling . . . and till then I send
you many kisses, Yours, Tibor.

Priska and Tibor marry in the synagogue in Bratislava 1941

The couple were married on Saturday 21 June 1941 at the twin-
towered Moorish-style synagogue in Bratislava. The bride, who was
twenty-five years old, wore a long white coat, a white pillbox hat,
pearls and white shoes with a patterned dress. She carried a bouquet
of white gladioli as she agreed to the *ketubah* or Jewish marriage

contract. Her groom, who was twenty-seven, wore a hat and smart suit with the fashionable baggy trousers of the time.

Priska's parents, Emanuel and Paula, who declared their son-in-law 'perfect', gave the couple their blessing and were delighted to have something to celebrate. Tibor's parents weren't at the wedding. His father had committed suicide at his farm near Púchov earlier that year, leaving his mother alone. Distraught, he'd returned home to be with her but then had to come back to Bratislava or risk arrest for being away from his registered address without permission. Priska and her parents became his new family.

It was a happy union and the newlyweds were well matched. 'We never even quarrelled once,' Priska said, describing her husband as 'sensational'. She liked that he spoke Slovak 'correctly', which many people didn't; often they blended it with German or Hungarian. 'He was wonderful to me and so impressed that I'd mastered all those languages. I have beautiful memories of my Tiborko. Such a good husband you couldn't wish for in your life.'

But the further reverberations of war overshadowed their happiness. On the day after their wedding, the Germans invaded the Soviet Union as part of Hitler's Operation Barbarossa to seize Russian territories. Still hoping for the best, and completely unprepared for what lay ahead, Priska and Tibor moved into an apartment at 7 Rybárska Brána, later known as Fischertorgasse, just off the main square of Hlavné Námestie. They lived there very happily in spite of the threats they continued to face. Eager to start a family regardless, Priska became pregnant straight away and the couple were delighted. With a child on the way, Tibor was even more grateful that he had a steady income. He even managed to keep his job in September 1941 when all Jews in Slovakia were faced with a list of nearly three hundred new rules to abide by, in something the Germans called the Jewish Code or *Židovský Kódex*.

This code, which officially defined Jews on racial grounds, reinstated a centuries-old practice of forcing Jews to wear humiliating emblems that had been instituted in places as far afield as England and Baghdad since the ninth century. Everyone of Jewish origin was obliged to have their passports and other documents stamped with a large 'J', for the German word *Jude*. They also had to buy armbands or stars, which were cut from huge bolts of pre-stamped cloth made in the very factories where many had once earned their living. Each emblem had to be sewn front and back on to all outer garments, but was primarily to be worn over their Jewish hearts.

Public persecution of Jews increased with their new visibility. Not only were their shops and businesses continually vandalised or looted, they faced danger each time they left the sanctuary of their homes. Many of Tibor and Priska's friends paid huge sums of money to acquire false papers but they were at enormous risk if caught. Tibor's employer managed to secure his exemption from wearing a star and many other restrictions, but Priska had no such protection. Each time they stepped out together after curfew or went somewhere Jews were banned, she'd hold her handbag or turn the lapel of her coat in such a way that none could see her star.

Then, not long after the imposition of the new rules, Jews were instructed to leave the centre of Bratislava and move to the poorer suburbs. Priska managed to find a job teaching in a primary school twenty kilometres away in the small town of Pezinok. Tibor commuted into Bratislava each day, leaving at 6 a.m. 'He loved his job and then he had to work because I was expecting a baby.' Priska's parents, grandfather and sister Boežka managed to remain in Bratislava in an apartment on the banks of the Danube where Boežka continued working as a seamstress. And so this close-knit family continued to cope and to hope.

Priska taught at the primary school until the day the authorities decreed that all non-Aryans were forbidden from teaching Aryan children. Having said a fond farewell to her pupils, she insisted she was fortunate because an Englishman who ran a local language school invited her to teach there instead, and she was able to earn more than before. 'I had options. I had very many private students who still came to me so it was as if nothing had happened. I did not suffer. They paid me and I had that to live on.'

Determined to help other families less fortunate than hers, she also continued to teach many of her former students for free, reading to them from German, French and English classics.

Then one day she lost her baby.

While the couple quietly grieved, daily life became steadily more difficult as the Nazi codes were ever more rigorously applied. The authorities forced Jews to catalogue all their silver, art, jewellery and other property, which they then had to deliver to local banks to be confiscated. Furs and their finest winter clothing followed. They were banned from keeping pets and had to deliver any cats, dogs, rabbits or caged birds to collecting centres, never to be seen again.

The Slovak State under Father Tiso became one of the first Axis partners to consent to SS *Aktionen*, deportations of Jews to new 'resettlement areas' or labour camps to aid the German war effort in the East. In return for the right not to lose its Aryan citizens to such places, the government agreed to pay five hundred *Reichsmark* for every Jew the Nazis deported across its border. In exchange, the Nazis assured the authorities that those 'parasites' that were 'resettled' would never return or make claim on any property they'd left behind. In the midst of this oppressive atmosphere, tens of thousands were rounded up by the Slovak *gardista* and other militia to be 'concentrated' at labour barracks within Slovakia – chiefly at Sered', Vyhne and Novaky.

Several thousand inmates remained in the new camps, manufacturing vital goods for the German war effort, but an estimated 58,000 were sent on to forced labour camps further east as part of what the Nazis called the *Osttransport*. By 'East', it was assumed the camps would be close to armaments factories within occupied Poland where inmates would work in return for food and shelter. Some were promised work gathering in the harvest or helping to set up new Jewish states.

Abandoned and helpless, the Slovak Jews resigned themselves to what seemed to be an increasingly bleak fate. They expected harsh conditions and general privations but prayed that once the war was over normal life could resume. Entire families volunteered to go with those sent ahead, thinking it would be better to remain together. Others promised to send money, letters and food parcels, fully believing that these items would reach their intended destination.

In March 1942, almost nine months to the day after her wedding and around the time that she had hoped to be celebrating the birth of her first child, Priska heard that her eldest sister Boežka had been rounded up in one of the *Aktionen* after the Slovak authorities agreed to supply 1,000 healthy single women. Learning of Boežka's fate, Priska hurried to the railway terminal in Bratislava to try to rescue her. It was an act that could very easily have cost her life. She found the crowded passenger train almost ready to depart but could see no sign of her sister amongst the sea of frightened and bewildered faces. 'I didn't know any of the *gardistas* but I begged them to let my sister go. They yelled at me and told me, "If you're single, get on the train! If you're married, then go home!" I was surprised they didn't just leave me (at the station) but they didn't.'

The feared Slovak *Hlinka* Guards in their distinctive black uniforms, many of whom had been trained by the SS, arrested Priska and locked her in jail overnight. Her distraught husband Tibor, who'd had no idea where she was, eventually received a message the following morning: 'Come and get your wife. She's a trouble-maker.' Tibor went to the police station and persuaded the authorities to let him take Priska home without penalty, but he was so angry at what she had risked that he refused to speak to her – although only for half a day, so upset was his young wife that she hadn't been able to rescue sweet Boežka.

Not long afterwards, Priska became pregnant again. Once more, even though their lives seemed to be disintegrating around them, the couple were overjoyed. Neither of them fully appreciated the danger they were in as, during the following weeks, the authorities continued to carry out lightning raids on Jewish homes to round up people for the transports, a thousand at a time. Once, when Priska's parents heard jackboots in the hallway, they leapt from a window and managed to escape.

On 17 July 1942, they weren't so lucky. Powerless against the chain of command that presided over life and death, Emanuel and Paula Rona were snatched without warning. Priska didn't even know that they'd gone until it was too late. They were in their mid-fifties and she never even had the chance to say goodbye. As with her sister, Priska couldn't save them. Nor could she save the second baby she then miscarried. 'I felt then that I should go East too,' she said. 'Nothing mattered to me.'

Tibor discovered that his mother, Berta, had also been transported from her home near Púchov to a camp in Polish Silesia. She was elderly and alone. For all he knew, he was now an orphan. Priska learned from childhood contacts such as Gizka that most of the Jewish population of Zlaté Moravce had vanished too, including friends and relatives.

It no longer seemed to matter that her parents had been able to give Gizka their most precious things for safekeeping. The best friend whom she'd tutored through high school had risked her life by hiding the family belongings. With her parents and sister gone and her other siblings scattered, though, Priska wondered what a few bone china dishes or silver cutlery would mean after the war if there was no one left to sit at their Sabbath table.

Her sister Anna had been helped by Gentile friends to escape to the relative safety of the High Tatra Mountains, where she worked as a waitress under her assumed name and lived with their mother's brother, Dr Gejza Friedman, a pulmonology specialist at a sanatorium for sufferers from tuberculosis. He also took in his eighty-three-year-old father David Friedman, Priska's grandfather, who'd been left alone after her parents were taken. Anna's son Otto, aged eleven, was hidden by Catholic nuns. Her oldest brother

Bandi was safe in Mandatory Palestine. Janko had defected from his Jewish work unit and joined the partisans to organise raids on the *Hlinka* Guards and take part in actions aimed at undermining the pro-German government. They had not heard from him in months.

Rekindling her early interest in Christianity, Priska considered being baptised in the hope that it might save her and her husband. Tibor, who'd been raised in a more observant Jewish household, didn't believe it would. Both of them continued to observe the basic Jewish traditions. In spite of the huge uncertainty surrounding them – or perhaps because of it – his wife became pregnant again, but miscarried this infant as well.

By the autumn of 1942, the transports East had been halted by the Slovak authorities. The political and religious elite and the Jewish underground had formed an organisation called the Bratislava Working Group, which placed enormous pressure on Tiso's government once they suspected that the majority of the 58,000 Jews it had deported had been sent to their death. More than 7,000 of them were children.

For the next two years, after the Slovak government reconsidered its position and refused to deport its remaining 24,000 Jews, those left behind remained relatively safe. There were frantic efforts by the Working Group to save the Jews for ever by bribing key figures in the regime. They even negotiated directly with the SS and with *Hauptsturmführer* Dieter Wislieceny, the Nazis' Slovak advisor on Jewish affairs, offering millions of Reichsmarks worth of gold. Called the 'Europa Plan', these negotiations stalled when Wislieceny was transferred. In the interim, though, they had created an easing of anti-Semitic laws and a reduction in persecution, although a sense of foreboding still pervaded.

Thanks to Tibor's job and Priska's tutoring, they were able to return to Bratislava and moved into an apartment in Edlova Strasse. Although they experienced rationing and restrictions on when and where they could shop, they were well fed compared with thousands across Europe. Whenever Priska's sweet tooth tormented her they would share a cake at their new favourite coffee house, the historic Štefánka Café.

Like most of their friends, Jewish and Gentile, they tried not to worry too much about the future and pinned their hopes on the war ending soon. By 1943, it certainly seemed to be swinging in favour of the Allies. The few radios allowed reported that there had been successful uprisings in Poland and that the Red Army was slowly taking control. The Germans had lost Stalingrad after a brutal five-month campaign. The Allies had seized Libya, forcing the Afrika Korps to surrender. Italy had declared war on Germany and Berlin was being evacuated of civilians. Could there be an end in sight, they wondered, or would the situation only worsen?

Priska and Tibor in Bratislava 1943

No one knew. Nor did they know what had happened to their loved ones, from whom they heard nothing. Rumours had been circulating in Bratislava for months about the camps Jews and others were sent to as word occasionally came back from some of the transports. People were being worked or starved to death or executed in brutal ways, it was said. News reports from America and Britain in 1942 claimed that Jews especially were being methodically murdered. These stories became wilder still after April 1944, when the Slovak prisoner Rudolf Vrba and escapee Alfred Wetzler emerged from a camp nobody had heard of in southern Poland to warn of mass exterminations involving the use of gas chambers and crematoria. The two men's detailed report on Auschwitz-Birkenau, complete with graphic illustrations, wasn't widely circulated for some time and many didn't credit it even then – although from then on, people became far more suspicious and avoided transports East at all costs.

Priska and Tibor couldn't allow themselves to believe the tales, which seemed too far-fetched to be credible. The general feeling among their friends was that such stories were either the ramblings of men driven insane by imprisonment, or exaggerated as anti-Nazi propaganda. In spite of all they'd endured, it was beyond their comprehension that Hitler really meant what he said when he'd promised to eradicate every human being of undesirable ethnic origin in order to create a master race. The Germans were, after all, one of the world's most cultured and civilised peoples. The nation that had produced Bach and Goethe, Mozart and Beethoven, Einstein, Nietzsche and Dürer couldn't possibly create such a monstrous plan – could it?

Maintaining their hopes of an imminent resolution to a war they didn't fully understand, the couple carried on with their lives as best they could. In the middle of June 1944, a week before their third wedding anniversary, Priska and Tibor decided to try again for a child. Two months later the relative calm they'd enjoyed for almost two years was shattered by the Slovak National Uprising, an armed insurrection intended to overthrow the puppet state. Priska's brother Janko was one of thousands of ordinary citizens and partisans who did their utmost to end the fascist regime under which they were forced to live.

The violent rebellion began in the Low Tatras on 29 August 1944, and quickly spread until German Wehrmacht forces were sent in two months later to viciously crush it. Thousands died. After that, everything changed. The soldiers who'd been sent to wreak revenge quickly occupied the whole country under the auspices of the Gestapo, who moved in to impose order on those who'd dared disobey the Führer. One of the first tasks of the security police they brought with them was to force President Tiso to resume the transportations of the remainder of the Slovak Jews. Desperate to avoid such a fate, thousands went into hiding or fled to Hungary or other countries where they hoped they might be safer.

Trying to remain optimistic in the face of what seemed an increasingly inevitable outcome, Priska and her husband chose to stay in Bratislava where they'd successfully managed to avoid capture for so long. Each day they went undiscovered felt like a gift, especially when each week brought more good news about the war. Paris had been liberated, along with key ports in France and Belgium. The Allies had begun an airborne assault on Holland. Surely Germany would capitulate soon?

On Tuesday, 26 September 1944, the couple celebrated Tibor's thirtieth birthday. It happened to fall that year on Yom Kippur, the 'Sabbath of Sabbaths', a twenty-five-hour period of fasting for the Day of Atonement and the most holy of Jewish observances. Having scrubbed their hands, as was their custom, they sat together and enjoyed a meal cobbled together from whatever was available. They were not only celebrating Tibor's birthday but the new life Priska had been carrying beneath her heart for a little more than eight weeks. Together they prayed that this, their fourth baby, might survive.

Two days later, their hopes for happiness were shattered when three members of the *Freiwillige Schutzstaffel* (Volunteer SS) – largely comprised of Slovak ethnic German paramilitaries – burst into their apartment and ordered them to pack their belongings into two small suitcases, together weighing no more than fifty kilograms.

'They were horrible,' Priska said. 'They were arrogant. They hardly spoke and I didn't say anything either … I knew how to stay calm in the face of adversity. I didn't start anything.'

On that fine autumn day and at a cost to the Slovak government of 1,000 Reichsmarks, Priska and Tibor Löwenbein were 'dragged' from their home and forced into the back of a large black van. They had to leave behind Tibor's collections of stamps, his pipes, shirts, well-stocked bookcase and precious notebooks containing years of writing.

The young couple were driven first to the large Orthodox Jewish synagogue in Heydukova Strasse. Kept waiting there for hours with scores of others sitting on the floor or on their luggage, they feared for their lives, while Priska was stricken by a bout of morning sickness – the first she'd ever suffered. Fighting waves of nausea, she clung to Tibor who kept telling her to remember their little one. 'My husband was just caressing me and saying, "Maybe they'll send us home, *Pirečko*." I was only thinking about my baby. I wanted that baby so very much.'

Later that day, they and 2,000 other Jews were transferred by bus to the small railway station at Lamač and then sent sixty kilometres east to the sprawling Sered' labour and transit camp in the Danubian lowland. A former military base, Sered' had been run by the *Hlinka* Guard prior to the uprising but then came under the supervision of SS officer Alois Brunner, assistant to Adolf Eichmann, the Nazi *Obersturmbannführer* (lieutenant colonel) and one of the chief perpetrators of Hitler's so-called 'Final Solution to the Jewish question'.

Brunner had been sent to Sered' to personally supervise the deportation of the last of the Slovak Jews after his success in overseeing a similar operation in Vichy France. Often seen wearing his favourite white uniform, Brunner is believed to have been responsible for the transportation of over 100,000 people to Auschwitz.

Jews being unloaded from cattle wagons at Auschwitz

Those who arrived in Sered' were herded into wooden barracks that were quickly overwhelmed by the sheer numbers. The prisoners' dehumanisation began with early morning roll calls, or *Appelle*, and a strict regimen of hard physical labour or domestic duties. Crammed into every available space, they were expected to exist each day on a half mug full of bitter 'coffee', some anaemic soup of questionable origin, and a little stale bread. Some of the more devout Jews used the hot water masquerading as food to wash their hands before they carefully sliced and shared out their pitiful rations.

On Yom Kippur, the day Priska and her husband had been observing in Bratislava, the Nazis at Sered' roasted a whole pig in the middle of the camp and laughingly invited the half-starved Jews to share it. Not one is reported to have stepped forward, in spite of their hunger.

The first transportations East from Sered' started almost immediately after Priska and Tibor arrived by bus, as Brunner supervised the 'liquidation' of the camp in readiness for the next influx of prisoners. On 30 September 1944, the almost 2,000 Bratislavan Jews were marched from their barracks by Slovak and Hungarian SS officers in the middle of the night, and lined up in military formation before being shoved into freight wagons. Between eighty and a hundred people were squashed into each boxcar, with barely room to breathe, let alone move. Once the heavy wooden doors were slid shut, leaving them suffocating in the semi-darkness, the smallest of the children were passed over the heads of the others, to be held on the laps of those who had a little room to sit on a narrow plank at the back. The rest could only stand or squat.

There was no sanitation other than an empty wooden bucket and a tin can full of water, and each wagon was soon stinking and unhygienic as the pail slopped its contents at every jolt. Some tried to empty it out of the tiny window but a barbed-wire grille prevented it from being tipped up completely, so people were forced to defecate or urinate where they stood, soiling their clothes.

Without food, fresh air or water, the sweating, despairing humans were crushed against one another. Those who could see through narrow cracks in the wood called out the names of the towns they passed as they continued on their three-hundred-kilometre journey northeast. By the time they crossed the Polish border, some of the eldest prisoners recited the Jewish prayer for the dead and then simply shut down. Those who died were hurled off at stops along the way, making a little more room for the living. Like thousands of Jews transported from Sered' in abominable conditions during the final months of 1944, these 1,860 Slovak Jews realised that they were headed somewhere they would almost certainly be treated most harshly and might well meet their deaths.

Priska and Tibor were as fearful as everyone else, but still they kept trying to reassure each other that all would be well and they'd return home with their child. Priska especially was determined not to give up, because 'I liked my life so much.' She reminded Tibor that her ability to speak a number of languages would allow her to converse with the other prisoners and even the SS, who might treat her with a little more respect. She had a brain and she knew how to use it, she assured him.

Priska's faith was always important to her and she relied on it during those dark hours as their locomotive pulled them ever eastwards. 'Belief in God is the most important thing in the world. When someone has faith they must be a decent person and know how to behave. Every night I greet my God before I fall asleep.' Having been christened as an evangelical, she rarely thought of herself as Jewish, an irony that wasn't wasted on her as she and Tibor were treated without a shred of compassion on account of their faith. 'It is terrible what they did to the Jews,' she admitted. 'Horrible. Like animals. Men are men, and a man to a man has to act properly. They treated the Jews terribly. We were stuck in a freight train and ... then thrown out of there. They behaved appallingly.'

The train journey lasted more than twenty-four hours as those squashed on board continued to wonder where they were heading and whether they'd be reunited with the loved ones taken from them two years earlier. Would Priska see her sister Boežka and her parents again? Might she be reunited with friends from Zlaté Moravce with whom she'd swum, sung and spoken English and German? Would Tibor be able to comfort his widowed mother at last?

An increasingly distressed Tibor didn't believe so and could hardly bear to see his wife suffer. Retching and without any water or fresh air, she struggled for breath in the dark, fetid wagon as he held her to him, kissed her hair and tried to console her. Hardly stopping to catch his own breath he spoke to her constantly, reminding her to think positively no matter what, and to focus only on joyful things. Just as in his letters he had spoken of her 'light piercing the dark clouds', so he tried to keep her hopeful for the future.

As the train trundled remorselessly on, though, his courage began to fail him. If this was how they were being treated now, then what further cruelty awaited them at their destination? Holding Priska closer still, he openly prayed that she and his yearned-for baby would at least survive. Realising that this could be their last chance, the couple decided to choose a name for their child in that unlike-liest of places. Whispering, they picked Hanka (more formally Hana) for a girl – after her grandmother's sister – and Miško (Michael) for a boy.

Standing next to the young couple in the dimly lit wagon was Edita Kelamanová, a thirty-three-year-old Hungarian spinster from Bratislava. She couldn't help but overhear their conversation and she was moved. Over the growling of the train, Edita told Tibor, 'I promise that if your wife and I remain together, I will take care of her.' From a wealthy, educated background, Edita not only con-sidered it her *mitzvah* or moral duty but hoped that if she did as she promised, then her prayers that she be saved and have a husband of her own one day might be answered. Tibor thanked the kind stranger as Priska, who recognised her accent, added softly in Hungarian, '*Köszönöm*' – thank you.

All cried out as the train jerked to a standstill at a central train depot at the border of Poland and the German Reich, where the prisoners were formally handed over to the new authorities. The doors to their stifling wagons didn't open and they had no idea what was happening as they waited in a siding. Then the train from Sered' gave a convulsive twitch and moved off again, until a few hours later it suddenly was buffeted sideways onto a dedicated rail spur and clanked violently to a halt at the railway ramp in the heart of Auschwitz II-Birkenau. It was Sunday, 1 October 1944. Beyond the sealed doors of their prison-on-wheels, the occupants of the

train immediately recognised the sounds of violence – men shouting and dogs barking – and knew then that they had reached their
destination.

'Everything will be fine, my Golden One!' Tibor promised his
wife moments before the wagon doors were thrown open with a
tremendous bang. Shuffling forwards to the brink of they knew not
what, he cried, 'Stay positive, Piroška! Think only of beautiful
things!'

## 2

# Rachel

Rachel Abramczyk

'Guten Morgen hübsche Dame, sind sie schwanger?' *(Good morn-ing pretty lady, are you pregnant?)*

*Rachel Friedman had been asked a similar question in the autumn of 1944, as Mengele gave her the special smirk he seemed to reserve* for the shaved, naked women paraded before him like mannequins at Auschwitz II-Birkenau.

Rachel didn't know what to say or where to look, so she kept her eyes lowered and her chin to her chest. Surrounding her were hundreds of other women in the same predicament, all of whom had been commanded to stand for hours on the open parade ground. Like them, she was mortified to be seen undressed in front of so many strangers. At twenty-five, she was suddenly grateful that her husband Monik hadn't been transported with her from their ghetto in occupied Poland and couldn't witness her humiliation.

Along with Priska Löwenbeinová – one of the thousands of women who shared her fate – Rachel had only a few seconds to choose how to respond to the high-ranking Nazi who would indicate with a casual movement of his hand if she was to live or die. She wasn't even one hundred per cent certain that she was pregnant with Monik's child – and if she was it could only be a matter of weeks. Nor did she have any idea what it might mean to admit that she was.

She'd heard a few horrible stories of what went on in some of the Nazi camps but she couldn't bring herself to believe them. And no matter how preposterous those rumours became, there'd been no mention of Dr Mengele, of the fate of pregnant women in his care, or of his brutal medical experiments on children – especially twins. That was to emerge later.

The only thing Rachel knew as she watched the impeccably groomed doctor personally examine scores of female prisoners was that his smile never quite reached his eyes. In fact, his whole demeanour was that of a diligent farmer closely scrutinising his livestock as he unashamedly appraised the physique of a blushing teenager, or roughly manhandled the breasts of a woman in her prime.

With his highly polished boots and crisp uniform, he bore all the hallmarks of a man who thrived on discipline and routine. While some of the fat-necked Nazis lolling around the perimeter of the muddy roll-call area appeared to be drunk or worse, Mengele didn't seem to need to deaden his senses. On the contrary, he seemed to enjoy *his work, sometimes whistling as he strode up and down the rows of inmates, breaking off only to dispense orders to prisoners wearing what looked like striped pyjamas.*

*Any women who were visibly pregnant or given away by telltale drops of milk were hauled off by these stony-faced men. The women weren't stony-faced, though. The look of fear in their eyes as they huddled together was enough to convince Rachel of her answer.*

*When Mengele asked her his question and then impatiently flipped his glove left and right, she cupped a hand protectively over each breast and said quietly, 'Nie.'*

*Mengele never laid a finger on the pregnant woman standing before him. As he moved on to his next victim, he didn't even give Rachel Friedman a backward glance.*

Rachel grew up as part of a large, 'happy and beautiful' family in which the children played, laughed and sang together, and for whom life should have been long and sweet.

She was named Rachel Abramczyk but called Ruze or 'Rushka' for much of her later life. The eldest of nine children, she was born one month after the end of the First World War on New Year's Eve, 1918, in Pabianice near Łódź – Poland's second-largest city.

Pabianice was one of the oldest settlements in the country and among its most prosperous, with a long history of manufacturing textiles. Even so, it was still relatively rural and there were only two cars in town, one of which belonged to the local doctor. Jews in this part of Eastern Europe had experienced prejudice since Prussian rule but by the 1930s they had assimilated much more and now comprised approximately sixteen per cent of the population. Orthodox and Hasidic Jews, who stood out in their black robes and hats, were persecuted far more than non-religious families like the Abramczyks, who described themselves as 'culturally Jewish' or as 'reformed' Jews long before the reformation movement officially started.

Although they spoke Yiddish at home and celebrated Shabbat

and other holy days with kosher food and candles, they rarely went to the synagogue and the children weren't raised to think of themselves as being especially observant – although they did attend a Jewish school.

Rachel's father Shaiah was a textile engineer in a company owned by his parents-in-law, one of the few industries open to someone of their faith. The family had their own looms and employed mostly relatives making tapestries and fabrics for curtains and soft furnishings. They lived well enough, thanks to the parents of his wife Fajga, and had a large third-floor apartment with two balconies and a large back garden.

Shaiah Abramczyk, who was forty-eight when his first child was born, was unusually well educated and considered himself an intellectual. Largely self-taught, he was a voracious reader who immersed himself in classic books on history, literature and the arts. He pushed his children to focus on their studies and encouraged them to become fluent in German, which was widely considered to be the language of cultured people.

Rachel respected her father and inherited his hunger for learning. A diligent student, she and her siblings walked a kilometre every day to and from school, come rain or shine. They studied from 8 a.m. to 1.30 p.m. but were then free to read or play.

As was often the custom then, her mother Fajga was a very young bride for her much older husband and was only nineteen when she gave birth to Rachel. She remained almost permanently pregnant throughout her eldest daughter's childhood. Although she adored her children, she was sometimes resentful of her husband's eagerness to improve his mind and openly expressed the wish to friends and family that he might consider more effective birth control.

A kind and gentle woman who was proud of her life and often told her children, 'Our home is our castle,' Fajga decorated their apartment with an eclectic mix of art, fine china and ornaments, and always fresh flowers for *Pesach* (Passover). Whenever friends or relatives came to call, they were impressed at how tidy the Abramczyks' home was and how well the children behaved. Much of that good conduct was down to Rachel, as her timid mother was no disciplinarian. As soon as she was old enough to hold a baby, Rachel effectively became the secondary maternal figure, helping with the cooking and chores as well as taking care of her younger siblings.

She prepared lunch when they came in from school and then she sent them out to play. The family had outside help once in a while but the eldest daughters did most of the work. Sala, the next in line and three years younger than Rachel, recalled, 'One of us was always holding one of the little ones or doing the washing the old-fashioned way, with washboards.' Their younger sisters Ester and Bala were recruited too, as soon as they were old enough. Their brothers Bernard, known as 'Berek', and her younger brother Moniek did what they could but the smallest children, Dorcka – known as 'Dora' – and her twin brother Heniek, born in 1931, plus their baby sister Anička – known as 'Maniusia' – born in 1933, were too little.

Rachel felt the pressure of her responsibilities. 'We were all very good kids and we didn't fight like other children,' she said, although she was the one her mother asked to make sure her younger siblings behaved themselves and did their chores. It was a disciplinary role she maintained throughout her life. Perhaps because of all her duties, Rachel was a skinny girl and sometimes spoken of as 'the weakling' of the family. Sala, vivacious and pretty, who sang and danced in local theatrical groups, said, 'Rachel always needed more feeding up than the rest of us.'

Largely financed by Fajga's well-connected parents, the family ate well, enjoying *pierogi* dumplings and meat dishes such as duck with apples or chicken with plums. Mealtimes were always a high-light and the mouth-watering memories of the food on their table would sustain Rachel and her family through the worst times of the war.

The four eldest sisters were popular amongst their peers.

Educated, well dressed and bilingual, they had a wide circle of friends of all creeds. Sala was considered such a beauty that she had her portrait painted by the art teacher at their school. 'It was a great honour but then I was always her favourite,' she recalled.

Although the family business was thriving and their home a modern and happy one, the Abramczyk way of life was constantly felt to be under threat as Jews in Poland experienced widespread prejudice, with often only their own community court or local rabbis to complain to. This concerned many and, amongst the younger generation especially, there was talk of leaving to start a new life somewhere without the constant threat of harassment. Zionism, founded in the nineteenth century, had enjoyed a surge in popularity across Eastern Europe during the 1930s. Its idealistic notions of setting up a way of life free from discrimination in the 'Land of Israel' – considered to be the Jewish homeland – held increasing appeal to those who felt largely powerless.

The older and more observant Jews dreamed of going to Palestine to die somewhere 'closer to God' – the ultimate status symbol. Some, like Rachel's father, preferred Azerbaijan, where Jews had been promised sanctuary. Their younger counterparts had little use for religion and just wanted to settle somewhere they could raise children safely, in a land where everyone could be equal.

Ever since she was sixteen years old, Rachel had been a member of the Jewish National Fund to raise money for land in Palestine. She too fantasised about moving there one day and living a life doing good works. Having spent her teenage years as little more than a nanny, Rachel privately made the decision to marry a wealthy man as soon as she could. By the time she left high school, she had done just that. His name was Moshe Friedman, also known as Morris or 'Monik', a good-looking young man born on 15 May 1916, who – with his widowed mother Ita and two older brothers David and Avner – owned a textile factory so large that it employed Gentiles, which was highly unusual.

It was Monik's indomitable mother Ita, born in Hungary, who
had kept the factory going after the death of her husband Shimon
from tuberculosis, a disease that almost killed her too and badly
affected her health. In spite of that, she became the 'boss of all she
owned'. A devoted mother who worshipped her three sons, Ita was
determined to improve the business so that her sons would have
something worth inheriting.

Rachel's husband Monik Friedman

Monik and Rachel married in March 1937, just after Rachel finished secondary school. Having filled out since her childhood she
made an attractive bride. Her new husband was only twenty-one and
Rachel, at eighteen, became a submissive, traditional Jewish wife. At
the time of her wedding, her long-suffering mother Fajga still had
six-year-old twins at home as well as four-year-old Maniusia. She
must have missed Rachel sorely.

Monik Friedman shared his bride's interest in Zionism, and the
couple had joined a youth organisation named Gordonia (after the

progressive Zionist A.D. Gordon) that promoted allegiance to the kibbutz way of life and the revival of Hebrew. In keeping with these beliefs, they'd asked for a simple wedding. Monik's influential mother expected her sons to live appropriately to their wealth, however, so her youngest son and his wife had an enviable lifestyle in the new home they moved to in Łódź. The post-war inflation that had ruined millions of lives across Europe had little effect on those savvy enough to invest in fabrics or gold.

'I married a very rich man and I didn't have to work,' Rachel admitted. 'We lived better than other people.' They deliberately didn't start a family straight away, as they wanted to enjoy each other's company and do whatever they could to help develop the business. Besides, Rachel had experienced quite enough of babies for a while.

Łódź, which had a chequered history of Prussian, German and Polish ownership, was one of the most densely populated industrialised cities in the world. An imposing metropolis with grand buildings, Parisian-style boulevards and beautiful public spaces, it had Poland's second-largest Jewish community after Warsaw, comprising over thirty per cent of the almost one million population. The rest were Polish Gentiles and a few minority Germans. With an estimated 1,200 textile businesses and more than two million spindles employed in manufacturing, Łódź had become the jewel of Poland's trading empire during the Industrial Revolution and a magnet for skilled workers.

There was much more for Rachel and Monik to do in cosmopolitan Łódź than there ever had been in Pabianice. Without chores or studies, Rachel was also able to focus on her fundraising while the Friedman family discussed opening another factory in Warsaw, one hundred and thirty kilometres away, where they already had an apartment. Their plans were stalled by world events, however. When Adolf Hitler annexed Austria and threw out all the Poles it became clear that the German Chancellor could no longer be ignored. After *Kristallnacht* they knew his threats were genuine. As

Jews across Germany, Austria and Sudetenland panicked and prepared to flee, Rachel and Monik also considered getting out while
they could. They were Zionists, after all, and many of their friends
were leaving for Palestine. But what would they do in the Levant,
so far from their loved ones? How and where would they live in
such a hot and hostile Middle Eastern climate?

Tempting as escape from extreme Nazi politics seemed, Hitler
and his fanatics were still some distance away and the hope was that
he would be satisfied with what he'd already seized. Even if his
influence did stretch as far as Poland, the family thought that only
religious Jews would be targeted, not wealthy assimilated ones such
as they.

After much deliberation, Rachel and Monik chose to stay in their
mother country. They looked German and spoke German. They
were better off financially than most and had many Gentile friends.
Until shiny black jackboots were marching through their city they
didn't think they were personally at risk. As Rachel said later, 'The
Nazi brutality didn't surprise me at all. The one thing I never
expected was that they would be German.' Besides, the couple
couldn't imagine that they'd find a better life than the one they
already had. The thought was that, whatever happened – even if
they lost property – they would 'muddle through'.

Those hopes were dashed when the Nazis invaded Poland in a
*Blitzkrieg* at dawn on 1 September 1939, showing off their massive
military superiority. Infantry invaded across the northern and southern borders and there were multiple bombardments, including an
aerial attack on Wieluń, just over an hour from Pabianice, which
destroyed ninety per cent of the city centre with the loss of 1,300
civilian lives. Entire communities fled on bikes, on foot or on carts,
praying that the Polish army might halt the German advance. Many
crossed the borders to Romania, Lithuania and Hungary. Then
Warsaw was pulverised by the Luftwaffe with aircraft targeting
civilian as well as military targets. Tens of thousands of people were
killed and many more injured.

Both Rachel in Łódź and her family in Pabianice heard the planes and ran to the shelters as sirens wailed warnings of fresh aerial attacks. By the time Britain and France declared war on Germany on 3 September, it was too late for the couple to flee.

When the bombardment eventually stopped, Warsaw was placed under siege for three weeks until Polish forces finally capitulated and 100,000 prisoners-of-war were taken. The following day, 1 October 1939, German Panzer tanks rolled through the streets as the Wehrmacht occupied the city. Hitler later announced triumphantly, 'The state to which England had extended its guarantee was swept from the map in eighteen days . . . the first phase of this war has come to an end and the second one begins.' He assured his jubilant followers that Germany was now the greatest world power.

After the initial shock of invasion came the first waves of anti-Semitism. From day one, the two families realised that their 'beautiful life' was over. Poland was carved up between the Germans and the Soviets, neither of which was an appealing prospect. Forced labour was immediately imposed on all Jews aged between fourteen and sixty and many of the Polish Germans who'd enthusiastically welcomed Hitler's army suddenly became German again almost overnight, instigating a campaign of racism and public humiliation against those they'd secretly despised.

Men of the Hasidic sect especially were subjected to random violence on the hostile streets. They were often stopped and abused, beaten with rifle butts, had their beards cut off (or sometimes torn out at the roots), and were forced to scrub the pavements with toothbrushes or their prayer shawls. Many were hanged for no reason. Homes were looted and the windows of businesses and synagogues broken. All Jewish holidays were cancelled, and the Germans seized Jews for forced labour while preventing them from doing their skilled work in the textile industry. Those who escaped being snatched away were compelled to hand over virtually every possession and cash transactions were banned.

Thousands lost their livelihoods and most of their belongings within days of the invasion. Former neighbours joined forces to storm Jewish homes and rob them of whatever they wanted. They stole china and linens, paintings and furniture. They even tore wedding rings from fingers. All Jews had to wear first yellow armbands then yellow stars, conspicuous emblems of their separateness.

German was declared the official language of their part of Poland, and city and street names were altered: Pabianice became Pabianitz, Łódź was renamed Litzmannstadt after a First World War general, and when its main street was renamed Adolf Hitler Strasse, Rachel and Monik knew that the Germans were there to stay.

Using the considerable means at his disposal, Monik managed to acquire false papers asserting that he was a *Volksdeutsche*, an Aryan Polish German. With his fairer colouring and green eyes, this gave him status even among the Aryan Poles who looked set to become the ruling class. He acquired similar papers for Rachel, which allowed them to travel freely between Łódź and his family apartment in Warsaw. It also kept them immune from the increasingly restrictive measures now being imposed. Ironically – and if not for their devotion to their business and families – the couple could have moved somewhere far safer if they'd chosen to do so, and might well have been able to stay undetected for the duration of the war.

Rachel heard through friends that her beleaguered family in Pabianice was still alive but any direct contact with them would have given her away. She also heard that a ghetto for Jews was being prepared in a small area of its old town and that some had moved voluntarily, hoping for safety in numbers. The authorities claimed the ghetto was necessary to protect Jews from Aryan attacks and to stop them 'collaborating with the enemies of the Reich'. They also said it was to keep them separate because of the risk of spreading the diseases that all Jews allegedly carried. In early 1940, Rachel's family was among thousands from Pabianice and the neighbouring countryside herded inside one of Europe's first ghettos with the threat of execution if they attempted to cross its heavily guarded boundary.

Entire families were given just a few days' notice and were only allowed to take bedding and a few belongings. By December 1940, the ghetto had grown from a few hundred inhabitants to approximately 8,000, squeezed into rooms or apartments allocated by the authorities. Luckily the Abramcyzks had friends who owned a property within the ghetto's tight grid of cobbled streets and were offered one large room to share. It had a little furniture and a small kitchenette. Others were less fortunate and many families were separated or forced to share tiny living spaces with strangers in derelict warehouses or bleak apartment blocks. Most had no electricity or running water.

Under Nazi rule, all food and fuel provided to the ghetto had to be paid for with goods and services, so everyone had to work. According to the terms of the Economic Communities set up by the Nazi-appointed Jewish Council of Elders, one day's work entitled them to one portion of soup, so unless they completed their shifts they faced starvation. Some people toiled in factories outside the perimeter of the ghetto while others laboured in their homes. Sala and her brothers Moniek and Berek worked in a factory that made clothes, uniforms and luxury goods. Fajga stayed home with her smallest children and Shaiah did what he could to provide food and make their home habitable. The family existed on pots of thin broth or stew and a little bread. They had to beg, scavenge or barter for extra vegetables and a little meat or eggs if they were lucky.

From 5 p.m. until 8 a.m. all the inhabitants of the ghetto had to remain within the confines of their homes, which were crowded and stifling in the summer. Without a working sewage system, people used wooden buckets that quickly overflowed and had to be emptied each day into stinking latrine tanks and mobile excrement wagons – wooden carts on wheels – that were pushed by the hapless *Scheisskommando* or 'shit detail'.

Rachel's family tried to make the best of their situation, praying that their ordeal would soon be over. They tried to keep morale up and kept telling each other, 'Just one more week and then we can be people again.' Weeks turned to months and still nothing changed. Everyone grew thinner and sicker as morale plummeted. Her sister Sala said, 'They took away our pride and we did the best we could but we weren't the same as before.'

By February 1940, a similar ghetto of approximately two and a half square kilometres was prepared for Łódź's 164,000 Jews in the run-down Bałuty and Stare Miasto quarters. Rachel and Monik decided to get out while they could and relocated to their apartment in Warsaw with his mother and two brothers. Even though the Luftwaffe had ravaged much of the city, Warsaw was by then in an area of Poland placed under the administration of a German governor-general named Hans Frank and the couple hoped they'd be less conspicuous. 'We didn't expect the war to last more than two or three months and then it would be over,' Rachel said.

They found the people of the capital extremely nervous. With refugees pouring in from all over the country seeking shelter, life was less easy than they'd hoped. More and more wooden carts pulled by men or horses arrived daily in the city, precariously over-laden with all they could carry, pots and pans dangling from them noisily. Food was in extremely short supply and even with false papers there was the constant threat of arrest, or worse.

By April 1940, construction began on the walls of the proposed Warsaw Ghetto into which all of the city's 400,000 Jews would eventually be squashed – making it the largest Jewish ghetto in Nazi-occupied Europe. In the ensuing months, widespread panic set in as people fled further east in the hope that they could escape to Palestine or somewhere safer. Rachel, Monik and his brothers also travelled to the border to investigate the possibilities. Along the route they encountered straggling lines of refugees taking with them whatever they could carry, all hoping for sanctuary in distant lands.

Monik's widowed mother Ita had refused to leave her home, while her health had deteriorated still further since the Nazi invasion. Like many sons of his generation, Monik felt that his first duty was to his mother and that they'd be better off if they stuck together. When he and Rachel realised what a strange, nomadic life they would have to lead they knew that escape with Ita wasn't feasible. 'It was very hard,' said Rachel. 'Too hard for her – so we came back and decided to stay.'

By November 1940, all the Jews in Warsaw had been rounded up and forced into the ghetto. Any escapees were shot. Behind walls three metres high and topped with barbed wire, its hundreds of thousands inhabitants existed from day to day squeezed into an area of just 2.09 square kilometres. The Friedmans' large apartment was already within the ghetto walls so, to begin with, little changed. 'Life was almost normal,' Rachel said. 'We didn't do much and we lived on my mother-in-law's money.' Food and other parcels were allowed in from outside and anyone with a supply of zlotys or Reichsmarks could buy luxuries on the black market. The months passed and life went on much the same, until the day when the family were ordered to leave their apartment because it was declared too large for four people. A customer of theirs from before the war kindly offered them a room in his flat, which they accepted gratefully.

With people beginning to drop in the streets and the death rate from starvation, exhaustion, and diseases such as tuberculosis and typhus growing to 2,000 a month, Rachel decided to organise relief for those less fortunate than her own family, especially if they hailed from Pabianice. 'A lot of people were very poor and very hungry so a few of us organised a kitchen so that they at least had a bowl of soup and a piece of bread every day. Some paid a few coins for their meal and with this we bought some more food and fed up to seventy every day.'

The Council of Elders or *Judenrat* who managed life within the ghetto found Rachel and her volunteers a larger kitchen in which to prepare their alms for the poor, but gave them no other material help. 'We did it for six months until we ran out of our money. Then we had to close it down.'

Rachel switched her focus to acquiring clothing for those most at risk of dying of cold in the winter. With fuel for heating and cooking in short supply, there were already corpses in the streets and the small cemetery filled so quickly that mass graves had to be dug. She was especially concerned about the ghetto children, many of whom had limited resistance as they were already half-starved and sick. She went with a couple of friends to see Janusz Korczak, the sixty-two-year-old doctor, educator and children's author, who'd first set up an orphanage in Warsaw in 1912. Korczak had turned down several chances to escape from the ghetto because he refused to leave his two hundred street children behind.

At his orphanage in Dzielna Street, the women offered their help and Korczak asked them to find warm clothes for his 'little ones', which they did. It was almost certainly those coats and dresses that the children wore when Korczak told them to look their best the day they left the ghetto the following year. Deportations East had begun by then and young, old and sick were some of the first to be summoned to the trains. Having announced, 'Where my children are going, I must go as well,' Korczak was with them as they were marched, two by two, to the *Umschlagplatz* (loading point) at the Warszawa Gdańska freight station, from which a train delivered them to the gas chambers at the Treblinka concentration camp. He died at their side.

Adam Czerniaków, the head of the *Judenrat*, who failed in his attempts to stop the Nazi demands to provide 6,000 deportees per day, swallowed a cyanide capsule rather than comply. He wrote notes to his wife and a member of the Judenrat in which he said, *They demand me to kill children of my nation with my own hands. I have nothing to do but to die ... I can no longer bear all this. My act will prove to everyone what is the right thing to do.*

The borders of the ghetto were heavily guarded but people could

pass through the gates if they had the correct papers. Deprived of
the goods they'd grown accustomed to buying from Jewish mer-
chants, the Gentiles of Warsaw relied on black market traffic. Those
sympathetic to the needs of the people trapped inside also risked
death to take in vital items such as food and fuel, while men and
boys crawled through tunnels and sewers to carry mail and other
goods.

Using his false documents, Monik occasionally risked travelling
beyond the walls to buy essential provisions or to seek news of
Rachel's family in Pabianice. Every time he left, Rachel knew there
was a chance that he might not return. It was always a relief when
he did and, lying together whispering into the night, they tried to
reassure each other that their nightmare would soon be over. Even
when the deportations began, they told each other, 'This too shall
pass.' And when the Nazis promised those who volunteered to be
'resettled' extra food and the chance to work on farms and live in
spa resorts, the family refused to be swayed. They were determined
to stay together until they were forced to leave. Still they clung to
the hope that the war would end any day.

It was clear that the screws were tightening, however. SS officers,
accompanied by Jewish police who wore special hats and uniforms
embellished with a yellow star, began to round people up and summarily execute anyone identified as 'subversive'. There were public
hangings in the main square. Families lived in terror of a knock at
the door, especially after curfew. Almost all the ghetto's smugglers
were rounded up and shot, cutting off contact with the outside
world. It became too risky to use false papers, and increasingly acute
food shortages hastened the deaths of still more Jews.

Monik, feeling increasingly helpless, knew that he and his young
wife had to escape. Using up virtually the last of the family
money, he hired a smuggler to get Rachel out of the ghetto, even
though the dangers were enormous. The smuggler, who was
probably a Gentile, arrived with a horse and cart. He collected
Rachel and another woman and calmly trotted them out through

the gates before setting off on the 120-kilometre journey to Pabianice. 'It took three days,' Rachel said. 'We didn't hide. We dressed
just like farmers with *babushkas*.' Two weeks later, he went back
for Monik.

Monik's mother Ita remained in Warsaw in the care of his
brother Avner. His other brother, David, fled east and was last heard
of in the Soviet Union. Avner later followed and ended up in Kiev,
but neither man is believed to have survived the war.

Rachel hadn't seen her own family for two years and there was
an emotional reunion with them in the Pabianice ghetto. Shaiah
Abramczyk was in his mid-sixties and his wife in her forties, but
they both looked much older. Frail and waxen, the light had gone
from their eyes and there was none of the joyfulness she remembered from her childhood. They were nevertheless keen to hear
Rachel's news and to tell her theirs, proudly recounting how they'd
managed to celebrate their twenty-fifth wedding anniversary with
a few small gifts and something a little better to eat than soup.

Happy as she was to be with her family, Rachel soon realised –
as did her husband – that life there was just as bad as in Warsaw.
Then word came that all the Jews in Pabianice were to be transported to the Łódź ghetto, where conditions were said to be even
worse. Leaving her family with a heavy heart, Rachel and Monik
felt they had no choice but to pay to be smuggled back into
Warsaw the same way they'd been spirited out. Once inside, they
each made their way to separate houses for safety. Monik was
taken in by friends, as arranged, but the door to Rachel's 'safe
house' was locked and its occupants too afraid to let her in. In
grave danger of being picked up by the police, she had no choice
but to persuade the waiting smuggler to take her back to her
parents.

Not long after she'd been returned, on Saturday 16 May 1942,
troops and police surrounded the Pabianice ghetto in order to
'liquidate' it. The authorities gave everyone just twenty-four hours'
notice to gather their most precious belongings. In the sights of Nazi

rifles, and with Alsatians barking at them menacingly, everyone had to assemble in precise formation. All eleven members of the Abramczyk family, Rachel amongst them, stuck close together as they were marched to the town's sports stadium to be herded inside and counted for a 'census'.

They sat there for a day and a night. They were given no food and some people were beaten or humiliated. Eventually they were told that they were to be sent to Łódź by bus and tram. As they stood in seemingly endless lines waiting to board the vehicles, German soldiers suddenly stepped in to decide who'd be viable for slave labour and who would not. 'We saw them taking old people and kids up to seven or eight. They were not letting them go on the bus,' Sala said. 'We were lucky because our youngest were eleven and we managed to keep them.'

Pandemonium broke out as hysterical women refused to leave without their children. Rachel and her family watched in horror as a Nazi grabbed a baby from its mother's arms and threw it far into the air. They didn't even see where the infant landed but they knew it couldn't have survived. 'I will never forget that,' said Sala. 'After that some mothers gave up their babies to the grandmothers to keep them safe, not knowing where they were going or what would happen.'

In the course of two days 4,000 children, the elderly and the sick were callously 'selected' before being sent to an unknown fate. The wailing of their relatives could be heard far beyond the stadium walls – as could the sound of gunfire as any who protested were executed on the spot.

While the family were waiting their turn to be transported, German officials called for strong young men to volunteer to travel with the children and the elderly for 'important work'. To their horror, Rachel's eighteen-year-old brother Moniek jumped up and offered his services. He insisted that the children might not be so afraid if he accompanied them. 'We said, "Don't go back! Stay here!" and he said, "No, I have to go and help." They took him away with the children.' Their last sight of handsome young Moniek was of him being driven away on a bus full of children, singing nursery rhymes in an attempt to calm them down.

The distraught family could have had no idea at the time, but those selected that day were transported to Chełmno, renamed Kulmhof by the Germans, a specialist SS killing centre less than a hundred kilometres northwest of Łódź. Approximately 150,000 people were to be exterminated at Chełmno during the course of the war – either shot as they were lined up beside burial pits or locked inside a specially adapted lorry that was then filled with exhaust fumes from the vehicle's engine as it was driven to a clearing in the middle of Rzuchów Forest. Some 70,000 of the victims came from Łódź. It was many years after the war before the family eventually discovered what had happened to their cherished Moniek.

'They sent them to a forest and they shot them all,' Sala said. 'My brother was one of the ones to clear the mess and after it was cleared they killed those young men too. They told him to remove his clothes and the authorities found his clothes after it was done. He was the first to be killed in our family.'

Unaware of Moniek's fate but still turned inside out by his loss, the Abramczyk family were in a sorrowful daze as they were transported – minus one – to Łódź.

Conditions in the new ghetto, situated in a slum area of the old town, were shocking for Rachel even by comparison with Warsaw, where an estimated 70,000 Jews had died of starvation between 1941 and 1942. She said she'd never fully understood what hunger meant until she arrived in Łódź. Large signs at the heavily guarded gates warned, 'Jewish residential area. Entry forbidden.' The soldiers posted every five hundred metres had instructions to shoot on sight anyone who tried to escape.

Inside the barbed wire barricades some 230,000 people were squeezed together in abysmal conditions in tenement buildings on mud or cobbled streets. Windowless apartments housed entire communities. The air was rancid with the smell of sewage and rotting people – alive and dead. The ghetto's scarecrow inhabitants seemed too catatonic to tend to their appearance any longer. Loose skin hung from them like cloth and many looked so insubstantial silhouetted against the light that it seemed as if the breeze might blow them away. Sala said, 'The ones that had been there the longest looked awful. They were undernourished and swollen with hunger. They could hardly walk and they had yellow faces hanging down. It was pitiful.'

Three steep wooden bridges spanned the ghetto's main streets, which were forbidden to non-Aryans, and trams passed beneath them, but their passengers weren't allowed off and could only watch helplessly as conditions in the ghetto worsened. Having come from homes filled with colour and vibrancy, all the Abramczyk family could see around them now were shadow people and monochrome hues, as if the very pigments of life had been bleached out by hunger and cold.

Łódź ghetto walkway for Jews to avoid Aryan streets

As with almost every ghetto they created, the Nazis insisted that the Jews pay for their own upkeep, so their chief purpose became industry in return for a chance to live. There were more than a hundred factories behind the fences that ringed the perimeter and everyone between the ages of ten and sixty-five had to work. Each day there were announcements on loudspeakers in the ghetto's largest open space – Fire Station Yard – on Lutomierska Street, informing newcomers where to report before the factory whistles blew. The Nazis set a 'Jew allowance' of approximately thirty pfennig a day per person for subsistence rations dispensed from communal kitchens, so each resident had to work to pay back their 'loan'. Rachel and her family were immediately employed making raw materials for the German war machine. These included textiles, shoes, rucksacks, saddles, belts and uniforms. In return, the Nazis provided just enough food for the population to survive (but not always) and a few basic services.

Once a worker had completed half their shift, they were entitled to a bowl of soup or 'swill' and a small piece of bread. Weekly, they queued for further rations such as beets, potato, cabbage, barley or onion, depending on what was available. If the authorities were feeling generous they might hand out a little sausage of dubious origin, a stick of margarine, flour, artificial honey or tiny (stinking) fish, which had to last a month. Milk was delivered through the gates occasionally, but in the summer it soon turned sour, while any fresh produce quickly spoiled.

It was up to individuals how they managed their provisions for the week; they might choose to barter shoes, clothes, cigarettes, books or other precious belongings for a little extra something like radish leaves to enhance a soup or root vegetables normally fed to cattle. Rachel's father Shaiah, a chain smoker, frequently traded his food for cigarettes and began to shrink inside his clothes.

What Rachel and her family remember most about the ghetto is 'working all the time and being hungry all the time'. Their eyes began to sink into their sockets and their hipbones to rub against their clothes. Belts were tightened and then had new holes punched in them, and the few clothes the family possessed soon became threadbare and stiff with grease. Their bellies ached and their legs were leaden. As in Warsaw, it was only the black market that helped keep people alive as the distribution points and potato depots increasingly fell prey to corruption and theft – known to all as 'skimming'. Hundreds suffered from pus-filled abscesses or swollen feet, legs and bodies – all caused by malnutrition. 'Some people could hardly walk because they filled their empty bellies with water and drank too much,' Sala recalled. 'There was a time when my feet wouldn't carry me so Mother gave me some dark oil and brown sugar as a kind of vitamin. I don't know why, but it worked.'

An estimated twenty per cent of the ghetto's population died of exhaustion, starvation or disease. In the frigid winters people froze to death in their beds. Some killed themselves by jumping from windows, by poisoning or hanging, in order to avoid the inevitable. A few parents killed their children and then themselves. Others 'went into the wire', which involved running at the barricades confident they'd be hastened to their end by a Nazi bullet. Later, in the camps, the most desperate prisoners were often to use this method of suicide, running at the electrified fencing in order to bring about a swift end.

Mordechai Chaim Rumkowski, a childless sixty-three-year-old Polish businessman, had been appointed the *Juden Älteste* – or 'Elder of the Jews' – by the Nazis. Just like Czerniaków in Warsaw, Rumkowski was put in charge of the day-to-day running of the ghetto from his headquarters in Bałuty Square. It was also his lot to decide the destiny of every man, woman and child. A former textile manufacturer and the director of an orphanage, Rumkowski was to become a controversial figure, regarded as a hero or a quisling, once he chose to co-operate with the Nazis.

White-haired and blue-eyed, he believed that in using the negotiation skills he'd honed as the director of the city's largest orphanage, he could help save the Jews of his city by trading on their 'currency' as skilled workers. Declaring the motto *Unser Einziger Weg Ist – Arbeit!* (Our only path is – work!), he insisted that if the ghetto remained highly productive then the Nazis wouldn't be able to afford to dispose of its valuable workforce. It was an achievement that some believed ensured their survival two years after the Warsaw ghetto and others had been destroyed.

But he also created a clear class structure within the ghetto, and many of the ruling elite associated with the man known as 'The Eldest' did well under the arrangement. These men and women who helped deceive, starve and exploit their fellow Jews lived in comfortable apartments, drinking vodka, and eating food destined for others. Some even had separate *dachas* or summer houses in the former allotment district of Marysin. They employed teachers of music and Hebrew for their children, enjoyed luxuries such as hot water and soap, shipped in goods from outside and even attended concerts and balls while the rest of the population sat in their hovels scratching at their scabs. In the winter, when only the soup kitchens and bakeries were allowed fuel for their fires, the elite had plenty while the rest of the population scraped out the dust from coal wagons or dismantled derelict buildings for their rafters.

Rachel and eight members of her remaining family, who shared one large room in a better-appointed apartment in an area renamed Pfeffergasse in the centre of the ghetto, were better off than many. Even so, they slept side by side on mattresses laid on the floor, both in order to keep warm and because of the lack of space. Rachel's brother Berek, who was immediately put to hard labour thanks to his youth and strength, was billeted elsewhere. The family received their ration of bread each week from a local grocery store and sent their youngest boy Heniek to queue for it in the hope that the shopkeeper might take pity on him and give him a slighter larger loaf. When Heniek eventually brought the precious bread home, Fajga carefully sliced it into nine segments, always giving the largest piece to their father as he was 'the king of the house'.

Each night when the older members of the family returned

home from work, Fajga would serve them soup cooked from what-ever scraps she could find. Sometimes they'd be allowed potatoes, although most that arrived in the winter were frozen solid and so black with rot when thawed that they had to be buried for fear of poisoning people. On other occasions, they might get turnips. Among the rations they were allowed was imitation coffee powder, which Fajga mixed with a little water to make soft patties to help fill her children up. The smell of coffee would ever after remind Rachel and her sisters of those innovative little patties.

'Hungry as we were we tried not to lose our happiness,' said Sala. 'We still thought that the day was near when everything would change.'

Slave labour in the Łódź ghetto

A surprisingly practical man with an inventive mind, Shaiah Abramczyk toiled all day in a workshop and then used his skills at home. He sectioned off one end of their room with a partition for privacy, mended his children's worn-out shoes, made shelves, and

somehow connected them to an electrical supply to bring them
light and power for a sewing machine. This was especially useful for
Sala, a talented needlewoman who made clothes and hats for
Germans. Once she'd finished her shift in a dimly lit factory she
would walk home footsore, her eyes gritty from the strain, eat her
soup, and set to making garments out of old fabric. She then
exchanged them with a family from the ruling elite for a little extra
food.

'My work ... was to make elegant clothes for ladies, which were
sent back to Germany,' Sala said. 'Sometimes I modelled them and
German people came in and watched me. Then at home I made
things out of nothing ... we had lots of green material once, I
remember.'

The requirement to work was not only necessary for food but
to ward off the ever-present threat of 'resettlement' to labour
camps, which had started in January 1942 before Rachel and her
family swelled the ghetto's numbers. Jews and Roma gypsies from
across occupied Europe had been shipped into Łódź from late
1941, and Rumkowski and his Resettlement Commission were
ordered to supervise deportations of 1,000 a day to make room. If
the elders didn't provide enough to satisfy the quotas, the Nazis
assured them that their wives and children would be substituted.
Repeatedly instructed to hand over his own people, Rumkowski
faced a monstrous moral dilemma but felt he had no choice but to
obey. He realised early on that those who were hell-bent on the
destruction of the Jews would only replace him with someone who
would do as they asked. He hoped at least to negotiate the numbers down.

As each new deportation began, German police accompanied
by the ghetto *Schutzpolizei* prowled the streets hunting for 'fresh
meat'. Salvoes of gunfire could be heard as any who tried to resist
were shot during the round-ups. Once a new batch of deportees
had been chosen from lists of names, men in uniform would
arrive in lorries and surround an apartment block. They would

then drag everyone out into the open, even in their nightclothes. If the occupants didn't open up voluntarily, their doors would be kicked in.

Those unlucky enough to be on the list were initially incarcerated in the ghetto prison in Czarnecki Street before being loaded onto trams to the main railway line at Radogszcz Station, Marysin, just beyond the ghetto perimeter. An estimated 200,000 Jews passed through what the Germans called the Radegast loading platform during the course of the war. While they were being held in Czarnecki Street, there was still hope. During those few hours or sometimes days, their loved ones raced desperately around the ghetto trying to find a 'connection' – a person of influence they might know – who could be begged or bribed to remove them from the transport lists. Invariably they failed, but if they did succeed it only meant that someone else would have to take the rescued person's place to fill the quota for what became euphemistically known as 'going to the frying pan'.

Although there were occasional lulls in the round-ups, everyone in the ghetto lived with the constant prospect of transportation and death. The growing feeling in Rachel's family was that hope was dwindling. Their sole focus was now on simply staying alive as long as possible and protecting those they loved. Increasingly fearful that he would lose some or all of his family to these random selections, Shaiah Abramczyk did something practical to protect them. The man whose children believed he was clever enough to have been an inventor, extended the partition wall of their room all the way across and built a wooden dresser up against the middle of it. He then created a secret door in the back of the lower cupboard, through which the family could squeeze each time they heard the police and SS arrive. 'There was just enough room for us all once we crawled through,' Sala said. 'Anyone who came into the room would think it was empty. Father even hung pictures up on the wall so that it looked solid.'

When the deportations from the ghetto resumed in September

1942, this secret hiding place proved invaluable. As the clatter of diesel trucks and the thunder of jackboots heralded the arrival of each new batch of guards, their neighbours were carried off to no one knew where. Each time, the Abramczyk family crept through the little door in the dresser and formed a tight human knot as they tried to close their ears to the pleas and cries of women, and the cackle of sadistic laughter. 'The Germans came in and started screaming at everyone, "Out of the house!" They selected people. They took fifty or sixty of them away in buses,' said Sala. 'That happened again and again and again.' All the family could do was say a silent farewell to friends and neighbours lost for ever.

Behind the barricades, few knew what was happening in the wider world or fully appreciated what would become of their loved ones who had been sent away. In effective quarantine from any news, they could have no idea that the only choice was between death by a bullet or suffocation by carbon monoxide at Chełmno. Hidden in the cracks of some of the cattle cars that came back from the East were found secret notes hinting at the horrors ahead and urging their fellow Jews not to board the trains. Clothing and possessions belonging to deportees from across occupied Europe were also sent back to the ghetto to be recycled for the war effort and some bore the names of people known to those left behind. Increasingly, the Jews of Łódź began to suspect the worst and came to believe the rumours about what 'the frying pan' really meant.

Fearing Nazi retaliation if their quotas weren't met, Rumkowski and his deputies repeatedly tried to assure the populace that those deported would be looked after in new camps and allowed to remain together as families. They would help with the war effort and enjoy better living conditions in military barracks, they promised. But as the transports continued relentlessly and no word ever came back from those sent away, few believed the reassurances. In the end, even Rumkowski stopped pretending.

His master plan was failing. Having set up what he'd considered to be a model work camp with its own schools, hospitals, fire service and police force, within a community in which he was the supreme ruler – he even conducted marriage ceremonies – his authority was being systematically undermined. Not only had thousands been sent away but the Nazis persistently failed to provide enough food in return for the labour his ghetto provided. Desperate to quell the increasing numbers of strikes and demonstrations by the hungry and the angry, Rumkowski became ever more dictatorial and threatened to arrest those who resisted his attempts to keep the ghetto working.

Determined to hasten the pace of Jewish annihilation still further, the Nazis broke their pact with him and demanded even greater numbers for the transports. Then they made their cruellest demand yet – the deportation of every child under the age of ten and every adult over sixty-five, which amounted to 3,000 lives every day for eight days.

The Abramczyks' hiding place was what saved them on 5 September 1942, when from 5 p.m. the *Allgemeine Gehsperre*, or *Groyse Sphere* (great curfew) in Yiddish, began. During that week more than 20,000 people were called for. Few families were left untouched.

Having spent days, hat in hand, pleading unsuccessfully with his masters to revoke the order or at least reduce the quotas, Rumkowski – who prided himself on his love of children – finally accepted that he could never sway the Nazis from their own master plan. A 'broken Jew', he summoned his people to Fire Station Yard the day before the great curfew began. That humid autumn afternoon he took a breath and announced to the vast gathering: 'A grievous blow has struck the ghetto. They are asking us to give up the best we possess – the children and the elderly … I never thought I would be forced to deliver the sacrifice to the altar with my own hands … I must stretch out my hands and beg: Brothers and sisters, hand them over to me. Fathers and mothers, give me your children!'

Amid screams and wails, he told his people that he'd only been able to negotiate a reduction in the original demand of 24,000 people, plus the preservation of children over the age of ten. He said the numbers of qualifying children and old people amounted to 13,000, so the rest of the allocation would have to be met elsewhere. He had agreed to hand over the sick, he said, 'in order to save the healthy'. If the deportations were met with any resistance he'd been assured that they would be carried out by brutal means.

Rachel's youngest sister Maniusia was eleven years old and just safe under the impossible edict. But that didn't diminish the horror of what was being demanded, or the manner in which the operation was carried out. Rachel said, 'We thought they were sending them to work until they started to take the children and the sick from hospitals. Then we knew they were taking them to kill them. They took away the children in such a terrible way. Children were thrown out of the windows down to the trucks so we knew nothing good would come of it.'

Already on the brink of madness because of the conditions they were forced to live in, some parents went insane once they lost the children they'd fought so hard to protect. There were rumours of mothers smothering their babies rather than hand them over to the Nazis, who prowled the streets with guns and dogs.

Sala said, 'We stayed in our hiding place whenever we heard the Germans looking for people and then we stayed there until we knew it was safe to come out.' When everything had quietened down after an hour or more, they crawled back through the dresser and wandered about their building to check on who'd been seized. The sight of an apartment door kicked in and swinging on its hinges meant that those neighbours wouldn't be coming back, so they helped themselves to any food or useful items left behind. 'That's how we lived through those few weeks . . . we took it and ate it like animals, not like people.'

The prisoners of Łódź continued to exist like this from day to

Radegast station, Łódź, from where Rachel
and 200,000 Jews were transported

day, sometimes from minute to minute, and certainly from meal to
meal. Polish *zlotys*, Reichsmarks, or the Litzmannstadt ghetto
money known as 'Rumkies' or 'Chaimkas' (in an early nod to
Chaim Rumkowski), became largely meaningless as the only currency became food. Rations remained unpredictable, not least
because the Nazis restricted deliveries whenever a fresh transport
was imminent in order to wear down any resistance. They would
then offer free meals to any who volunteered to be resettled elsewhere. For those who stayed, the daily calorie intake was also cut
by two-thirds at a time when growing corruption meant that many
supplies were being illegally diverted anyway.

Those worst affected by malnutrition, often barefoot and in rags,
their bodies misshapen, were known as 'hourglass' people. It was
common for these cadaverous souls with swollen bellies and legs to

take to their beds, eyes gleaming feverishly, and die within days. Epidemics of scabies, typhus and TB carried off hundreds more. As conditions worsened, an increasingly beleaguered Rumkowski vowed to keep the lamp of industry burning in the ghetto. In another speech, he promised, 'I can't save everyone so instead of having the entire population exposed to a slow death by hunger, I'll save at least the top 10,000.'

With people collapsing in the street to be covered by swarms of blowflies in the summer or for the ice to claim them in winter, the need for food became all-consuming. Getting hold of even a few vegetable peelings or a rotten potato became an obsession in the ghetto.

Rachel, a young wife from a once wealthy and prominent family, was more fortunate than many because of their connections. But she still had to work – twelve hours a day in the office of a straw factory that made footwear for soldiers on the Russian front. These huge overshoes were so rigid that they were almost impossible to walk in but they protected Wehrmacht toes against frostbite. Three of her sisters worked in that factory too – even the youngest.

Beyond the ghetto walls, Rachel's husband Monik continued to try to find ways to rescue his wife. Risking everything after escaping from Warsaw with his false papers, he travelled to Łódź to try to see her. 'He thought I was too weak to live in that ghetto on my own, but he couldn't get me out,' Rachel said. 'My brother Berek who was working in a nearby camp saw him going back and forth on the tram. In the end he risked his life and came through the barbed wire with the Germans all around just to be with me in the ghetto because he was sure I would have a better chance. He didn't want to live through the war without me . . . so he came in to be with me.'

Giving up his opportunity to escape for ever, Monik moved in with Rachel's family, into an already overcrowded room. His biggest problem was that he was now an illegal alien within a meticulously regimented Nazi system that didn't feature his name on any of its lists. Before the war Rumkowski had been a personal acquaintance of Monik's mother Ita, so the family called in a favour. The 'king of the ghetto' told Monik that the only place nobody would ask questions about where he came from would be in a division of the Jewish *Sonderpolizei* or special police. He readily agreed and was put into quarters with the rest. 'He did whatever they told him to do,' Rachel said. Like all those fighting for survival under Nazi rule, he didn't have much choice.

Monik also became a volunteer fireman with Rachel's brother Berek in what had, by necessity, to be a self-regulating community with its own emergency services. Those who were lucky enough to get government posts such as theirs were billeted together in the police headquarters or the fire station, where they were slightly better fed. Then Rachel was allocated a small room to herself in an apartment on a nearby street. It was somewhere she could finally enjoy some privacy with her husband, whenever he was able to join her.

There were other surprises too. 'Someone who was a representative from our company before the war took us to a big stockroom and helped us to some clothes and blankets – because we came with just the clothes on our backs.' With the ghetto in the grip of winter and blizzards coating everything in deep layers of snow that lent even the most squalid streets a deceptive air of innocence, an extra blanket meant the difference between life and death.

Everyone did what they could to keep up morale by organising musical and cultural events. There were jazz bands and classical concerts, plays, and pantomimes for children. Sala – who'd danced and sung in amateur theatre productions since childhood and in the Pabianice ghetto – featured prominently in several of the performances. Education wasn't forgotten either and in Rachel's factory, teachers were employed alongside children to give them lessons while they all worked. 'They taught them without books or papers, just by mouth, or by listening or spelling and telling them stories.'

From September 1942 until May 1944, the 75,000-strong work-force of *Judische Arbeitskräfte* (Jewish slaves) was so productive for the SS that it earned the ghetto a respite from transportations. But the tide of war was turning and Allied bombers now began to target German cities for the first time, including a mass bombing of Hamburg and the Ruhr industrial region that killed or injured thousands. Then in May, Heinrich Himmler – the second-most powerful man in the Reich – ordered the liquidation of the ghetto. In the next three months 7,000 Jews were sent to their death at Chełmno, but when the special death vans couldn't keep up with the numbers, transports were switched to Auschwitz. The hapless ghetto postmen whose task it was to deliver the notices to those expected to report for a transport became known as 'Angels of Death'.

With food in such short supply, there was a need to reduce the number of mouths to feed, so more of the remaining children and the elderly were put on trains to the unknown. By rights, the youngest of Rachel's family should have been sent away then, but still they managed to keep safe behind their false wall. Then some of the able-bodied men were taken. Berek and Monik escaped that transport because of their roles within the police and the fire brigade, but they couldn't protect their family much longer. There was nowhere left to hide.

For all those years, Rachel and her family had managed to remain together and evade capture. Then one day in August 1944, Berek – 'the best brother in the world' – a man who'd done everything he could to keep his family alive and together, visited his family to tell them the 'good news' that the transports had ended.

The authorities assured the firemen that the relatives of key workers would be saved. They just had to come out of hiding and assemble in Fire Station Yard so that the authorities could make a note of who they were and work out how many mouths they had left to feed. Like so much else in Łódź, though, the promise was hollow.

'We were on our way back home from the fire station when guards dressed in SS uniforms caught us,' Sala explained. 'Mother had stayed home with some of the young ones so I told one of the Germans, "My little sister Maniusia needs to run home and tell my mother that we've been taken." I hoped she'd be able to hide with the rest of the family but Mother came hurrying back with them and so we all went together. We were taken to the trains. We didn't talk. We didn't know where we were going or what they were going to do with us. I was holding my little sister like a baby. Then they opened the doors of the wagons.'

Inside a goods wagon used to transport enemies of the Reich

Amongst some of the last Jews to leave the Łódź ghetto – which was the last of its kind in Poland – Rachel Friedman was twenty-five years old the day she was transported to Auschwitz II-Birkenau on Monday, 28 August 1944. She hadn't seen Monik for several hours and had no idea if he'd been seized for the same transport and was in another wagon, or whether he was hiding somewhere in the ghetto. They were never given the opportunity to reassure each other or say goodbye.

Her brother Berek, who could have remained in Łódź as part of the special squad of seven hundred and fifty Jews designated to clear and recycle everything left behind, elected instead to go with his family. He was young and strong and knew that he could help their father Shaiah survive the worst privations of a hard labour camp. He almost managed it.

Accompanying them on some of the last trains out of the city that August night were Chaim Rumkowski, his wife, and three other members of his family. Some claimed he'd volunteered to go with the last deportees, hoping for the best. Every other ghetto in Poland had been liquidated by then and the 'king' of Łódź (whose forename was taken from the Jewish toast 'To Life') had, by whatever means, managed to keep his people safe for longer. His fate was either to die in the gas chambers to which he'd inadvertently sent thousands, or at the hands of other Jews who blamed him for the deaths of so many. Nobody can be certain.

Of the more than 200,000 people registered as living in the Łódź ghetto, less than a thousand survived. It was one of the Nazis' greatest triumphs in the destruction of European Jewry. Herded into closed goods wagons like animals to the slaughter, Rachel and her family managed to stay together. Pressed against each other in a dark rear corner with very little space, no food and not a drop of water, they waited to find out where they were being sent. 'We were all so scared and afraid to talk in those enclosed trains with not even a place to look out,' she said. Without any privacy, the Jews of Łódź suffered together as the waste bucket in the wagon quickly overflowed and was then accidentally kicked over with a clatter; the spilled ammonia made their eyes water. Desperate for a little fresh air, they all realised they might have been better off if they'd stood closer to the slit of a window threaded with barbed wire.

By the time the train shuddered to a stop in Auschwitz, the children were crying and the elders praying. Breathing shallowly, pressed together in the crushing darkness, they heard the metal clasps unlocked and then the doors slid open on their rollers with a bang, letting in a welcome blast of air. Spilling out of the wagon into dazzling searchlights, they were met with an insufferable din of yelling and were prodded and pushed into separate lines. That, they agreed, was the worst moment of all. 'You don't think. You don't talk. You just go like an automaton,' Rachel said.

Dr Mengele was on duty again that night, standing by the *Rampe* as his latest shipment was delivered. His wife Irene, the mother of his only son Rolf, had recently arrived to visit him in the camp – a stay that would last almost three months, as she was taken ill and had to remain in the well-equipped SS hospital for a time. During her visit, her husband told her that his work in Auschwitz was the equivalent of serving at the front and that his duties there had to be carried out with 'soldier-like obedience'.

Whenever a transport came in, some of the officers of the special SS-*Totenkopfverbände* ('Death's-Head Units'), responsible for administration in the concentration camps, were overheard complaining about the quality of the 'new stock'. Mengele rarely commented but instead looked each new prisoner up and down as he asked a few questions, sometimes quite kindly, before directing them to the right or to the left – to life or to death.

Rachel's family was split up within minutes of their arrival. A wide-eyed Fajga clung to her three youngest children, the thirteen-year-old twins Heniek and Dora, along with 'baby' Maniusia, as they were shoved one way, while Rachel and her sisters Ester, Bala and Sala were pushed another. Huddled together as each group was marshalled forward, their heads swivelled anxiously on their necks as they tried to snatch a last look at their loved ones before being shouted back into line.

Shaiah Abramczyk, the sensitive, book-loving intellectual and inventor who'd encouraged his children to learn the language of the Reich, watched what was left of his beautiful family scattered to the Polish winds as he and Berek were forced into a group earmarked for hard labour. 'They were too far away,' Rachel said. 'There was no sign of my Monik. We didn't see our mother with the younger children ... We saw our father and he showed us with his fingers that two went through and one didn't.'

They didn't realise it, but that was to be the last time Rachel and her sisters ever saw their parents and younger siblings.

# 3

# Anka

Anka's identity card

'*Are you with child, lady?*' *the infamous doctor of Auschwitz II-Birkenau asked Anka Nathanová in German when it was her turn to stand naked in front of him at* Appell *that October night in 1944.*

*A well-endowed twenty-seven-year-old Czech who'd long been embarrassed by her breasts, she attempted to cover them with one arm while the other tried to shield her private parts. Looking around, stupefied, Anka could hardly believe she'd been foolish enough to volunteer to follow her husband Bernd to this place. After surviving three years in the Terezín ghetto one hour north of Prague, she'd naively imagined they would be settled somewhere similar. With the rest of her family already sent East, she thought it would be best to stay together.*

*From the moment her train came to an agonisingly slow stop on its dedicated rail spur through Birkenau's arched 'Gate of Death', she realised her mistake. Terezín was a paradise compared to this.*

*As soon as the iron latches of the goods wagons were unlocked, the heavy wooden doors crashed open with an ominous clang. Bewildered men, women and children plunged out into the night, tripping and lurching over each other as if intoxicated.*

*'We came to hell, and we didn't know why,' Anka said. 'We were disembarking but we didn't know where ... We were frightened but we didn't know what of.'*

*Pulled down into that hungry mouth that devoured transport after transport into the most efficient of the Nazis' industrialised killing centres, Anka was in shock from the outset. In the stark lights from the watchtowers all she could hear was the clamour of dogs barking, all she could see was men wielding cudgels shrieking 'Raus! Raus!'*

*Impeccably dressed German officers stood around like marble statues as their prisoner minions beat, pushed or frightened the pitiful crowd into submission. All were cruel and hostile and a cacophony of languages could be heard as guards bellowed orders, women and children wailed, and men protested in vain.*

*With no time to comprehend what was happening, everyone who lurched off that train experienced the sudden horrible sensation of being in a place of acute danger as they were expertly separated into two long lines. With women and children on one side and men and older boys on another, the Jews of Terezín were pressed into a seething mass of humanity towards the SS officer whom Anka was to meet again later.*

*The smirking doctor, in whose hands their fate lay, stood with his legs apart watching them approach. He was the only one who didn't look straight through them as if they didn't exist. Interrogating each rapidly and asking if there were any 'Zwillinge' or twins, he waved a riding crop indicating to which side they should go. 'Links' meant left and 'rechts' meant right; he sent at least two-thirds of the new arrivals, including men, women and children, left, but indicated that Anka should keep right.*

*As she passed close by him she felt an almost palpable air of excitement in his bearing, as if selecting the choicest specimens from his latest delivery was the best part of his day. Beyond him, flames as high as houses blazed from the tops of two enormous chimneys. A double ring of barbed wire and electrified fencing precluded any possibility of escape. Hanging heavy in the air was a strange, sweet smell that no matter how hard she tried to breathe through her mouth, Anka was never quite able to expunge from her nostrils – or from her memory.*

*Less than an hour after entering what she called this 'Dante's Inferno', the ever diligent Mengele was standing in front of her again, this time on a sodden parade ground expecting her to admit that she was carrying a child.*

*Avoiding eye contact and staring down at his knee-length boots, she noticed that they were so highly polished that she could see her own naked reflection in them. Pressing her eyes shut against her humiliation she, too, shook her head and told him, 'Nein,' before he sighed in apparent exasperation and moved on.*

Some of the happiest days of Anka Nathanová's life were when she was a carefree young law student at the medieval Charles University in Prague just before the outbreak of the Second World War.

Strikingly beautiful and fluent in German, French and English with a smattering of Spanish, Italian and Russian, Anka revelled in the rich life of one of Europe's most vibrant, multi-cultural cities. Prague was prosperous and progressive with cafés, theatres and concert halls, and it attracted some of the world's finest minds and greatest artistic talents.

Anka loved classical music, especially the works of the composer Dvořák, and concerts featuring Beethoven and Brahms. She especially liked the Czech opera *The Bartered Bride*. Popular with the boys, her greatest joy however was to be taken to the cinema where she lost herself in the stories of other lives and enjoyed films such as *The Good Earth*, *The 39 Steps* and *The Lady Vanishes*.

Anka was born Anna Kauderová on Friday, 20 April 1917, in the small fourteenth-century town of Třebechovice pod Orebem, some thirteen kilometres from the city of Hradec Králové in what was once the Austro-Hungarian Empire. Hradec Králové, whose name translates as 'Castle of the Queen', is one of the oldest settlements in the Czech Republic and lies at the fertile confluence of the Elbe and Orlice rivers. It is a city also known for its grand pianos, manufactured by Antonin Petrof.

Cheerful and – by her own admission – a little spoiled, Anka was the baby of the Kauder family by several years and utterly adored by her parents, Stanislav and Ida, her older sisters Zdena and Ruzena, and her brother Antonin, known as 'Tonda'. Another brother, Jan, aged three, had died of meningitis two years before Anka's birth and her mother never quite recovered from the loss.

The family owned Kauder & Frankl, a successful tannery and leather factory in Třebechovice pod Orebem. It was co-owned with a relative of Ida's named Gustav Frankl. Anka was three years old when her family relocated from a flat in Hradec to a large apartment at one end of the factory.

Kauder & Frankel was a sprawling C-shaped construction on a large plot of land. A new building, its tannery had a tall brick chimney that Anka, as a little girl, was always afraid was going to topple over and kill them. Their apartment had a garden and a patio with a gazebo and an outdoor oven for summer dining. They grew vegetables and tomatoes and plucked fruit from their own trees. The grounds were so big, in fact, that after her sister Ruzena married, she and her husband Tom Mautner hired renowned Prague architect Kurt Spielmann to design and build them a Bauhaus-style villa on the plot, where they lived happily for many years with their infant son Peter.

An avid reader, Anka would slip away into the family garden to devour her favourite Latin books and the classics, which she read in various languages. She shared her passion for reading with her brother Tonda, who was kind to his little sister and took her everywhere with him, especially to the football matches he was such a fan of and always returned from hoarse. 'We had a marvellous relationship,' she said. 'He had a car and he took me on outings. Whenever we went dancing and my mother didn't feel like going, he came with me and was always in the background and never intruded. I was taken care of because I had my brother with me.'

Anka's mother Ida was unusual for her generation in that she worked behind the till in the family factory. A warm, chatty woman, she thrived on gossip shared with her largely female customers, who enjoyed confiding in her. With the matriarch at work every day, the family employed several staff including a maid, a cook, a gardener and a washerwoman. Ida made sure that they kept a clean house and took good care of the children.

'My mother would have done anything for me,' Anka said. 'We had a beautiful relationship. Only the best was just good enough for us at home.'

Athletic, healthy and a strong swimmer, Anka became the schools junior backstroke champion for Czechoslovakia and swam in the local river – occasionally nude. Naturally bright, she was raised to think for herself and do as she pleased. At eleven years of age she left her idyllic childhood home to become one of the few Jews to attend the Girls Lyceum in Hradec Králové. She went on to do well at the Gymnasium where she took extra classes in Latin, German and English. 'I lived in a *pension* in Hradec and went to the

Gymnasium and I was as happy as a lark. I had a lot of boyfriends and went dancing and to parties and everything went smoothly.' Anka also learned to play the piano and to dance, as well as taking part in sports such as tennis and rowing.

Her father's factory manufactured handbags and other goods for the mass market, and although Anka and her sisters often spurned his offers of free bags because they thought them too old-fashioned, she was proud of the new leather satchel she was given every few years – which was big enough for her school atlas.

Stanislav Kauder, who was forty-seven when Anka was born, was 'an unbeliever' and a committed Czech. He did not agree with the concept of Zionism and was intensely patriotic. Jewish by birth, the family was not at all observant and considered themselves free-thinkers. 'I was brought up without any religion whatsoever,' Anka said. 'I went to school in a very small place where there were Jewish children and a Jewish teacher came sporadically to teach us about history, but I never learned how to read Hebrew and in my parents' house kosher wasn't kept.' In defiance of tradition, the family frequently enjoyed the Czech national dish – roast pork with sauer-kraut and dumplings – even on the Sabbath. And Anka's brother Tonda once ruined his chances of marrying an eligible young Jewess by lighting his cigarette from the family menorah as her parents looked on, appalled.

Stanislav loved his children but was a self-contained man who rarely spoke to them. As was the custom, he let his wife take charge of the children's upbringing. He adored his wife, whom Anka described as 'an angel'. Ida Kauderová was slightly more observant than her husband and was driven ten miles to the syna-gogue in Hradec Králové on the highest Jewish holidays. It was, however, more out of 'piety for her parents' and to please her large family – she was one of twelve children. The best part, she always said, was to go to the local Grand Hotel afterwards with one of her sisters for coffee and cake. And she never forced her religion on her children.

'We happened to be Jewish and that was that,' said Anka. 'It didn't hinder me in any respect.'

There were only a handful of Jewish families in Třebechovice but she experienced no anti-Semitism amongst her friends and could do pretty much as she pleased.

As the political situation in Europe began to worsen, those around Anka became increasingly nervous. When her German-speaking mother heard Adolf Hitler's inflammatory speeches on the radio, the normally optimistic woman became overwhelmed with fear and insisted to any who'd listen that no good would come of him.

Like so many of her friends, though, Anka was blasé almost to the point of ignorance and felt that they lived too far away to be directly affected by Nazi ideology. 'We never thought anything would happen to us. We felt invincible,' she said. She was the first of her family to go to university, something that made her parents very proud, especially her mother Ida, who was bilingual and a frustrated academic especially fascinated by history.

Anka couldn't wait to move to Prague, which was two hours away by train. It was a city she knew well, as she would stay there as often as possible with her aunt Frieda, a milliner who had an apartment on Wenceslas Square. Whilst studying at Charles University, Anka lived there too.

Even after she moved to the city in 1936, she continued to remain largely immune to growing concerns about Hitler. Funded by an allowance from her father, she was on holiday skiing in the Austrian Tyrol with friends in March 1938 when the *Anschluss* happened. Overnight, Austria was in the hands of the Nazis and Czechoslovakia was surrounded. Red flags bearing *Hakenkreuze* or swastikas appeared on the streets of Salzburg, and Anka watched in amazement as Austrians greeted Hitler as a hero while the country's Jews became outcasts. This first direct contact with the Nazis was 'something that we couldn't grasp'. She added that although she personally didn't see any attacks on Jews, 'it was in the air somehow'.

Still, she didn't think that the German Chancellor with the funny moustache (whose birthday she happened to share) would directly affect her gilded life. Only when her first serious boyfriend, Leo Wildman, announced that he'd decided to move to England to join the British Army did she begin to reconsider. Leo's father had already been arrested and imprisoned as a subversive and his family feared for the future. She was sad to see Leo go and waved him off at the railway station. Just as the train departed, his father – who'd just been released from prison – ran up the platform to say good-bye to his son, but he was too late.

Although the couple had been quite serious about each other, it never occurred to Anka to go with Leo, even though she'd been given the chance. 'Two English ladies came to Prague to offer work to Jewish girls as domestics or in nursing. I applied for a job in nursing and got it. They provided me with a valid visa and exit papers and I could have gone then but . . . I procrastinated so long . . . I had all the papers in my hand and then war broke out in Europe . . . and I couldn't have been happier that I [had] managed to prolong it so long that I couldn't go any more . . . How stupid was that?'

Others given a similar *Durchlassschein* or special exit permit did leave, but they were in the minority. Among them was Tom Mautner, the husband of Anka's sister Ruzena, who seized the chance to flee to England on one of the last trains to London. He'd pleaded with Ruzena to go with him and bring their son Peter but she'd refused to leave her home and family. 'It was so much nicer to stay there than go to England so she stayed, and she paid dearly for it,' Anka said sadly.

Like Ruzena, many more remained, hoping for the best. Soon afterwards, she must have regretted her decision. Hitler seized control of Sudetenland after the signing of the Munich Agreement, adding more than two million Germans to his domain. It seemed that nothing could be done to stop his march across Europe. Later that same year he repeated his intent with the vow: 'I will continue this struggle, no matter against whom, until the safety of the Reich and its rights are secured.'

Jewish refugees from the border towns flooded into the city, bringing with them only what they could carry, as Hitler's intentions became frighteningly clear. With no help from Britain or their allies, the Czechs felt terribly betrayed.

Then in March 1939, German tanks rolled into Prague. Just as in Austria, Anka looked out onto the streets one day to find them teeming with soldiers while people stabbed the air with salutes. She wasn't the only one who watched aghast as wave after wave of steely-eyed Nazis marched through Wenceslas Square that grey day. 'It was the height of winter with snow on the ground, and it was a catastrophe.'

Nazis invade Prague, 1939

From the ninth-century Pražský Hrad or Prague Castle, Adolf Hitler proclaimed the partitioning of Czechoslovakia as they knew it into the Protectorate of Bohemia and Moravia and the (first) Slovak Republic or Slovak State. While Hitler waved to crowds from the windows of the castle high above the city, twenty-one-year-old Anka and her family suddenly found themselves citizens of a Nazi-administered territory and part of the Greater German Reich. 'I didn't have a care in the world until Adolf Hitler came,' she said. 'You don't give [your home and your country] a thought until it disappears ... which it did after twenty years and it was the biggest shock.'

Initial student demonstrations against the occupation were quickly crushed as troops stormed the university where Anka studied law. Nine student leaders were executed and 1,200 professors and students rounded up and sent to concentration camps before all the universities were closed. Following further random arrests, the imposition of the Nuremberg Laws began, restriction after restriction systematically stripping the 'enemies of the Reich' of their fundamental human rights. People had no choice but to grow accustomed to the gradual loss of freedoms they had previously taken for granted.

Among numerous strictures, Anka's family car was taken. A commissioner appointed by the Reich took over the factory of Kauder & Frankl and threw Anka's parents out of their apartment. They were allowed to move into Ruzena's villa in the garden with her and Peter while the authorities decided what to do with them. Whenever Anka went home, that was where she stayed too. Then the family's assets were frozen and they were forbidden to withdraw more than 1,500 crowns per week from their own bank account. Their citizenship was taken away and they were only allowed in segregated areas of restaurants and a few hotels.

In Prague, Jews were banned from using public baths and swimming pools and from entering the popular cafés that lined the River Vltava. Pushed to the back of the second car on the city's crowded trams, they were also prevented from owning bicycles, cars or wireless radios.

Denied access to the university, Anka's studies came to an end after just one year – which she always joked was a blessing in disguise, as she'd done very little work because she'd been enjoying herself too much. There was little enjoyment to be had under

German occupation, however. 'It got worse and worse but as you get used to everything in life, so you got used to that as well,' she said. 'First we were not allowed this and then we had to give up that and you just did it. We talked about it . . . and there was a possibility to get out but unless you knew what was waiting for you it did seem very difficult to let everything go and leave everything behind for the unknown.'

The one Nazi measure that hurt Anka the most was that she was banned from going to the cinema. This seemed to her to be an unnecessary torment to someone who loved the movies. So when a film came out that she desperately wanted to see, she decided to go anyway. Setting off without telling anyone, she was – she admitted later – 'a complete fool'. As she sat on her own deep in the middle of the cinema, the screening was halfway through when it suddenly flickered to a stop. The houselights came on and members of the Gestapo burst in to check everybody's identity papers, row by row. As the Nazis drew closer Anka sat frozen to the spot, terrified of how they would react to the 'J' stamped in her documents. Looking around frantically, she wondered if she should try to make a run for it but decided that would be worse. Then suddenly the Gestapo stopped one row in front of her and, apparently bored, abandoned their inspection.

Allowing herself to breathe, she sat in her seat until the credits rolled in order not to draw attention to herself. When she told friends what she'd done, they were appalled and told her, 'They could have shot you!' To her dying day she couldn't remember the film she'd risked her life to see, but it may well have been *Gone with the Wind* – which had been one of her favourite books as a teenager and was released in 1939. It was a movie she watched so often after the war that she could quote entire passages from it, and which had such significance later.

As the restrictions on Jews tightened still further and more people made plans to flee, Anka and a girlfriend were approached in a café by some English journalists. 'My friend said, "I'm going to marry one of them!" and she was married within six weeks,' Anka recalled. 'He had a friend and I was introduced to him and in ten minutes he said, "Marry me?" I thought he was insane and funny but I wasn't interested at all.' Flattered, she turned him down, still not appreciating the chance to escape from the danger she was in.

Instead, she became apprenticed to her aunt as a milliner at her salon in the city's historic Black Rose Passage and her social life continued behind closed doors. It wasn't mere bravado that kept her from fleeing, however. She had one other very good reason for staying in Prague. In November 1939 her cousin had introduced her to Bernhard 'Bernd' Nathan, a devastatingly good-looking German Jew who'd fled Berlin in 1933 after Hitler came to power. Among the hundreds of thousands German Jews who'd emigrated by 1939, he'd mistakenly believed Prague was far enough away to be safe. His younger brother Rolf had fled to Holland and then Switzerland, where he joined the US Army and remained safe. His younger sister Marga also escaped to Australia and survived.

Bernd Nathan

Born in 1904, Bernd was thirteen years older than Anka. An architect and interior designer, he worked at the famous Barrandov Film Studios, one of the largest and best-equipped in Europe and a place that would become known as 'the Hollywood of the East'. With his own workshop and staff, he had a lucrative sideline in furnishing shops. He also worked for Nazis, who had no idea he was Jewish and commissioned him to equip their bars, nightclubs and coffee houses.

Bernd considered himself German first and Jewish second. He was not at all religious, and as German was his native tongue he was better able to flout the restrictions and pretend to be Aryan. 'He looked like them . . . and he spoke like them because he was from Berlin,' Anka said. 'They kept on inviting him to come out with them . . . We were doing rather well, even under Hitler.'

Bernd's father Louis had won Germany's highest military award – the Iron Cross (1st Class) – in the First World War and was *kriegsblind* (war-blind) by mustard gas, something that gave him a heroic status. In spite of his disability, Louis was a womaniser and eventually divorced his elegant wife Selma – Bernd's mother. It was Selma who ensured that her eldest son received a private income of 2,000 crowns a month.

With his captivating looks, Bernd was a natural ladies' man like his father and had a way about him that melted women's hearts. When Anka first spotted him at a swimming pool in Barrandov, hers did a backflip. 'I thought he was the best-looking man I'd ever seen in my whole life.' A few weeks later, they were formally introduced at one of the nightclubs he'd recently refitted. 'It was love at first sight,' she said of the handsome architect with the light brown hair, dazzling blue eyes and ready smile who was brought to her table. 'We got to know each other and we clicked and . . . behaved like complete idiots.'

After what she described as 'a whirlwind romance', they were wed within a year, on Wednesday, 15 May 1940, eight months after the start of the war. Anka had just turned twenty-three and Bernd, still listed by the authorities as a German immigrant, was thirty-six. 'Hitler had reigned over Czechoslovakia practically from the Munich Agreement,' she said. 'Even then we didn't realise the deadly danger we were in.'

Bernd and Anka at their wedding, 1940

Their simple wedding took place at the German *Oberlandrat* or regional office in Prague, next to the art deco Grand Café Slavia. It was attended by just two witnesses. As Jews weren't allowed to own gold or diamonds, Anka's engagement ring was a pretty rectangular amethyst in a silver setting, along with a plain wedding band. In a hat and dark suit over a crisp white blouse and with a shell comb in her hair, Anka posed with her besuited husband for photographs. Carrying a spray of lily-of-the-valley, she was beaming with joy.

She only plucked up the courage to contact her parents in rural Třebechovice to inform them of her marriage the following day. They were not at all pleased, chiefly because Bernd was German and they worried that this might cause her unnecessary trouble. Even when they met him, they didn't particularly like him. Anka's mother thought he was a philanderer and claimed to see 'straight through him and out the other side'.

The day they were married, Holland surrendered to the Nazis. Twelve days later the Allies had to evacuate their troops from the beaches of Dunkirk in France. On 28 May, Belgium surrendered. On 10 June, Norway followed suit and Italy declared war on Britain and France. Almost a month to the day after they took their vows, Paris fell. Then began what they dreaded most of all – resettlement transports.

SS *Obersturmbannführer* Adolf Eichmann set himself up in a requisitioned Jewish house in Prague to oversee the Central Office for Jewish Emigration. He demanded multiple transportations (to the Dachau concentration camp) by 1940 and if the community elders didn't comply, he threatened to have his troops clear Prague of three hundred Jews a day.

The world they had once known was changing beyond all recognition.

Deeply in love, the newlyweds moved into Bernd's airy apartment high in the eaves above a synagogue in U Staré Školy or Old Synagogue Street. It had a cupola and along one wall was a curved glass window – like in an artist's studio – that was impossible to black out for night-time safety. Without a curtain, they'd sit by candlelight after curfew and listen to their favourite music on a phonograph, or enjoy the harmonies wafting up from the prayer ceremonies below.

Snuggling up in the roof was, Anka said, 'terribly romantic'. With his flair for interior design, Bernd had decorated the apartment beautifully. They were surrounded by furniture he'd made, including a clock with a lovely chime and a pretty carved face. He'd also hung some pale apple green silk curtains, which Anka considered wonderfully indulgent.

Thanks to her allowance, she had a housemaid who made 'marvellous' doughnuts that Bernd especially enjoyed, and whenever they went out she had a choice of good clothes plus her pick of hats from her aunt's shop.

Having been prevented from leaving the city without a special permit, Anka hadn't seen her family in more than a year when in June 1941 she received the news that her much-loved older brother Tonda had died of a brain aneurism. He was thirty-three and had suffered a stroke two weeks earlier. Praying that no one would ask to see her documents, she travelled by train to attend his funeral and console her grieving parents, especially her mother, who had sat like a sentinel by Tonda's bedside for two weeks and was devastated at the loss of a second son.

'[My brother] was the first dead person I'd seen and looking at my mother was unforgettable – how she had to watch him die. That I don't wish on anybody.' As they sat quietly in the family home after the burial, the atmosphere was deeply melancholy. Anka's father Stanislav was even quieter than usual. Her older sisters Zdena and Ruzena were there, along with Zdena's husband Herbert Isidor and Ruzena's son Peter, but there was no joy in their reunion.

All of a sudden German soldiers banged on the door and then flung it back against its hinges before marching in uninvited. A neighbour had tipped them off that Jews lived there, so they started ransacking the place and opening cupboards and drawers. Anka's mother Ida had an ample bosom, just like her youngest daughter, and she quietly stuffed the family cash into her brassiere when the Germans' backs were turned. Then, quite calmly, the grieving woman asked her unexpected guests if they'd like some coffee and cake. Surprised, they said yes, sat down, and had a perfectly polite conversation with the family they were supposed to be terrorising.

Flirting with Anka, the young soldiers asked why she spoke such good German, so she confessed that she was married to an architect from Berlin living in Prague. They joked that they should drive her home and dump her in his bed. Their faces suddenly serious, they warned her never to risk coming to see her family without a permit again and then they left – without arresting her. It was another lucky escape.

Back in Prague, people were increasingly wary of what might

happen next. Hitler had declared that all Jews must be eliminated from the Protectorate. Faced with the threat of deportation, they learned to trust nobody and keep their own counsel. People hid or hoarded as many valuables as they could and many still tried to get out of the country, though rumours abounded that those who'd fled were now living unhappily in strange lands where they had no funds, couldn't speak the language, and felt unwanted.

Yet again, Anka had a chance to escape. She and Bernd heard through friends that it was possible to get out by train across Siberia to Shanghai, where the occupying Japanese had unexpectedly welcomed 23,000 Jews from across Europe and given them sanctuary in a ghetto. Still the couple hesitated before finally electing not to go. When Germany invaded Russia in June 1941, they lost their chance but were again relieved.

The people who'd offered to help them weren't the only ones who went out of their way to save Jews. An international group of multi-racial sympathisers had already helped entire families, and especially young children to escape to safer Great Britain in what became known as the *Kindertransports*. A similar programme entitled The One Thousand Children transported some 1,400 children to the United States between 1934 and 1945. An estimated 10,000 Jewish and other children from across Europe were rescued in this way when the transports were stopped. For those who could no longer be helped, the future looked increasingly bleak.

The synagogue above which Anka and Bernd had lived so cosily was closed, so they were forced to vacate their apartment and move to another in an old house in the district of Jindřišská. Still, Anka made the most of their two unheated rooms with a little kitchenette. 'The anti-Jewish rules meant we weren't allowed to do this or that, but it was all bearable,' she said, describing the restrictions as 'pinpricks' on their happiness. The regulations tightened 'very cleverly' but they continued to endure the changes. 'People took it and kept on saying, "If it doesn't get any worse ..." We had to give up radios and that was bad, but one could still read the newspapers . . . you found something else . . . You never know how far you can go – lower and lower.'

When all Czech Jews over the age of six were instructed to sew a yellow Star of David to each of their outer garments in September 1941, everyone was apprehensive about how non-Jews might react to them in the street. There had already been numerous incidents of Jews being randomly picked on, arrested or beaten, and with a star marking them as social outcasts there would be no chance to hide.

The first time Anka donned her star she deliberately chose her smartest outfit – a dark green tartan skirt and a rust-coloured suede jacket – to set it off as an accessory. She said that of all the anti-Jewish measures, the star worried her least of all. 'I felt very proud of my yellow star and thought, "If they want to mark me, they can mark me." I couldn't care less. I put on my best clothes. I did my hair, and I went out proudly with my head up and not crawling about. That was my attitude.' The people she met ignored her new emblem. Nobody spat at her or was rude to a young woman full of self-confidence who refused to be bowed or cowed by it.

So much so that when she met a friend one day, bent over double and 'creeping along the pavement' trying to hide her star, she told her crossly, 'Why give them such satisfaction? . . . Stand up straight! Be proud to be Jewish. So, we have to wear a star? So what? Don't let them grind you down.'

Once when Bernd had a Gentile friend called Otto visiting from Germany, he decided to show him the sights of Prague after curfew. He removed his star and told Anka to do the same, so that they could all go out together. 'If anyone stops us, keep quiet and let us do the talking,' he said, because he and Otto both spoke *Hochdeutsch* (High German), the equivalent of BBC English. They were never challenged, but the experience frightened them too much to ever try it again.

By then, most of the city's Jews had been forced out of the best areas and into tenements. They were banned from working in the arts, the theatre or the film industry and Bernd could no longer risk making furniture for the Germans. Unemployed and trapped in Prague, the couple lived on Anka's allowance and whatever her aunt could pay her for making hats.

In September 1941, SS *Obergruppenführer* Reinhard Heydrich, the head of the Gestapo, was named acting *Reichsprotektor* of Bohemia and Moravia and the atmosphere changed almost overnight. Within less than a month 5,000 men, women and children under his 'protection' had been rounded up and sent to the Łódź ghetto. Among them were Anka's aunt and her family, none of whom ever returned. 'That is when we started to get ready and prepare ourselves for something we couldn't define – something nobody reckoned with ... We thought people were just panicking ... We didn't know they were sending people to their death on a conveyor belt.'

After a lull of a few weeks, Bernd received a notification from the Nazi-appointed *Judische Gemeinde* (Jewish Community) in Prague assigning him a number and informing him to report two days later to an assembly point in the *Veletržni Palác* or old Trade Fair Palace building, renamed by the Germans the *Messepalast*. It was in the district of Holešovice, not far from the mainline Praha-Bubny railway station.

It was November 1941.

His time had come.

Anka's beloved Bernd was among a thousand young men who were to be transported away from his wife and their happiness. It was hopeless to resist.

Those who arranged the *Umsiedlung* (resettlement) assured this latest consignment that they were 'pioneers' being sent north to set up a 'model ghetto' in the Czech garrison town of Terezín, a short train ride away. Built by Emperor Joseph II and named after his mother Maria Theresa, Terezín comprised two impregnable fortresses surrounded by high walls, ramparts and a moat. Designed – prophetically – in a shape similar to the Star of David and covering a little over one square kilometre, it would be a perfect holding pen. The Germans, who'd already set up a Gestapo prison in the town inside what was known as the *Kleine Festung* (Small Fortress), reinstated Terezín's Austrian name of Theresienstadt.

Losing Bernd to the unknown was a horrifying prospect but at least Terezín was still in Czechoslovakia and not 'East', which they all dreaded without being certain why. 'It was only fifty miles from Prague so it was still "home" . . . and that was better than being sent out of the country,' Anka said. 'I didn't want him to go and I didn't want to go but they could do with us what they wanted.'

Heydrich had originally conceived the idea of setting up a ghetto for Czech Jews in the protectorate of Bohemia and Moravia in order to placate growing international concern that Jews were being mistreated at the hands of the Germans. In September more than 33,000 Jews had been lined up and shot dead by the Nazis in Kiev, and in Auschwitz doctors had tested the gas chambers for the first time. News of these developments was kept strictly secret, but rumours were harder to control.

In the coming months Heydrich was to announce that Terezín would be open to the '*Prominenten*' – wealthy German and Austrian Jews over sixty-five, including any disabled or decorated war veterans, and anyone of sufficient social standing to encourage outside scrutiny. Hailed 'as a gift' from the Führer to the Jews 'to prepare them for a life in Palestine', the new ghetto was sited in a pretty pastoral landscape against a backdrop of the purple Bohemian mountains. It was designed to be largely autonomous, with SS supervision – for as long as it suited them.

But first, the ghetto had to be made ready for the expected arrivals. The Nazis demanded that 3,000 able-bodied men and women aged between eighteen and thirty-five report for *Aufbaukommando* (construction detail). Sent in three batches of 1,000 each, they were to help transform the run-down garrison designed to house 7,000 men into a camp that could hold an expected

100,000 Jews. The Nazis promised that if these first few pioneers did a good job, they would never be sent on anywhere else.

Bernd, as a skilled carpenter, was ideal material for the pioneer list. He and his wife knew that there was no way of escaping the summons. 'One simply obeyed,' she said. When he was told that in his allotted fifty kilograms of luggage he could take pots, pans and warm clothing, they both hoped that this meant he'd be labouring outdoors and could cook for himself. Swallowing her tears, Anka helped him pack. What to take though? Should he use up the limited baggage allowance with luxuries, books and his tools, or would it be better to take canned food or medicines? Would he need a bedroll, and how about some of their favourite records?

After a last bittersweet night together, Anka eventually waved her husband goodbye, quietly confident that she'd see him again soon. Bernd Nathan left Prague on the second of two transports of the construction detail from Praha-Bubny railway station on Friday, 28 November 1941. Soon afterwards, his young wife received a similar notification to report for transportation. 'I was delighted I was going and I was sure that I would see him. It never occurred to me that I wouldn't.'

On a frosty December morning, with her best handbag, hat, and a small suitcase, she handed over the keys to their flat to her maid and asked her to keep their most precious belongings safe there. These included all her family photographs, their furniture, curtains, and Bernd's clock. Then she joined the disorderly progression of Jews heading for the *Veletržni Palác*. Instead of taking something 'necessary and useful' like tinned fish or packet soup, Anka carried a large hatbox tied with string. In it were three dozen of her maid's delicious sugar-coated doughnuts, Bernd's favourite treat.

Before long, she found herself inside the dilapidated six-storey building that had once housed trade fairs. Each floor was crammed with hundreds of men, women and children, all jostling each other and vying for space on the dirty floor. There were limited and already stinking lavatories and only a little food and water, which

was served in mess tins. Czech marshals with armbands shepherded them into groups and handed out lettered transport
numbers that had to be written on suitcases, pinned or sewn to
bedrolls and clothing, and hung from a string around each trans-
portee's neck.

Everyone seemed fascinated by Anka, who – amidst the chaos,
noise and heat – was beautifully dressed in her finest green suit and
a hat. As people around her became neglectful of their appearance
in a place where it was impossible to look after themselves, the
young bride kept brushing her hair and reapplying her make-up.
They were even more intrigued when she knelt on the floor in her
fine stockings to use her eyelash curlers. 'I just wanted to look my
best for the man I loved.'

After three sleepless days and nights locked in the building,
trying to sleep curled up on the floor, even Anka almost gave up
trying to look presentable. More and more people arrived, although
there was no room for them. Her box of doughnuts became soggier
and heavier, and still she resisted the temptation to eat its contents
or give it up. Eventually, they were mustered into columns and
marched the thirty minutes or so to the railway station. On the
pavements stood Jews and Gentiles, silently watching them go and
wondering who'd be next. Unable to witness the humiliating spec-
tacle, many turned away in shame and embarrassment, their cheeks
wet with tears.

The route was lined with scores of young Nazi officers. Anka was
accompanied by a girlfriend named Mitzka, who pleaded with one
of them to help Anka with her hatbox, which was in danger of slip-
ping from her arms. Only just out of his teens, the baby-faced
soldier snapped, '*Es ist scheiss egal ob die Schachtel mitkommt*' ('I
couldn't give a shit if that box comes or not'). His words sent a
shiver down Anka's spine as she sensed that it wouldn't matter
either way.

The train to Terezín pulled second-class carriages into which its
1,000 passengers were inhumanely forced for transportation to

Bohušovice nad Ohří station on the main line north from Prague. From there they had to march two and a half kilometres to the ghetto, trudging through snow and past frozen fields, flanked by a cordon of armed Czech and SS guards. The heavier bags were loaded onto wooden carts by a special transport squad pulled by young men, but most of the luggage – especially hatboxes – had to be carried, and 'on the double'.

Terezín, with its imposing redbrick ramparts and impenetrable perimeter walls, loomed vast and sprawling ahead of them. 'It was well suited to the purpose the Germans wanted it for,' Anka said. Behind the high wooden fencing and menacing rings of barbed wire, the town itself was extremely dilapidated but still rather handsome, with a symmetrical grid of wide boulevards around a grand central square called the *Marktplatz* (marketplace). To begin with, the area was out of bounds for Jews and covered incongruously by a circus tent that hid a production line in which slave labourers filled engine parts with anti-freeze. The surrounding streets were lined with crumbling four-storey barracks, ideal for swallowing huge numbers of people, with street after street of smaller houses, garages and stables beyond.

Within minutes of passing through one of the four main gates that separated them from the rest of the world, the transportees arrived in an outer courtyard to be counted, catalogued and searched by German guards and the one hundred or so Czech gendarmes or police. These early newcomers were allowed to keep most of their belongings and allocated housing by the ghetto's Jewish administrators.

Men were separated from their wives and billeted in eleven *Kaserne* (garrisons), all named after German cities such as Hamburg, Dresden and Magdeburg, while children were placed in *Kinderheime* or children's homes. In dusty, unheated buildings infested with vermin, they were placed in three-tier bunks twenty to a room and given palliasses, musty straw mattresses, to lie on in a space of precisely 1.6 square metres each. There were no cupboards, so people stashed their belongings under the bunks or hung their clothes from nails. Wet washing was strung between bunks, never to properly dry. As in the occupied world beyond, all were subject to restrictions and a curfew.

Bunks in the Magdeburg barracks, Terezín

Anka was young, strong, healthy and optimistic when she arrived in Terezín on Sunday, 14 December 1941. Her initial reaction to her crowded first-floor room was that the place 'wasn't too bad' and that they could survive. They had a pump that brought (polluted) water from a well, cooking facilities, latrines, kitchens, and a basic system of administration. After making enquiries, she found out that Bernd was in the all-male Sudeten barracks in the western bastion, not too far away. Just as she was carving out a space for herself, a few girlfriends already living in the ghetto found her and Mitzka and cried, 'You can't stay here!' They grabbed her things and moved her to their room of just twelve in the Dresden barracks so that they could all be together. Surrounded by such friends, Anka felt as if she was on an adventure.

Best of all, later that night she was reunited with Bernd when the men were given special passes and allowed into their section to welcome their wives. Triumphant, she was finally able to present him with the well-travelled doughnuts, which were by then stale and soggy. 'He still ate them happily!'

Nobody was allowed out of their barracks unless they had a signed permit or a police escort, but just as Anka and Bernd had flouted the laws in Prague, so they did now. Punishments included imprisonment in the ghetto jail or floggings, but the couple still managed to find ways of meeting. By each discovering where the other would be working and making short risky detours, they were able to spend a few clandestine moments together.

The *Ältestenrat* or Jewish Elders placed in overall charge of the alphabetically lettered streets within the fortress walls allocated jobs for every person over fourteen. Hundreds worked an average seventy-hour week on construction, in the kitchens, the laundry or the administrative offices. Others made Nazi uniforms or clothes for German civilians. Some had the unenviable job of cleaning the latrines or were formed into disinfecting brigades to try to reduce the risks of infection. Within a year, bricklayers were set to work building a crematorium for the hundreds who were expected to die, even though cremation defied the Jewish faith, which considers it a desecration of the body and decrees that burial only is allowed.

Bernd – assigned to the carpentry division – was given the task of building more bunks, as well as of transforming derelict barracks and converting houses. He was also signed up to be a *Ghettowache* (ghetto guard), a job envied by many because of its special privileges.

Anka wasn't assigned a job at first and then she became too ill to work. She broke out in a rash and came down with scarlet fever that put her in quarantine for six weeks. When she finally recovered she was given a job in the department responsible for handing out milk, bread and potatoes after tearing coupons from people's ration cards. 'I was standing with a bucket ... and giving everybody a ladle-ful of milk,' she said. Her position meant that she was able to barter for an extra piece of bread or a vegetable to try to add flavour to the watery grey soup they were given every day.

It was while dishing out the milk that she first came to know the conductor Karel Ančerl, his wife and son. Ančerl was later to help organise music events in the ghetto and became the leader of the Terezín String Orchestra. 'I happened to give him more milk than I should have – for the child ... I liked them and they liked me and we became friends ... If anybody had caught me I would have paid for it.'

In the coming months transports continued to arrive – at their height they brought in another thousand people every third day. Sixty thousand of the old, young, sick and hungry filled the over-crowded garrisons – an influx that placed impossible demands on the kitchens and the ancient sewage systems. The rationed water in the ghetto was contaminated and had to be boiled. Inmates were only allowed to wash their crusty clothes every six weeks. Holes were broken through the ceilings to utilise valuable loft space, damp catacombs beneath the ramparts opened up, even the stables were converted.

The latest influx were in a pitiful state and many died within days of arrival. They were poorly equipped for transportation in rickety trains and not at all prepared for what confronted them. The stink of rotting human waste pervaded everything and there was a dismal greyness about the place.

The trains that arrived between September and December 1942 disgorged the crumpled figures of Anka's parents Stanislav and Ida, her sister Zdena and her husband Herbert Isidor, and her nephew Peter. They had been transported from Hradec Králové, the town where Anka had gone to school. Peter's mother, Anka's sister

Ruzena, was sent to a Czech internment camp at Svatoborice as punishment for her husband Tom becoming a 'traitor' by fleeing abroad. Separated from her son, who'd remained with her parents, she became very despondent, and by the time she was sent to join them in Terezín she had virtually lost interest in life.

Then Anka's parents-in-law Louis and Selma, who were divorced, arrived separately. Louis, sixty-four, came first; then his ex-wife arrived from Westerbork, a camp in Holland established largely to accommodate Dutch Jews. Selma was accompanied by her second husband, who (much to Bernd's embarrassment) was younger than him. The Nathans had never met their daughter-in-law before and the first words Selma spoke to Anka – referring to the private allowance she'd had from her father – were, 'You know Bernd only married you for your money, don't you?' It was an inauspicious start.

By the time further relatives arrived, including the parents and brother of Anka's cousin Olga (who was safe at first because she'd married a Gentile), the young bride found that she had no less than fifteen mouths to feed daily. Selma fully expected her new daughter-in-law to take care of her, her husband and her ex-husband, as well as a woman who cared for him. There was also an elderly aunt who depended on her completely for food and became so afraid of starvation that she would wait up for her every night in the hope of a little extra something.

'It was jolly!' Anka joked, even though all she could find for them to eat was an 'inedible dark grey mess' of boiled barley with the consistency of wallpaper paste. 'I seemed to spend my entire life going around with my cauldron or cooking pot, desperately trying to find things to cook ... for my aunt and my uncle, my mother-in-law and my father-in-law. I felt I had to support them by hook or by crook ... If they'd had to live only on what they were given they would have starved.' Many did. Her sisters were young, so they would have managed, but not her parents, especially her seventy-three-year-old father Stanislav – 'such a gentleman' – who never adjusted to having to sleep on a cold stone floor with other men his age. He became so dependent on his sixty-year-old wife Ida that she couldn't even leave him to get a job, which would have meant more food for them both. 'In the camp [Mother] was always cheerful . . . my father would have died the next week if it hadn't been for her. He clung to her all his life . . . but in the camp he wouldn't let her out of his sight.'

As well as milk and a few basic vegetables and grains, the ghetto had a canteen. So young and old alike stood in line at 7 a.m., noon and 7 p.m. with aluminium plates, mugs or pots to receive a small piece of bread plus a ladleful of watery coffee or soup. Those who were assigned hard labour – the *Schwerarbeiter* – were given the largest portions, while regular workers had medium-sized rations, and the *Nichtarbeiter* or non-workers (mostly the old) were put on a starvation diet.

'From the bottom, please?' the hungriest would plead, hoping for something substantial. Anyone recovering from an illness was given a special ticket which allowed them a slightly larger allowance, so many feigned or prolonged their symptoms in order to get more. Whatever their status, the food they were allocated was never enough; hunger became a constant torture and the struggle to find food a daily chore. Many became listless and depressed. Destiny had forced once-proud people from beautiful homes and prosperous lives into unwanted intimacy with vermin-infested strangers. They had nothing in common but Jewish blood. Given no other choice but to breathe in air thick with the smell of unwashed bodies, fear and hunger reduced them to a bitter existence.

New jobs were handed out every day, along with ration books and basic provisions plus a few root vegetables – many of them rotten. These were supplemented at first by items including salami or canned goods that arrived in the mail from well-wishers back home. Friends and family also sent cash, which was immediately pocketed by the Germans and swapped for coupons or fake 'ghetto money' which could be used on the black market.

The men did most of the hard labour while the women tended to the health and welfare of young and old. Both sexes were assigned to the *Landwirtschaft* agricultural division, which was responsible for growing vegetables and keeping chickens for the Nazis, as well as sorting the potatoes, onions and root vegetables that the prisoners were allowed. A small hospital was established to deal with the many cases of pneumonia, scarlet fever, sepsis, typhus and scabies, and there were makeshift schools for the children.

Although they were permanently hungry and it was so cold in winter that they had to chip ice from the inside of the windows, Terezín's early residents remained stoical and were secretly grateful that it wasn't worse. Not long after they'd arrived, though, something happened that made them all realise the 'grim truth' of where they were and who was in charge of their destiny. 'We were in good spirits until the executions started,' Anka said.

The Germans who formed the *Lagerkommandantur* summoned the Jewish elders and a few select witnesses to assemble in the square near the Aussig barracks where gallows had been erected. Then they publicly hanged a group of nine young men who'd 'insulted German honour' by trying to smuggle 'unauthorised correspondence' to their families. Further hangings followed, including those of seven young men who were executed for a variety of minor misdemeanours like the theft of sweets and the possession of cigarettes.

Shaken, Anka said, 'There were about six punishments like this and that brought us back down to earth with a bang and made us realise that it wouldn't be easy to survive. From then on we started to be much more careful and worried ourselves sick because we didn't know what was going to happen.'

As an 'avalanche' of people continued to arrive from Germany and Austria, the regulations passed by the Nazi command became increasingly stringent. A fresh wave of prohibitions forbade the inmates from being in certain parts of the ghetto at certain times of day or from doing everyday activities. More fences and security barriers were erected and sentries posted. Main streets had to be kept clear and people could only use the back alleyways. Those who infringed the rules could be beaten or shot. Others were taken to the Small Fortress, rarely to return.

To save electricity, people were often confined to barracks for *Lichtsperre* – lights out – and could only undress by touch or read by the light of candles, which were in short supply. Lying on a dirty mattress, itching from bites, the air around her unendurable, Anka could not help but recall the romantic candlelit nights she and Bernd used to enjoy in their Prague apartment. There was also a plague of fleas and bedbugs to contend with, as well as the gnawing hunger. Once winter came it was a struggle to find wood to light a stove in order to heat a room or warm food. Rations of coal were only allowed if the temperature dropped below zero. 'People started to die like flies because of malnutrition, bad housing, lack of washing facilities,' Anka said. 'It was fatal for old people.'

In this place of famine, the food situation became unbearable for many and animal instincts took over. Survival often depended on how accomplished a thief one became. 'Everybody who could, stole,' Anka said. 'If anyone tells you that they didn't steal, don't believe them.' Those who worked in the kitchens hid potatoes or even peelings which they later sold or bartered. Anka learned how to make soup from nettles and constantly took the opportunity of grabbing something from the kitchens, and then trying to exchange a single blackened potato for a soggy onion.

Her luck changed once when she accidentally received a parcel of Portuguese sardines destined for another woman named Nanny Nathan who had perished. Anka pointed out the error to the Jewish post office, but was told she could keep the parcel anyway. 'I gladly accepted it but we had so many sardines that we couldn't even eat them any more. My husband would ask, "Sardines again?" . . . One gets so ungrateful!'

Even though so many had died, there was never enough room for newcomers – especially those expected from Austria and Germany –

so in January 1942 the transports East began, each made up of between one and five thousand souls. As in Łódź and the other ghettos, people ran around trying to beg or bribe officials to remove their loved ones from the lists, but it often had little effect and they watched their numbers melt away. The first deportees from Terezín were sent initially to a ghetto in Riga, Latvia, then to ghettos in occupied Poland, but few had any idea where they were going. 'It was just dreadful when you saw those people on stretchers, old and incapable of going from here to there, being transported God knows where ... Thousands of people arrived only to be sent further East in a few days ... Thousands came, thousands died, thousands went off. 1942 came and went. 1943 carried on in the same way.'

The transports became a kind of terrorism – a threat that overshadowed everything. Nobody knew what the next day would bring and the fear ground down their already sinking morale. Of the 140,000 Jews sent to Terezín, an estimated 33,000 people were to die and more than 88,000 were sent to death camps as Jewish life in Czechoslovakia was all but eradicated. Fifteen thousand were children, including 1,260 who'd been promised safe passage to Switzerland and had volunteers to escort them, almost all of whom were executed in Auschwitz.

The 'pioneers', like Anka and Bernd, still clung to the hope that the promise made to them meant they would avoid such a fate, but they had no guarantees. 'You never knew when you might be sent or at what interval,' she said. 'Today? Next week? Next month? All we knew was that "East" meant something dreadful and everyone tried to avoid such a transport.'

As conditions worsened, the Gestapo sold imaginary plots of land and 'admission rights' for privileged German Jews to move to Terezín, which they variously dubbed a country resort with free housing and medical care, a *Reichsalterheim* or state old people's home, and a *Bad* or spa. Many paid extra for a room 'with a view' or a penthouse apartment, not appreciating until it was too late that they had been swindled. Those who arrived expecting a pleasant resort where they could safely sit out the war were shocked by the conditions. Imagining a rich social life with like-minded people, they brought tiaras and top hats, jewels and sequinned gowns, which quickly became crumpled and stained. Instead they found grubby scenes of Dickensian hopelessness punctuated only by the ever-present fear of what lay at the far end of the railway tracks.

'That was the first time I came across old people who should have been in [a] hospital ... who travelled I don't know how long and we had to take care of them. It was just inhuman. There wasn't any room for them,' said Anka. 'They didn't know where to stay ... they were packed into the lofts of those little houses that were made into dormitories ... and they had to climb up and down and they couldn't.'

Plagues of flies descended in summers that fell hot and heavy without a breath of wind. Epidemics of encephalitis, diphtheria and dysentery wiped out hundreds who lost control of their bowels and died lying in their own excrement. Wagons carried away the dead, whose bony feet stuck out beneath their shrouds. Special delousing stations were set up to disinfect clothes and belongings with insecticide.

In spite of their worsening situation, or perhaps because of it, the remaining inmates created a rich artistic life within the ghetto walls. Terezín was filled with some of Europe's finest artists, intellectuals, composers and performers who devised increasingly innovative means of warding off their growing despair. Children and adults staged plays and recitals, and were encouraged to express themselves through art and poetry. Materials were begged, borrowed or stolen, and young and old shared splinters of charcoal or the nubs of crayons to draw on pages cut from ledgers or the endpapers of books.

Their imprisonment seemed to spark a flurry of creativity. Some made collages from scraps of cardboard and cloth. One young man named Pavel Friedman wrote a poem on a flimsy piece of copy paper: 'I never saw another butterfly ... Butterflies don't live here.

In the ghetto.' He was twenty-three years old when he was sent to his death in Auschwitz. Artists who'd secretly made drawings depicting the worst conditions in the ghetto were taken to the Small Fortress to be tortured and have their fingers broken. Many were shot or sent away to concentration camps.

In spite of the constant threat of reprisals, the cultural revolution went on. Mini-exhibitions, musical reviews and concerts were secretly arranged. The impromptu theatrics began quietly in basements and barracks but became so popular that they were later staged in warehouses or exercise halls. The Jewish administration, which had to approve each performance, began to issue tickets; these became highly sought after and were often exchanged for food on the black market.

When the Germans didn't step in to crush such activities – they even allowed musical instruments – people became bolder and began to stage major productions. Architects and set designers were put to work and seamstresses enlisted to make costumes. Writers were encouraged to pen satirical plays and cabarets, including one called *Posledni Cyklista* (The Last Cyclist) by playwright Karel Švenk, which depicted a world in which people with bicycles were persecuted by inmates who'd escaped from an asylum. Sadly, it was never performed in Terezín, having been banned at the dress rehearsal by the Council of Elders for fear of reprisals. But after the war – which Švenk didn't survive – it was recreated from memory by survivors and continues to be played to audiences around the world.

Other less controversial shows were allowed to go ahead, including operas such as *Aida*, featuring famous soloists from across Europe. There were more than fifty performances of an opera for children by Hans Krasa called *Brundibar*. This was put on thanks largely to the producer František Zelenka, the most influential and innovative Czech set designer of his era. After helping to stage more than twenty plays in Terezín, including works by Shakespeare and Molière, Zelenka was to perish in Auschwitz aged forty-two.

Anka watched a memorable dress rehearsal of *The Bartered Bride*, a comic opera she'd first seen as a carefree student. Even though she thought the woman playing the bride was too old for the role, it was still 'fantastic' because of its optimism. 'When it was first composed no one knew it would be used at Terezín but in it were quite a few songs and sayings that had everything to do with being there ... There is one sentence where she asks him, "And what will happen in the end?" and he answers, "It will be all right!" ... It was so symbolic. Moments like that were unforgettable.'

For the hour or two that these performances lasted, those in the audience were no longer prisoners whose only thoughts were about food or fears for their own survival. Instead they were free to laugh and cry, feel hopeful and sad, transported as they were to happier times by music, dance and song. 'It all helped to ease the atmosphere,' Anka said. 'Through [the] arts you could let go.'

One of the most remarkable artistic achievements in Terezín was created thanks to a dedicated amateur choir under the direction of the Romanian conductor and chamber musician Rafael Schächter. Between them, this prison chorus put on no fewer than sixteen performances of Verdi's most demanding work – *Requiem*. The fiery Catholic funeral mass was learned by rote – note by note, Latin word by Latin word – in a cold, dank basement. Using only a smuggled score, one piano (with missing legs), and a cast that frequently changed as the transports wrenched more of its voices away, Schächter told his choir, 'We will sing to the Nazis what we cannot say to them.'

One of the lines in *Libera me* (Liberate me) is 'Deliver me, Lord, from eternal death ... when you will come to judge the world by fire.' Another states that 'Nothing will remain unpunished' on the Day of Reckoning. It was a defiant message of holy judgement on all sinners. Anka, who was at one performance attended by senior Nazi officials, said it was the most heartbreakingly moving thing she ever heard. When it was over, the Jews in the audience sat breathless, waiting for the Germans' reaction. Once the SS began to clap, everyone else did too, their faces wet with tears.

As part of their ongoing artistic resistance under the supervision of the *Freizeitgestaltung*, or Administration for Free Time Activities, the people of Terezín also organised lectures and classes, sewing bees and improvement programmes. If they weren't taking part in one of the artistic or educational events for their own intellectual nourishment or that of others, they were trying to upgrade their quarters.

In open defiance of the threat of death that hung over them, the Jews chose life. As part of their private rebellion, they sang, they danced, they fell in love, they married, and – desperate for love and some sort of physical contact – they tried to find comfort wherever they could.

Bernd worked in a specialist workshop and timber yard in the *Bauhof* or Block H, which was within the ramparts beyond the barbed wire. One of his jobs was to make fine furniture for the Nazi officers, just as he had done in Prague. When he finished work he would sneak into his wife's barracks to visit her. There was no privacy but neither was there any shame. They weren't the only ones who felt that way, and many couples rented private rooms from the privileged few who had access to them. Others had to make do with whatever time they could find together and, on some nights, when a few men were able to creep into the female barracks, Anka said she could feel the whole place shaking. 'We were twelve women in a room and sometimes there were twelve men who slept in there at the same time and nobody took any notice,' she said. 'It was one of the few pleasures left and it kept us alive.' It was quite a risk, but one they considered worth taking. They were young and in love, and lying together for a few hours gave them hope.

The departure of so many others on the transports, while they remained behind, convinced the couple that the Nazis' promise about the 'pioneers' being safe would be kept and that they would most likely remain in the ghetto for the duration of the war. Even though a dedicated rail spur had been built right into the heart of the ghetto in June 1943, Anka still believed – as so many did – that the war would soon end.

At twenty-six years of age and having been married for three years, Anka didn't want to wait to be a mother until she was too old, but nonetheless she and Bernd decided against having a child in the circumstances. Although it was never specifically stated, the Germans had decreed a strict segregation of the sexes and it was feared that the 'crime' of falling pregnant might be punishable by death. However, when Anka found out in the summer of 1943 that she was expecting a baby, she was secretly delighted. Her mother Ida, who by then shared the same barracks with her daughter, asked incredulously, 'How? When?' and when Anka shrugged her shoulders, Ida laughed. Anka convinced herself that perhaps the baby was meant to be. Nine months felt such a long time and anything might happen by then. Through illegal radios and gossip from the Czech police, snippets of news reached the Terezín grapevine. Sicily had been invaded, Mussolini had been ousted from power and Italy had surrendered to the Allies. There had been a mass uprising in the Warsaw ghetto and the German Ruhr had been heavily bombed. For many, it seemed that the end was finally in sight.

But it wasn't over yet. A typhoid epidemic in the ghetto killed more than a hundred people a day. The same wagons that delivered the mildewed bread were used to cart away the corpses. Coffins were in such short supply that the dead were wrapped in shrouds and stacked in corridors, and the crematorium had to cope with a thousand corpses a month.

Then in the autumn word came that Anka's sisters Ruzena and Zdena, aged thirty-six and thirty-nine, her eight-year-old nephew Peter, and her brother-in-law Herbert were to be sent East as part of a transport of 5,000 souls. Her cousin's parents would also be going, as would other family members. 'When someone you love is going on the next transport you try to move heaven and earth to save them,' Anka said. 'Obviously I tried everything without any results whatsoever. I tried to … bribe the right people … but it didn't help. It was also a dreadful risk. There were so many people who could get hold of something to bribe somebody. The Germans said a thousand people had to go and a thousand people had to go. You were lucky or you were not.'

Scores of people killed themselves, or tried to, rather than face that journey into the unknown. There were a reported 430 suicides and 252 suicide attempts in Terezín between 1941 and 1943 – most of them during the transports. Those who couldn't face leaving their loved ones jumped from windows, slashed their wrists, hanged themselves, or took overdoses of barbiturates stolen or bought from the infirmary.

One of Anka's final memories of her latest relatives to be sent away was of her elderly aunt, 'composed and coiffured', sitting on her suitcase. 'She shook hands with me and said, "So, see you soon," as if we had been meeting in the Grand Hotel in Hradec Králové . . . not "Goodbye for ever" but "See you next week!" She didn't know about the gas chambers but she knew it would be dreadful.'

Forcing a smile, Anka waved them off as they were marched to the spur line, the tramp of their thousand footsteps sending up clouds of dust. She prayed that she'd see them again soon and that they'd find enough to eat without her.

As the months passed and her belly swelled, Anka became excited at the prospect of being a mother, even though she had lost a lot of weight and had very few nutrients in her food. 'We were looking forward to our baby like mad,' she said. 'I remember being four and a half months pregnant and the baby started moving. I was sitting in an office where I was working and I felt the movement and I ran into the main office and told my boss, "It started moving!" I was beside myself. What a miracle that was!' But her joy soon turned to fear, especially as there was no further good news about the war and the transports East accelerated.

When the latest SS camp commandant, *Obersturmführer* Anton Burger, discovered that some of his prisoners were pregnant, he ordered them to immediately report their condition. To be Jewish and expecting a baby was a crime against the Reich. He decreed that every foetus under seven months be aborted. He also threatened to punish those who hid their pregnancies, along with the communities from which they came.

Anka and Bernd must have chosen not to disclose her condition until it was impossible to hide it any more. Then they were summoned to the commandant's administrative offices along with four other couples. They had no choice but to obey. There – as the angry Nazi waved a gun at them – they were each forced to sign documents agreeing to hand over their newborn babies for 'euthanasia'. In spite of her mastery of languages, Anka had no idea what that word meant and had to ask someone afterwards. When they informed her that it meant her baby would be executed after birth, she almost passed out.

'I never imagined that I would have to sign a paper giving [my baby] up to be killed. Nobody had ever heard anything about that before ... How can you sign a thing like that? But we did. They said, "*Sie unterschreiben!*" [Sign it!] and we signed ... The presence of the SS man with a revolver behind you was enough ... Of course you sign!'

In November 1943, when Anka was six months pregnant, the Germans held a census to make sure that the requests for supplies matched the remaining numbers of prisoners. As a result the entire ghetto was emptied. Bernd was in the infirmary with a fever, so he was left behind, along with the rest of the sick and any infants. Anka was evacuated from the ghetto without him and accompanied instead by her parents and 36,000 other prisoners.

Fearing the worst, they were marched in the snow by armed guards to a huge open meadow in an area known as Bohušovická Basin. From 7 a.m. to 11 p.m. they were counted and recounted, half-expecting to be shot. No one was allowed to sit or relieve themselves, so they had to go to the toilet where they stood. The cold and sleet was too much for the weakest amongst them and many fell to the ground, never to recover. When they were finally forced to run back to their barracks, Anka was enormously relieved to discover that those in the infirmary – including her husband – hadn't been murdered.

Then in December, the summons came for her elderly parents, Stanislav and Ida, to go East. Her once-proud father, the respected entrepreneur of Třebechovice who'd built a successful leather factory and provided well for his family, had been reduced to living 'like a pitiful beggar' and was suffering from ill health. An SS officer had struck him across the face, breaking his only glasses so that he could no longer see. 'That hurt me the most,' Anka said. 'He . . . became a little old Jew who hung on my mother . . . It was so terribly sad to see it because he . . . couldn't take a step without her.'

In spite of their consuming hunger and deteriorating health, however, her parents had never once 'burdened' her with complaints and remained cheerful to the last. 'When my parents went I was very upset. I said goodbye to them but I didn't realise that it was the last time I would see them. It was very short – "Goodbye, see you again". They knew I was pregnant and they took it in their stride. They had so many other things to consider and we thought that somehow we would all manage.'

Bernd also watched his mother Selma and other relatives depart. His blind father Louis was saved, he believed, because of his Iron Cross.

Neither Anka's parents nor her sisters were around when her son was born a few weeks prematurely in Terezín on 2 February 1944, a few weeks after the bombing of Berlin by the Allies. The ghetto by then had a working hospital and operating theatre with modern, sterile equipment and hundreds of qualified prisoner-doctors. Anka, who had her choice of gynaecologists and paediatricians, nevertheless went through the usual agonies of childbirth that no one could save her from. 'It hurt. I thought it was dreadful and that I would never have another child if you paid me,' she declared, although she added, 'Our little boy was gold!'

After the delivery, Anka cradled her longed-for child in the *Säuglingsheim* or infant home with the other mothers and babies, expecting him to be snatched from her at any minute. 'He was a normal baby and he had plenty of food,' she said.

She and Bernd named their son Jiri (George), which made her father-in-law very happy as he'd had a brother named George. But the Germans refused to allow any non-Jewish names, so they had to strike that out and rename him Dan – 'not Daniel but Dan'. Still no one came to take their baby away to euthanise him, and they never knew why they had been so pardoned. They were just grateful that they had.

It was only after the war, in the hidden diaries of another prisoner at Terezín named Gonda Redlich, that the mystery may have been solved. Redlich's wife Gerta, whom Anka knew, was another who was also pregnant. She and her husband were also forced to agree to 'infanticide' in November 1943. Redlich wrote poignantly in his diary that on that day 'I signed an affidavit that I would kill my child.'

In a later entry in March 1944, after the birth of his son (also named Dan), Redlich wrote to his boy: 'It was forbidden for Jews to be born, for women to give birth. We were forced to hide your mother's pregnancy. Even Jews themselves asked us to slaughter you, the fruit of our womb, because the enemy threatened to levy punishment on the community for every Jewish birth in the ghetto.' His child was saved by a 'miracle', he said, when the wife of a German officer gave birth prematurely to a stillborn baby. 'Why did they cancel the order forbidding births when you and the others were born?' he wrote. 'Jewish doctors saved the woman. Our enemies felt for the bereaved mother and allowed your mother and other mothers to give birth.'

Anka knew none of this and focused only on caring for her infant. She had some torn-up rags for nappies and enough milk to feed him with. She shared her 'good fortune' with the other pregnant women who had also given birth in the ghetto, one to twins, although three of the babies later died and one of the mothers succumbed to TB.

At a month old, though, and despite having been saved from his death sentence, Dan Nathan started to weaken. Anka said, 'He didn't look like the other babies born at the same time.' Within a few weeks her tiny firstborn developed pneumonia. He died on a Thursday – 10 April 1944. 'My little boy wasn't killed. He just wasn't strong enough,' she said. 'My little boy died in my arms. It was a natural death . . . I didn't expect him to die so it hit me when he did.'

Gonda Redlich wrote: 'A child died from among those whom the Germans permitted to be born. Just think of a mother's sorrow, who by a miracle gained a child only to lose it.'

Bernd attended a short service for his son's cremation before his ashes were placed in a little cardboard box. It was stored with thousands of other cremated remains in the ghetto columbarium until November 1944, when most were dumped in the fast-flowing River Ohře.

Memorial to the ashes of the dead scattered in the river at Terezin

Anka couldn't face the cremation. She rarely spoke of her son again. She said later, 'It was dreadful but so many dreadful things happened afterwards that one forgets it ... One gets over it somehow.' Later she asked a cousin why she couldn't mourn baby Dan and the cousin's explanation made perfect sense to her. 'We can't afford to mourn because we will all go mad.' She added, 'You started thinking about what happened and why it happened, so you had to find some way not to think about it.'

One of her favourite maxims for life came from the lips of Scarlett O'Hara in *Gone with the Wind*. It was, 'I'll think about it tomorrow.' Anka repeated that mantra again and again throughout her time in the camps. She admitted that what she called her 'Scarlett O'Hara theory' sounded 'stupid' and 'irrational' but claimed to have used it to good effect all her life. 'If I push something off when it is happening and sleep on it then perhaps the next day it will be better. Thus far it has worked ... It is a characteristic of human nature that people think they are going to survive somehow ... Those who gave up and neglected themselves physically died the sooner.'

So much had happened to systematically chip away at their reality and all sense of stability in the previous few years. There was no chance of escape and no means of controlling their own destiny. 'The way I protested was by surviving,' she said simply.

After her son's death, Anka suffered from a severe case of jaundice that almost killed her. She was placed in isolation in the infirmary, where Bernd was forbidden from visiting her. One day he picked a single flower from somewhere and showed it to her through the window. Much as she appreciated the romantic gesture, she said later that she was so hungry she would have far preferred a piece of bread. Eventually, though, Anka pulled through and was reunited with her husband once more.

In the months that followed, and as the Allies prepared to invade Europe, the first Danish Jews arrived in Terezín. Representatives from the Danish government and Danish Red Cross immediately began to press the Nazis about the whereabouts of the almost five hundred Danes, and question them about the growing rumours of mass exterminations of Jews and others in Nazi camps. The Danes, of all the occupied nations, had protested most vehemently about the Nazi treatment of the Jews and managed to save the majority of their own Jews by hiding them or helping them to safety. Those they couldn't save were monitored so closely by the Danes that the Nazis afforded them special treatment.

Anxious to quell the uproar, the Germans agreed to allow the International Red Cross, accompanied by Danish officials, to visit Terezín, but only once they had turned it into Hitler's 'showcase' camp. To clean the place up some 5,000 Jews were transported East in May 1944, including all the orphans and most of the sick, especially those with tuberculosis. A further 7,500 followed. The rest of the gaunt or sickly were hidden from view and the rougher quarters kept strictly out of bounds.

The commandant planned the precise route the handful of Red Cross delegates would take and ordered a mass beautification of the buildings along the route, whose streets were reassigned pretty names such as 'Lake Street'. Under his *Verschönerungsaktion* (embellishment action), fresh turf was laid, roses planted, and park benches brought in. Everything was painted, including meaningless signs that read 'school' or 'library'. Flowers filled new window boxes, and playgrounds, a merry-go-round, bandstand, community centre and sports pitch were created. Those barracks to be visited were decorated and entire streets of gaily painted shops were opened, 'selling' goods seized from the prisoners' belongings.

Threatened with death unless they complied, the prisoners rehearsed what to do, where to be and how to behave. They were instructed to wear their best clothes and make sure they were well groomed. Deliveries of fresh vegetables and newly baked bread were carefully orchestrated and timed. The Red Cross visit took place on 23 June 1944.

The Ministry of Propaganda of the Third Reich, under the direction of Joseph Goebbels, had the six-hour visit filmed and added to other stage-managed images intended to be broadcast around the world in a film titled *Der Führer schenkt den Juden eine Stadt* (The Führer Gives the Jews a City). The carefully edited clips, set to upbeat music such as Offenbach's 'Infernal Galop', the most popular music for the Parisian can-can, captured images of healthy-looking young men and women working outside the ghetto in forges, potteries or art studios. They were shown making handbags, sewing or doing woodwork, before walking arm in arm back to the ghetto to enjoy leisure activities such as reading, knitting, playing cards, or attending recitals and lectures. There were shots of an energetic football match, scenes of old couples chatting on park benches, and sun-tanned children eating bread thickly smeared with butter – the first they'd seen in years.

Facetiously, communal showers were shown with naked men soaping themselves down. Men, women and children were seen watering the commandant's vegetables in the walled garden. Anka and Bernd were two of many Jews filmed sitting in a Viennese-style *Kaffeehaus* drinking 'coffee'. As the ciné cameras whirred, they did as they were told, smiling into the lens and sipping from mugs filled with oily water served by smiling waitresses in white aprons. In what proved to be the recording of a remarkable moment in history, Red Cross officials were also filmed sitting alongside senior SS officers from Berlin enjoying Verdi's *Requiem* – performed by a greatly reduced choir.

Everyone in the ghetto prayed that their visitors would see beyond the charade, ask probing questions or demand to divert from their designated route. It wasn't to be. The event was a triumph for the Nazis. Dr Maurice Rossel, the head of the International Red Cross delegation, stated in his report, 'In general, nobody who has arrived here will be deported any further.' Effectively giving the Nazis an alibi against all charges of mass murder, he and his colleagues announced that the Jewish quarters were 'relatively good' and 'comfortable' with rugs and carpets. They said that there was nourishment, clothing, a postal service and culture, and that the youth homes were of a 'remarkable educational value'. He concluded: 'We were extraordinarily amazed to find in the ghetto a town which lives almost a normal life. We had expected to find worse.' He stated that his report would be 'a relief to many'.

The inmates knew nothing of the Red Cross report and hoped that the outside world would finally come to know of their existence. No matter how much the ghetto had been embellished, surely the delegates could see that this was still a prison occupying a square kilometre that had been cruelly severed from the rest of the world?

After the visit everything attractive or pleasurable that had been placed in the ghetto was destroyed, dismantled or taken away. Terezín and its inmates were returned to their former dilapidated state and even had their rations cut for two weeks because of the 'extra' food and luxuries they'd been allowed. Smiling children who'd been filmed on rocking horses or in theatrical productions were among 5,000 deported to Auschwitz in the days after the filming ended. They included Verdi maestro Rafael Schächter, along with the Jewish producer of the propaganda movie, and Anka's friend the conductor Karel Ančerl and his family. Schächter – who'd brought hope to thousands and played the last music many of them would ever hear – was eventually killed after surviving three camps. Ančerl survived but his wife and child didn't.

The Czech police who guarded Terezín continued to smuggle in reports from outside whenever they could, and informed the delighted prisoners that the Allies had landed at Normandy and were moving across France. 'The news spread like the wind and we thought then that we had won!' Anka said. 'And we told each other that we'd be home in a month.' Quite deliberately, she and Bernd decided to try for another baby – 'mad as we were'. She added, 'That first pregnancy wasn't planned, but it happened. My second pregnancy was planned because we thought, "Now we have been here three years . . . how long can it still take?"' Her reasoning was that if they arrived back in Prague with a baby they'd manage somehow, but if they didn't then they would have to wait until they had money and jobs, and that would take so much time they might never do it.

With numerous transports still taking people East, some of the attics in the barracks suddenly became empty, so Bernd build a secret compartment in what he called the 'hay loft' of one of the buildings where he and his wife could meet. These became known in the ghetto as *kumbalek* or cubbyholes. Later, Bernd extended the space to a private one-room apartment in which they could live. 'We adapted it for our use very prettily,' Anka said.

There was always the risk that the Germans would make one of their periodic raids and find them, but Bernd and Anka took their chances. France had been all but liberated, including Paris, and the Allies were embarking on an airborne assault on the Netherlands. The summer of 1944 was long and hot, and while many of those around them – especially the old – died from poor sanitation, disease and starvation, Anka and Bernd were happy in their stolen moments of togetherness.

It was difficult for Anka to know if she was pregnant or not, because her previous pregnancy, coupled with her illness and general lack of nutrition, had interfered with her menstrual cycle. The women called it 'prison syndrome' and it affected many in captivity. She still had no idea if she was expecting a baby when in the autumn of 1944 – as the Allies drew ever closer and entire German divisions were forced to surrender – the Nazis decided to deport most of the inhabitants of Terezín.

Fearing a rebellion, and in an act of calculated planning, the Germans first demanded the transportation of the most able-bodied men to a new camp 'somewhere near Dresden' in Germany. They declared that for the next four weeks another thousand people would be sent every other day. All the promises to the pioneers that they would be saved proved worthless as Bernd received one of the dreaded pink slips ordering him to report for a new *Aufbaukom-mando*. When the elders complained to the Germans that the pioneers had been promised immunity, they were told that all such exemptions had been 'abolished'.

Under the regulations of the ghetto, Bernd had to surrender his ration card so that his food supply would be cut off and he was expected to report for deportation within twenty-four hours. 'There was no warning that he was going away,' Anka said. 'Suddenly an order came for all men to leave for a different ghetto. We thought it would be similar to Terezín, somewhere in Germany. It might be worse but it would still be a sort of ghetto ... One didn't associate it with any catastrophe or horror.'

Nevertheless Anka fought to control her emotions once more as she helped Bernd pack a few belongings for his unknown destination. The men were assembled in one of the courtyards in the barracks and their loved ones allowed to take bitter leave of each other. After she hugged and kissed him goodbye, they promised to see each other again soon. Without knowing that his wife was pregnant, Bernd was then marched to the rail spur on the fringes of the camp and loaded onto a crowded passenger train. It was 28 September 1944, just short of three years since he'd been sent to Terezín.

Without his comforting presence, the days melded into one for Anka. Despondent, she lived in a world of sorrow, hunger and dread. With so many prisoners deported and the demands of the Nazi war machine ever more persistent, she was transferred to a factory within the ghetto where she was put to work cutting strips of processed mica laminate for aircraft spark plugs. 'They called it *Glimmer* and it came in small transparent platelets. We used very sharp knives to split it into thin layers.' This *Glimmer spalten* was considered a vital product for the Luftwaffe and safeguarded many from the transports, including Anka.

Desperately lonely and miserable in her new job, in which she could no longer acquire extra rations for herself and her one remaining relative, her blind father-in-law, Anka wondered how she would manage. Then the Nazis announced that they needed a thousand more people to work in the new German labour camp. Her friend Mitzka's name appeared on the list, along with many other friends from Prague who'd also been pioneers. Anka was exempted because of the war work to which she'd been assigned. To quell the pervasive unrest, the German high command made a further announcement that anyone could volunteer to follow their friends and family to the new camp near Dresden if they wanted to. They encouraged the hope that to be sent for useful employment would give them a guarantee that they'd be saved.

Anka's heart leapt at the news and her decision to follow Bernd was sealed. 'By then I knew I was pregnant, but my husband didn't know it ... Totally mad.' She said that, rightly or wrongly, she thought that as she had survived with Bernd in Terezín, so then could she exist in some other place, even if it was worse. She still had no idea where he was or what the conditions might be like, but she was determined to be with him regardless. 'Germany was, at least, a civilised country where one could live,' she thought, describing her decision to volunteer as 'the biggest foolishness of my life'. She and Bernd had survived three years together; they had lost their son and most of their family. She didn't believe that anything worse could happen. She prayed that they'd be reunited straight away and then put to work somewhere she might even see her parents and sisters, and that they could all remain together until the war was over.

She also feared that if she waited, she might be transported somewhere else and never find them again. She packed up her few belongings – this time with a far more practical mind than when she'd arrived in Terezín three years earlier carrying a box of doughnuts – helped by a friend who was staying behind. 'I hadn't told anyone I was pregnant,' Anka said, 'but when I packed a dress someone had made for my first pregnancy she said, "Why do you take this with you?" and I didn't answer. She said, "Oh God, you are pregnant!" and she practically fainted. She said, "Are you mad? Why would you go of your own free will?"'

A few days later, on Sunday, 1 October 1944 – not long after American troops had reached the Siegfried Line in western Germany – Anka left Terezín for good. Climbing up into crowded third-class passenger carriages, she, Mitzka and her friends were packed in 'like sardines'. As the doors were locked behind them and the blinds pulled down, the train gave a piercing whistle before moving off. Anka tried not to panic and hoped that the journey taking her to her husband would not be too long.

Her prayers were answered in as much as she did follow Bernd, just as she'd hoped. Cruelly, their train even pulled into Dresden station, which they thought meant that they'd arrived. Relieved, she and the others expected to be let out there to join the new camp and looked forward to being reunited with their loved ones. Exhausted, hungry and dehydrated, they waited and waited in the locked train until it suddenly moved off again. To their horror, the next station they stopped at was Bautzen, sixty kilometres east of Dresden. And that was when they knew that they'd been lied to. 'Slowly but surely it dawned on us where we were heading,' she said, describing seeing Polish station names as 'a bad moment' as their train clanked morosely on.

'Going East really meant only one place, which we knew nothing about but its name – Auschwitz. It was a camp: a dreadful camp. But we didn't know anything more about it.'

Anka couldn't possibly have known, but had baby Dan lived, and had she arrived with him in her arms on the infamous *Rampe* of Auschwitz II-Birkenau on that Sunday in October, she and he would almost certainly have been sent straight to the gas chambers. Instead, she was carrying a new life in her belly, its tiny heart beating against all the odds.

No stranger to hiding a pregnancy, none but Anka knew she was with child again as – after two days – the train doors were unlocked and she came face to face not with the smiling face of Bernd but with what appeared to her to be hell on earth.

# 4

# Auschwitz II-Birkenau

*Priska*

In the unearthly chaos that followed Priska's arrival at the second of the three vast camps of mass extermination known collectively as Auschwitz, the latest consignment from Slovakia were snapped at by hounds and yelled at by striped prisoner functionaries known as *Kapos* as they were pulled violently from the wagons. A grim phalanx of SS sentries stood a little to one side, their weapons raised. 'We didn't even know what Auschwitz was,' she said, 'but we knew what it was the minute we jumped down off that train.'

Stunned into silence by a surreal world of high-voltage barbed wire fences, watchtowers manned by soldiers armed with machine guns, and the sweeping beams of searchlights, she and Tibor found themselves immediately assailed on all sides by aggression and cruelty as whips cracked and commands were barked at them – '*Alle heraus!* [Everyone out!] Hurry! Leave your luggage! *Schnell!*'

Young and old, equally defenceless, poured from the train and were shoved into closely patrolled lines. Swiftly separated from each other while they were still reeling from the confusion, their precious suitcases lay abandoned in muddy puddles. Some of the women became hysterical as they tried to cling to their loved ones or shield their children from the hostile hands of strangers.

Priska was wrenched from Tibor's arms and almost thrown to the ground, but Edita managed to catch her before she fell. Crying out and looking around for him desperately, she could no longer see her young husband as he was swallowed up in the swarm of people crowding all around her. Stumbling forward, she suddenly came face to face with the senior SS captain she would later learn was called Mengele. To her, though, he was just another Nazi officer with cold, impersonal eyes.

Dr Josef Mengele

Wearing the smile that seemed permanently fixed to his pale face, Mengele asked her, 'What's the matter, pretty one?'

Straightening up, Priska lifted her chin and replied defiantly, 'Nothing in this world.'

'Show me your teeth,' Mengele instructed.

She hesitated for an instant but then dropped her jaw.

'*Arbeiten!*' (Work!) he commanded sharply.

Rough hands pushed her towards a line on the right. Amid the vast sea of suffering she found herself drowning in, no one was allowed to stop or look back. Tibor had vanished in the waves of bewildered humans that stretched for hundreds of metres, and she wasn't even certain if Edita had been able to follow her.

Wielding batons and yelling '*Schneller!*' (Faster!), the *Kapos* and the uniformed SS guards marched the women five abreast through a corridor of sticky mud lined with deep ditches and ringed with high barbed-wire fences. Taken to a remote brick building on the periphery of the camp, they were squeezed into a long room with windows and immediately ordered to strip naked in order to be 'disinfected'.

Stunned, many of these women who'd never been seen undressed even by their husbands, faltered. If any were slow to disrobe or begged for something to cover their nakedness they were felled with blows until they complied. Their discarded clothes, watches, money and jewellery were quickly piled into mounds to be sorted in the commercial heart of Auschwitz – a warehouse named *Kanada* after the country rich in natural resources. There, the *Kanadakommando* of approximately a thousand mostly female Jewish prisoners were closely supervised as they waded through a gigantic jumble of clothing up to three storeys high.

It was their task to put aside any warm or good-quality clothing to be steamed, disinfected and sent to the Reich. They had to search seams and linings for gold, banknotes, precious stones or jewellery. Sifting through the pockets of the doomed, they came across lovingly preserved photographs of family celebrations and loved ones, which were thrown into a pile to be burned (although some were bravely saved).

Once the new arrivals were completely naked, they were hurried along a corridor to a small room where skilled fingers examined mouths and other orifices for hidden gold or gems. Those who'd

feared the loss of everything they owned had their dentists hide diamonds in their fillings. Others secreted jewels in their vaginas. Most
were found. Once thoroughly checked, the women were then fed
like sheep to the shearers who wielded scissors and electric clippers
to hurriedly shave off all their hair.

The women hung their heads and sobbed as their precious
locks – once so carefully tended and curled – were swept away to
be collected in large sacks. Their hair had been their crowning glory
and an integral symbol of their femininity, so when their fingertips
gingerly explored their unaccustomed baldness they felt truly
degraded and enslaved. Then they were pushed on to the next
guard to stand on little stools and have their underarm and pubic
hair removed, although in the rush to process them not all of the
women, including Priska, had everything shaved off.

Designed as a measure to identify them immediately as prisoners should they escape, and to reduce the risk of lice, this shaving
with semi-blunt razors was the most shocking element of the
process of dehumanisation that the women from Slovakia were
now locked into. Stripped of their clothes, their hair, their identities
and their dignity, they were often left with painful nicks, and with
scalps that hadn't been completely shaved and sprouted irregular
strands. Friends and relatives huddled together and gripped each
other in tight embraces, afraid to lose physical contact because they
suddenly all looked the same and 'no longer human'.

Since there were too many of them to be further examined
inside the building, the women were bullied outside onto a large
open parade ground for their first *Appell* and another inspection by
Mengele, the chief physician of the women's camp at Birkenau. The
shock of the cool air on their naked heads and bodies made them
gasp. Unable to look each other in the eye, they were lined up in
rows of five to be scrutinised, their degradation complete. Cringing
in the mud, the women felt that the world had tilted on its axis as
the life they'd once known had been snatched from them for ever.

Where were their loved ones, gobbled up by the night? What had happened to their once carefree existence? In the madness and mayhem of Auschwitz, and with that infernal smell ever lingering in her nostrils, Priska wasn't the only one who felt on the brink of lunacy.

As Dr Mengele approached, she watched as he pulled women from their rows if they looked unwell or had any obvious scars or injuries. Sometimes he seemed to select them just because he didn't like their faces. Having overheard him addressing several prisoners before her, she knew that he would ask if she was pregnant. Trying to appear outwardly dignified, inwardly she had never felt more humiliated or afraid.

Then suddenly he stood before her smiling, so close that she could smell his aftershave. She lifted her head. Incongruously handsome in his uniform, Mengele looked her up and down appreciatively, seemingly impressed at how healthy she was compared with the scores of scrawny women around her, many of whom were all bones and boils.

Yet Priska knew she couldn't trust him. She and Tibor had been conveyed to the camp like animals. They'd been denied water and food, screamed at, beaten. Having been sundered from the only man she'd ever loved, she had then been deprived of all dignity and shown nothing but contempt. If Hitler truly intended to keep his promise to make Europe *Judenrein* – pure of all Jews – then that would surely mean that the unborn child of a Jew wouldn't be spared either.

As Mengele studied her with unblinking eyes, there was just a fraction of a second to decide. But in the small space after he'd asked her in German if she was pregnant, Priska looked back at him directly.

'*Nein*,' she replied, unwilling to admit to any further mastery of the language that he and his cohorts arrogantly assumed they all understood. Her heart beat wildly beneath her ribcage. She knew that if she was later exposed – as she undoubtedly would be if she remained a prisoner – then the consequences could be severe. After a pause, though, the physician with a PhD in anthropology who harboured deep-rooted ambitions to become a great scientist, passed nonchalantly to the woman next in line.

Once that first *Appell* was over, Priska and the rest of the women were herded back into the brand-new *Sauna* with its many windows and efficient T-shaped layout, specially designed to process the small percentage of prisoners earmarked for labour. Still naked, they were taken to a concrete shower room where the *Kapos*, who gestured violently and spoke roughly in order to curry favour with their watching masters, harassed them into standing under a complex grid of copper piping and large metal showerheads. There was an agonising delay while they waited, clustered barefoot on the slippery floor.

The showers at the Sauna, Birkenau

All of a sudden steaming hot water gushed onto them from above as they cried out in shock and disbelief. They threw back their heads and opened their mouths to try to slake their thirst, but the water in Birkenau wasn't fit to drink and they quickly spat out the salty, contaminated liquid. There was no soap or towels but the *Kapos* sprayed their heads and underarms with a stinging disinfectant that found its way into every sore and nick. The water was cold and then hot and came in spurts, but the women did what they could to wash the stink of fear from their skin.

Sopping wet, they were hurried by the continually yelling guards into another room where they were given a few moments to dry off. Marched along a parallel corridor to the one they'd entered by, they were pushed into a space almost as large as the undressing hall, and then into a small latrine without a door located off to one side.

Commanded to squat over holes in the floor five at a time, the women recoiled at the stench of ammonia that rose from the gulley below. Prodded with batons and without any paper, few were able to perform before they were hurried out again. Frightened and confused, they were pointed to the door of another small room off the main hall in which there was a huge pile of discarded clothes. As each woman entered, some inmates threw her an item or two of leftover clothing.

Making no eye contact and sifting through the absurdly mismatched garments with grubby fingers, those whose choices could mean the difference between life and death tossed Priska some footwear from a random pile of shoes and a baggy coat dress of sturdy black material, for which she was eternally grateful. Many of her less fortunate companions were handed incongruous items such as dresses that were far too small, items of male underwear, or even full-length satin gowns. The sartorial effect might have been amusing if they'd been anywhere else. Instead, they pulled their ridiculous prison garb over damp skin and stared at each other with a growing sense of foreboding.

The women from Sered' were then frog-marched – five abreast – through an exit door across another parade ground and then pushed along a corridor of barbed wire that led to another building. Still on the fringes of the female camp, it was known as the *Durchs* (transit) block or as 'Lager C', where row upon row of wooden huts or barracks, each thirty metres by ten, housed thousands of frightened women.

The geography of death at whose centre Priska found herself was an immense network of three camps and the deadly hub of more than forty satellite camps. Not far from Oświęcim, the remote southern Polish town that the Nazis renamed Auschwitz, this place was to become the most potent symbol of the Third Reich's decision to commit assembly-line genocide. Originally an Austro-Hungarian cavalry garrison which was later taken over by the Polish army, Auschwitz I was initially intended to be a 'Class 1' prison camp for mostly Polish Jewish and non-Jewish criminal and political inmates. In May 1940 it was officially designated a concentration and *Vernichtungslager* (destruction or extermination camp) under the authority of the commandant, SS captain Rudolf Höss, who had previously served at Sachsenhausen and Dachau.

The wooden accommodation blocks at Auschwitz II-Birkenau

Auschwitz II-Birkenau, built early in 1941 by Soviet prisoners-of-war, of whom it was to hold 100,000 (most of that number later died), was three and a half kilometres away on the site of a former village named Brzezinka, renamed by the Germans Birkenau, which means 'birch trees'. On a marshy plain at the confluence of two rivers, the spot was chosen for its central location within the Reich and its proximity to a major rail network.

As soon as the Nazis decided to expand their operations in Poland, the 1,200 hapless villagers of Brzezinka were ordered to abandon their homes, which were then razed to the ground. Thousands more were evacuated to create a no-man's-land of twenty square kilometres where the camp could remain hidden away from the rest of the world. Bricks from the houses were used to build the camp's arched gatehouse, guards' quarters, and a few early prisoner blocks. As more blocks were needed, so they were made of local wood. Birkenau was reclassified as a concentration camp in March 1942.

Auschwitz III, at a place the Germans named Monowitz, was built in 1942 as an *Arbeitslager* or work camp specifically to provide slave labour for the German chemical company IG Farben. At Farben's Buna Werke factory manufacturing synthetic fuel, it had a workforce of around 80,000 by 1944. Auschwitz I and Auschwitz II-Birkenau began taking in Jews in early 1942, the first transports coming from Bratislava and Silesia. To ease congestion, the camp was expanded with the construction of wooden blocks as far as the eye could see. Then it began accepting transports of Jews from camps such as Drancy in France and Westerbork in the Netherlands, before harvesting inmates from Terezín.

Josef Mengele arrived at Birkenau in May 1943, a member of a German contingent of medical experts in genetic and other experiments. With the devotion to duty of a workaholic, he quickly rose to a senior position. Although he was often cited as the one who carried out selections and came to represent the personification of murder for many survivors, it may not always have been Mengele who inspected the new *Häftlinge*. What is certain is that he showed tremendous zeal for the job and appeared eager to preside over the railhead *Rampe* to 'welcome' as many transports as he could.

The SS officers were also given extra rations of cigarettes, soap, schnapps and food for 'special actions' such as the selection and execution of prisoners. These extras supplemented the generous meals prepared for them daily by chefs in the Waffen SS Club, who offered menus featuring roast chicken, baked fish, frothing tankards of beer, and unlimited quantities of ice cream and sticky desserts.

A short distance away, thousands of terrified half-starved prisoners rolled into Auschwitz every day, each of them a fresh candidate for execution. An estimated ninety per cent were murdered within hours of arrival. As soon as they had been identified as worthy of *Sonderbehandlung* or 'Special Treatment' (marked in the records as 'SB'), they were sent to their deaths. In the early days, the camp was a kilometre from the railway sidings and those destined to die were transported directly to their fate in canvas-topped trucks.

The SS had tried all manner of means to kill the Jews and other enemies of the Reich, from starvation and shooting to suffocating with carbon monoxide, but these practices were largely inefficient and time-consuming, while the disposal of the bodies by burning them in trenches wasted valuable fuel. The Nazi command was keen to find a method that would eliminate large numbers simultaneously, using minimal staff and at minimum expense. Many prisoners at Auschwitz were killed by an injection of phenol to the heart, but later arrivals experienced the SS's new preferred practice – gassing in special chambers.

At the core of Birkenau were two pretty brick cottages that had survived the destruction of the original Polish village. Known as 'the red house' and the 'white house', they were disguised as showers where the prisoners were told that they would be washed and disinfected. A lorry marked with the symbol of the Red Cross was often parked outside, an emblem of reassurance. It was, in fact, the vehicle used to transport the canisters of Zyklon B *Giftgas* (poison

gas) to those entrusted with exterminating the prisoners. An effective pesticide that had been used to control vermin in the ghettos,
Zyklon B consisted of tiny crystallised pellets that released deadly
hydrogen cyanide once they reacted with moisture and heat. Soviet
prisoners-of-war had been the subject of merciless experiments in
the basement of a prison in Auschwitz I during 1941 until Nazi
doctors had fully perfected the system.

Those to be murdered were handed towels and small pieces of
soap by men in white coats in an effort to further delude them,
and were herded naked inside the cottages with their walled-up
windows and gas-tight doors. Most had no concept of what was
about to happen. The Germans would then allow several
agonising minutes to pass for their body heat to warm the enclosed
space. This was found to make the gas take effect far more effi-
ciently. Only once they were huddled together in the sulphurous
darkness might the sweating prisoners have begun to suspect their
fate. All would have hoped for water to gush out of the false showerheads, while others hugged each other, praying, or reciting
'Shema Israel' from the Torah. When a precise amount of time had
elapsed, uniformed soldiers would don gas masks, climb ladders,
and empty the pellets through special vents in the roof or via
openings in the walls to work with the heat and sweat to release
their lethal vapour.

Foaming at the mouth or bleeding from the ears, the victims
could take up to twenty minutes to die depending on how close
they were to the vents. Those who administered the gas often heard
them screaming, shouting and pounding on the doors as they struggled for every breath. Only when they fell silent and enough time
had elapsed for the ventilation system to suck out the gas would the
prisoner Sonderkommando (special unit) be sent in. These skilled
operatives of streamlined mass destruction were forced under
threat of death to dispose of the corpses. In groups of four to nine
hundred men they were also known as Geheimnisträger, 'bearers of
secrets'. Kept in strict isolation from the rest of the prisoners, it was

their task to open the gas chambers, pull out the dead, and begin the gruesome task of washing away the faeces, vomit and blood in preparation for the next 'batch'.

Sometimes, these prisoners came across members of their own families. Faced with such horror, several committed suicide – their only means of escape. Each unit was killed off and replaced at intervals of between three months and a year, depending on their efficiency. The first duty of any new *Sonderkommando* would be to dispose of the bodies of its predecessors. Few survived the war but, knowing their impending fate, some recorded their experiences in writing and hid the evidence to be discovered after their deaths.

The gas chamber at Auschwitz I

The indignity both for these prisoners and for those whose corpses they handled didn't end with their deaths. Little was wasted in the Nazi human recycling machine, where the ancillary products of murder were salvaged for the Reich. The luxuriant curls and braided plaits of hair that had been lopped or shaved from the female prisoners' heads were used to make cloth or netting, or as insulation and watertight padding for German war machinery. Not yet cold, every corpse would have its mouth yanked open so that teeth could be torn from jawbones with pliers, a task also undertaken by the *Sonderkommando*. A particularly fine set of teeth might be saved to make dentures. Any gems found implanted into fillings would be given to the SS ostensibly to cover the accommodation, food and transportation costs incurred in carrying out their extermination programme. Gold from teeth was melted into huge nuggets of 'dental gold'.

Later, with deportation trains rolling in day and night, the four camp *'Krema'* (crematoria) numbered II to V were specially built as extermination factories with a much greater capacity. These modern concrete edifices were a hundred metres long and fifty metres wide and contained fifteen ovens. They were not only far more efficient than the cottages but had subterranean undressing rooms that sloped straight down to the soundproof gas chambers designed to look like showers, which in turn were fitted with special electric lifts that hoisted the corpses up to the ovens once the job was done. Between them they were capable of gassing and cremating more than 4,000 people from each transport. At their peak, they gassed 8,000 men, women and children in a single day.

In the early days, the hot ashes of the dead were scattered in a series of deep ponds at the fringes of the camp, but once the water clogged with human debris, they were barrowed into a glade of silver birch trees and shovelled across the forest floor. They were also used as fertiliser in nearby fields as the area became the world's largest Jewish graveyard. The easterly winds often caught the grey ash and sent spiralling whorls of powdered bone across the plain, which worked its gritty way into each crevice of human skin and left thick dust on every surface and on the lips. Those inmates who had somehow avoided such a fate ended up inadvertently breathing in the charnel dust of their loved ones – day in, day out.

Priska, fresh from Bratislava, was unaware of any of this in the first few hours after her arrival at Auschwitz II-Birkenau. All she sensed in the airless, windowless shack into which she'd been locked with far too many other human beings was that she and her unborn child were in a place of the utmost danger. Mercifully, she had been reunited with Edita, who then never left her side. It was only when the women who'd been in the blocks for a while started to whisper in the dark that Priska began to comprehend how deadly it was. Veterans of almost every nationality, bald and with sunken eyes, would sidle up to the newcomers to ask if they had anything to eat. Disappointed, they would begin to tell them what went on in the camp, arguing with one another all the while. They were all condemned, claimed one ominously. They'd been brought there to die – worked or starved to death – their situation hopeless. No, they were only in quarantine, insisted another, as the different factions bickered amongst themselves. Why else had so many been sheared and some branded with tattoos? They should all pray to be selected for *Arbeit* because that was their only chance for survival, explained a third.

But where was everyone else, the newcomers asked plaintively. What about their families? Could they be in another hut, or had they been sent somewhere else to work?

'See that?' the skinny wretches would murmur with a twisted smile, pointing at the thickening smoke over the chimney they could see through the cracks in the walls. 'That's where your loved ones are – and that's where we'll all end up!'

The Nazis' promises about annihilating the Jews on a grand scale had always seemed impossible to believe, but once Priska heard about the gas chambers and started breathing in the nauseating stink of roasting human flesh and scorched hair, she was in no doubt that the prisoners spoke the unspeakable truth. The smoke from the dead hung all around them like a shroud. 'Daily events made it very clear what would happen to women and to the children of those who were pregnant,' she said. 'Logic convinced me that the rate of survival in this hell was very slim.'

In that place of suspended belief, all she knew was that she had to try to save her baby – and that meant not starving to death like the rest of them. Within hours it became apparent that all they would have to live on was liquids, starting with the 'dishwater' the Germans called coffee – made from marsh water and burned wheat – which they were given morning and night. At midday, unspeakable soup made from rotten vegetables was slopped out with their only solid food, a small square of black sawdust bread. On such a diet, Priska had too little in her belly to suffer from morning sickness any more.

Following animal instincts to learn the art of survival, she and Edita noticed that the other inmates roused from their stupor in the dark rushed to the fifty-quart kettles of soup the minute they were carried into the block by fellow prisoners. Arguments broke out between cliques and nationalities, while *Kapos* with cudgels or rubber hoses meted out brutal punishments to those who licked at spillages in the dirt or fought like jackals over every revolting morsel. The hungriest endured the blows in order to fish around in the soup with grimy hands for anything substantial. With every scrap they could get vital to their survival, the hand-cleansing rituals of their past were abandoned. Priska saw that it was best to get a ladleful that had been tilted at an angle in the bottom of the kettle, but everyone wanted that and all had to wait their turn.

Once their unwashed bowls had been licked clean and the only light came from the blinding searchlights that swept through the camp at night, she and those she was with attempted to sleep six or more across, lying on their sides on pallet beds in a windowless block that let in rain and wind through every gap in the planking. They had thin mattresses or just dirty straw to lie on, and a thin coverlet between them. They kept their shoes or boots on all night

A women's block in a concentration camp

for fear of theft, and clung to any precious bowls or spoons they might have been given as if they were life rafts.

Those who slept on the bottom of the three-tiered bunks had the best position, but they were still pestered by the rats that scurried around in the damp earth and gnawed the dead skin from their feet. Those in the middle suffered terribly from heat and a lack of oxygen during the summer months, and those on the top burned up in the heat and were drenched in the winter, although they could at least eat the snow or lick at the rainwater. Whichever level the women were on, they all woke with stiff muscles and bruised bones.

With no work to do and nothing to think about but fear, hunger and unbridled thirst, Priska and the other prisoners dreaded each new hour and waited anxiously to learn their fate. Trapped in the foul air of the hut, each half-lit day seemed to stretch endlessly and the enforced idleness only demoralised them still further. Many women had gone mad and wailed with longing for lost children, parents or loved ones. Their despair was contagious and death was seen as deliverance. Others – broken and indifferent – retreated into themselves, becoming mute and ghostlike as they blindly followed orders in a state of permanent mortal dread.

All were overseen by *Kapos* known as *Blockältesten* (block elders), who were either career criminals who'd earned themselves privileged status, or those who'd proved themselves capable of the kind of brutality the Nazis demanded. Some of these *Häftlinge* had been in Auschwitz for years and had learned early on that their only means of long-term survival was to mimic the incendiary hatred of their masters. Like all the prisoner functionaries in the Nazi system, their tenure depended on their competence. If they were seen to be too lenient, then they risked severe punishment and even a quick journey to the gas chambers. Those who displeased the SS were stripped of their rank and thrown into the very barracks they'd presided over, often to meet their death at the hands of those they'd terrorised. In this way, the *Kapos* helped ensure that order was maintained, especially after dark when there were no SS in the camp. In return for their collaboration they were allowed separate rooms just off the main block, better beds and food. They also had fuel for winter fires. The women in their charge weren't supposed to talk or collaborate in any way and risked a beating or worse for the most minor infringement.

The prisoners did speak, though, whispering to each other at night in whatever language they shared about friends and family, husbands and lovers, children and their lost lives. Thoughts of children, parents and husbands tormented them. They yearned for colour and laughter, birdsong and flowers. Occasionally they would recite poetry or quote favourite passages from books. If they dared, they'd sing together quietly – often numbers from shows or soppy laments that sparked floods of tears.

Most of all, though, they talked about food. No matter how hard they tried not to, they tortured themselves by conjuring up from memory great feasts with recipes that featured only the finest imaginary ingredients. Salivating together in a stinking human tangle, they would recall family kitchens filled with the aroma of freshly baked bread, tables groaning with food, and the taste of sweet red wine. Only when it became too much to bear would someone yell at them to stop their fantasies and they'd fall silent again.

When they finally succumbed to mental and physical exhaustion they were pressed up against each other so tightly that they were forced into immobility. The SS guard dogs had bigger kennels. Jammed elbow to elbow, on their sides, if one woman had to turn over to relieve a hipbone pressed against the wood or climb down to use the bucket, then they would all have to turn. Their awkward, fitful slumber was punctuated by nightmares, the urgent call of nature, or heartbreaking dreams of home.

Every morning at around 4 a.m. the women were rudely woken with a shrill bell or the banging of a gong, accompanied by shouts and the pummelling of their feet as the female *Kapos* hurried them to and from the *Appell* to stand in lines and be counted and then counted again. Blinded by floodlights and stumbling in the mud, they had to stand five abreast for up to twelve hours in all weathers in the designated *Appellplatz* as they were repeatedly accounted for. Those who felt faint were propped up by their friends, as anyone with poor teeth, scars, or who was too weak to stand was in acute danger of being condemned.

Breathing through their mouths to avoid the ever-present stink of death, they were often naked in the biting winds and ice storms that swept in across the plain. Frequently it was Mengele who, with the quick professional eye of a doctor, decided if they should die that day or be worked to death in a factory for the Reich. So keen was he to do his duty that he often carried out such selections even when it wasn't his shift.

One day he shocked Priska by walking up to her and roughly squeezing her breast. 'I was very afraid that I would have milk, but thank God I did not,' she said. Staring at her with his hazel eyes, the doctor who'd won an Iron Cross for his role in the Ukraine campaign contemplated her for a moment before moving on.

A prisoner whose breast was similarly squeezed was horrified when Mengele cried, 'Milk! Pregnant!' Like a director signalling an actor stage left, the slightest motion of his hand had her flung aside and sent to a female prisoner-doctor who told her after a cursory inspection that she was expecting. She denied it but the doctor insisted, so when she went to fetch a guard the woman took the chance to escape and ran back to the *Appell*, an action that saved her life.

Even Mengele had to sleep sometimes; so other medical personnel including Dr Fritz Klein, who patrolled with his dogs and a condescending expression, conducted some of the early morning *Selektionen*. After asking the women their names, ages and nationalities, he inspected their bodies for eczema, blemishes or deformities and then indicated with a jerk of his finger whether they would endure another day's grace or soon be sucking on gas. A virulent anti-Semite who examined the women before him with obvious distaste, at his subsequent trial for war crimes Klein publicly declared that Jews were 'the inflamed appendix' of Europe that needed to be surgically excised.

Every night at dusk, the women went through the same deadly routine as their fates were evaluated once again. Those prisoners who'd given up or whose diarrhoea, disease or dehydration rendered them unable to remain upright were carried off – rarely to be seen again.

Edita remained close to her pregnant charge, helping her to stand up straight and sleeping alongside her to protect and warm her. Occasionally, and always at night, she would press her lips to Priska's ear and whisper, 'Open mouth.' Priska would do as she was told and a miraculous sliver of raw potato or a tiny piece of black bread would be slipped between her chattering teeth – 'the most delicious thing I ever tasted'. She had no idea where or how Edita acquired these life-saving morsels in that desolate wasteland but without them, Priska is certain she wouldn't have survived.

Day and night, the women were bitten by lice that hid themselves in every seam, nook or cranny, and multiplied too quickly to be eradicated. Hunting down and squashing the lice between forefinger and thumb whiled away a few hours. Without medical attention or the chance to remain clean, the bites that the prisoners felt compelled to scratch became infected, often fatally. Further weeping sores were caused by the lack of anything soft to sleep on and the gradual breakdown of the skin through dirt and malnutrition.

With up to eight hundred women in each block, disease rampaged unchecked through their defenceless bodies, with dysentery and diarrhoea a daily scourge. The washing facilities comprised a long trough in a separate barracks with two pipes that sputtered suspicious brown water, and there wasn't a toothbrush or sliver of soap in sight. The women who had been there longest showed the newcomers how to use sand or grit to scrub themselves, and some used their own urine to clean their sores.

The women were only permitted to visit the block latrines once or twice a day. These comprised two oblong slabs of formed concrete fifty metres long, with fifty holes cut into each of them built over a shallow trench. Having been pushed en masse through the mud onto the faeces-smeared holes, the women were allowed only a few minutes each and had no choice but to wipe themselves with their hands, with dirty straw from their bedding, or on scraps torn from their clothing. The few women who were menstruating had limited means of soaking up the blood. That was one thing Priska didn't have to worry about as her baby somehow stayed alive inside her shrinking body.

Latrine block at Auschwitz II-Birkenau

With cries of '*Weitergehen!*' (Keep moving!) they were quickly marched back to their blocks until the next *Appell*, struggling to lift their feet and fighting to keep their life-saving shoes from being sucked into the greedy mud.

Each time they were allowed out, an increasingly desperate Priska scanned the camp right and left, praying for a glimpse of her Tiborko. But all she could see were hundreds of unused chimneys from the row upon row of other blocks, scores of wooden watch-towers known as 'storks', and the ever-present plume of oily smoke pouring from the furnaces.

Tibor had told her to think only of beautiful things, but what was there to see in this colourless marshland with its horizon of barbed wire where not a single blade of grass pushed its way through the yellow clay? The stagnant air reeked only of death in that camp that stretched far into the distance. Birch trees swayed under vast skies but the sun was too pale to pierce the eternal gloom, and the birds had abandoned this forgotten corner leaving only a clamorous silence. Where was the rest of the world?

In that complex that specialised in the dismantling of the human spirit, the faces of the shapeless spectres around her were gaunt, their expressions catatonic. Transported East to nothingness and reduced to an inhuman existence, they'd become shadow people, half-mad or half-dead already. There wasn't the faintest glimmer of hope in most of their eyes. Death seemed unavoidable and inmates often woke up next to a corpse – a fact they often tried to hide in order to claim an extra share of food.

Achingly homesick and longing for the faintest hint of beauty and gentleness, Priska began to grasp that her hopes of survival were ridiculously naive. Tormented by hunger and thirst, itching from her sores and barely able to stand her own smell, she could hardly believe what had happened to her since she and Tibor had been seized from their home. Where was the lovely life she'd known growing up in Zlaté Moravce? When she'd tutored her friend Gizka or gobbled up flaky pastries on the patisserie steps? What about her happiest moments with Tibor eating *Sachertorte* in the smoke-filled cafés of Bratislava, surrounded by vital, intelligent people? Or sitting quietly alongside him as he scribbled in his notebooks and puffed aromatic smoke from one of his pipes? Hitler's unconscionable master plan had swallowed up her past and now she could only fantasise about such days.

Numb and deeply afraid as she was, there was a point when Priska considered giving in to the hopelessness all around her and allowing destiny to take her, along with the rest. But after losing three babies, the will to survive and the determination to bring her growing infant into the world was surprisingly tenacious. She had no idea if they would make it but whatever happened, she longed to see her husband for one last time.

Male prisoners were kept well away from the women's camp at

Birkenau, housed in huts on the far side of the sprawling complex. Although a few of the men in striped uniforms were occasionally detailed to clean the latrines or carry out menial work in other sectors, those selected were usually wearing the pink triangles that identified them as homosexuals, so Priska's quest seemed utterly futile. She began to fear that her suave journalist-cum-bank clerk of a husband had already 'gone up the smokestack' or been transported somewhere far away. As the days passed, so her hopes faded.

Then one afternoon, the God that she greeted every night before she closed her eyes finally answered her prayers. Through the coils of barbed-wire fencing she suddenly spotted Tibor in a small cluster of men passing her section of the camp. She recognised him immediately even though he looked so different – thinner than ever and almost transparently pale.

Hardly believing her own eyes and risking being shot or beaten to death, Priska ran through the mud in her clogs to the electric wire – being careful not to touch it – and was able to exchange a few words with him before they were discovered.

Tibor – who just weeks before had celebrated his thirtieth birthday with her – looked twice that age. He was, however, overwhelmed to see his 'Piri' and told her how fervently he'd been praying that she and their baby would survive. 'That's what's keeping me alive!' he cried.

'Don't worry. I will return. We'll make it!' Priska told him with renewed resolve, before they were forced apart and dragged back to their respective zones sporting fresh bruises.

The miracle of seeing Tibor that day and knowing that he was still breathing was enough to lift Priska's spirits. The thought that she might see him again became a tremendous solace to her. His words of encouragement echoed in her ears and, as she lay sandwiched between Edita and the other women on her bunk that night, she began to feel even more passionate about saving her child. Surely the war would be over by the time little Hanka or Miško was born?

Shortly before she and Tibor had been deported, the news bulletins they'd been secretly following on a friend's wireless had assured them the tide was turning against the Germans. France was free and the joint Soviet and American forces were closing in. It could only be a matter of weeks before they were liberated and then she, Tiborko and their unborn son or daughter could return to their home and pick up their cruelly interrupted lives. Pressing her palms flat against her belly she silently worked out when her baby would be born. 'I got pregnant on 13 July 1944, so I knew exactly when nine months would be up,' she said.

Her due date was 12 April 1945. Setting that day firmly in her mind, Priska decided there and then that – no matter what – she would protect the baby she carried and keep herself alive at least until he or she was born. Having been able to remain relatively unscathed in Bratislava for the first five years of the war, she was healthy and strong. She had a husband who was alive and who loved her and was counting on their survival.

She had promised him that they would make it – and so they would.

It was a dream Priska clung to until the grey dawn on or about 10 October 1944, approximately two weeks after her arrival in Auschwitz II-Birkenau, when she and the other prisoners were rounded up once more and roughly paraded in front of Dr Mengele, with his fickle power over her fate. Smiling as always, and this time tapping a riding crop against his polished boots, he casually flicked it *links oder rechts* as he selected the healthiest of them for hard labour. Priska was still bright-eyed and blooming compared with those who'd spent years in ghettos or camps. She was of prime stock. Before she even understood what was happening, she'd been directed to one side by the flick of Mengele's crop before being pushed into a group of other women deemed suitable for *Arbeit*.

After being given a morsel of bread and a ladleful of slop doled out from a kettle, the women were unexpectedly loaded back into the closed goods wagons of a huge train, which squatted broodingly on the tracks.

As she inwardly cried out her husband's name, the doors were slammed shut with a dreadful finality on Priska's dreams of seeing Tibor again. With a hiss of steam, the big black locomotive hauled her away from the hellfires of Auschwitz to a new and unknown destination.

## Rachel

With little variation in the day-to-day mechanics of the murderous Nazi machine, Rachel and her sisters were treated similarly to the rest of the women transported to the end of the line at Auschwitz during the late summer and autumn of 1944.

After the train from Łódź pulled to a halt on the dedicated rail spur in Birkenau with a screech of metal against metal, the doors were flung open and the light dazzled their eyes. Their limbs stiff after their enforced immobility, they were pulled from their wagon to find themselves frightened out of their senses in a desperate crush of screaming, weeping people. Before they knew what was happening, they'd been hived off to one side and jostled to the *Sauna* where they were ordered to take off their clothes. Spurred on by whips and curses, they were forced to leave all vestiges of their old life behind.

'They shaved our heads, they washed us with some disinfectant, and then we went out the other side of this big room,' Rachel said. 'They were walking around looking at women – and *how* they looked – as they selected healthy younger ones. There were no babies. No mothers. Only healthy women who could work.'

As they stood with their arms in the air, earrings were ripped from their earlobes with pliers and rings prised from fingers by greased hands. 'You won't need watches where you're going,' the prisoner-functionaries sneered, so those were taken too. Then their ears, mouths and private parts were poked and explored before they were shorn. Naked, hairless and utterly humiliated, the young women looked almost identical as they were assessed for their suitability to be worked to death. They were of a similar age, height and build, without any obvious disabilities or blemishes.

Sala said, 'We were scared little sheep. I didn't even recognise my own sister after a female SS guard shaved us. I told her we don't even look like people any more . . . I was wearing a little necklace that my friend made for me and, stupidly, I didn't even try to hide it so one of the guards grabbed it from my neck. They didn't even talk to us. It was all so cruel. Then we were paraded outside, for all to see our shame.'

Waiting in line for her turn to be judged, Rachel watched as the good-looking SS doctor she'd first seen on the *Rampe* squeezed every other woman's breast. Any who were visibly pregnant were dragged from the line. She suspected that she might be carrying her husband Monik's child, but she couldn't be sure. Either way, she sensed instinctively that to admit her condition would be a fatal error of judgement. Trembling with cold and fear, the comely wife who wasn't even sure she wanted a baby of her own yet must have felt some shame in denying the existence of her unborn child.

As Mengele passed by without challenging her, Rachel realised with a wrench that she'd never even had the chance to share her news with her husband or her lovely mother Fajga. And now she didn't dare tell her sisters for fear that it might have repercussions for them too. Somewhere in the rows and rows of shivering manne-quins, Sala, Bala and Ester went through the same clinical process of selection as more of the weak and undernourished were weeded out and marched away. Even after their years in the Łódź ghetto, the women were safeguarded by their youth, looking far more vital than those whose bones could be mapped beneath their skin.

Earmarked by an ever-cheerful Dr Mengele, all four sisters were directed to a group destined for immediate transportation to a slave labour camp. Hastened back inside the building with whips, they were thrown bizarre items of mismatched clothing from a loose pile that appeared to be all that remained of the last human cargo – as if they had just stepped out of their garments. As with everyone else who passed through the *Sauna*, the choice was wildly random and size or shape never a consideration. These tangible vestiges of broken lives included teenagers' dresses, workmen's overalls, feathered hats, even baby clothes. Some prisoners were given backless cocktail dresses to wear accompanied by huge men's boots. Others were tossed nightwear or summer blouses. A few were fortunate enough to be flung some underwear or cloths that could be used as such, but the majority had no undergarments at all – an experience that was completely alien to them. Their feet slopped around in oversized shoes, black 'Holland' clogs, or were squeezed into heels that would soon become instruments of torture.

'I was very lucky,' Rachel said. 'They threw me a big black dress that must have come from a cripple. It had a detachable yoke and was as big as a tent. I knew straight away that I could hide my pregnancy in that. Nobody would know what was going on under that dress. Then they threw me a pair of shoes that I couldn't bear, but I still wore.'

Once again, the sisters managed to stay together, only this time they were marched outside and beaten into a semblance of order. Commanded to stand five deep in the roll-call area to await the next phase of their nightmare, they stood stiffly to attention in their ridiculous attire, and watched as the rest were herded off to another block or somewhere worse. As the Polish winds began to bite, heralding the start of one of the harshest winters in European history, the women wondered what was to become of them and whether they would ever be able to escape from this bitter purgatory.

Fortunately for them, there was no time to lose. The Germans knew that they were losing the war and, with most of their men enlisted, the scarcity of labour for armaments and industry was a major problem. As in the ghettos, the Nazis realised that the healthiest prisoners – even Jews – could be economically useful before they were killed. The factory the women were destined for was vital to the continuation of air attacks on the Allies – a field of combat in which the Germans had been very successful. Advances in technology had made aircraft on both sides of the war capable of unparalleled devastation, but the Luftwaffe had initially gained air supremacy over western Europe using its Messerschmitt, Junkers, Heinkel, Stuka and Focke-Wulf planes. Hitler considered his bombers to be the 'flying artillery' that supported his ground forces, but once the Allies achieved supremacy thanks to the Battle of Britain, the German air force suffered a series of catastrophic losses. During the defeat at Stalingrad especially, the Nazis lost nine hundred planes, so more needed to be built – and fast. Anyone deemed physically capable of doing work was appraised and those who didn't make the grade were simply thrown away.

Unaware of the fate that had been decided for them, the bewildered women in Birkenau in late 1944 waited with parching thirst as the light faded and the temperature dropped still further. In the distance they could hear dogs barking, the cries of the desperate, and sporadic bursts of machine-gun fire. Filled with incredulity and terror, they were commanded not to move and the *Kapos* and female SS guards struck or slapped anyone who became unsteady on her feet, pleaded for water or asked to use the toilet.

Eventually, they were allowed to sit down in the cold mud and each given a small portion of some watery substance. It quickly became apparent that the bowls they shared had been used as chamber pots. The salty liquid slopped into these vessels was evil-smelling and inedible but the women pinched their noses and forced it down in a futile attempt to quench their thirst. 'We got some soup but without spoons, so we ate it with our hands,' Rachel said, her mind raging against the profanity while her body cried out for food.

They then sat for hours in the dark watching the strange crimson glow in the sky from the camp's chimneys whilst trying not to breathe in what smelled like burning meat that left a caustic taste in their throats. One by one, veteran prisoners approached them to whisper sadistically, 'See those chimneys? They gas people here and then they burn them. If your mother went to the left, that's where she is now.'

To begin with, their battered minds simply refused to process the information. The words being spoken seemed too fantastically evil to be true. But then came the chilling suspicion that these withered creatures with mad eyes and shuffling feet were speaking the truth.

Choking on the realisation that almost their entire family had been marched to the charnel house to be gassed and incinerated, the acrid smoke made them gag. Rachel, numbed, suddenly thought that if the Nazis could do that to innocent men, women and children, then what on earth would they do to a newborn baby? Fear stabbing at her womb, she could barely breathe.

Her foreboding of what might happen if her pregnancy was detected was fully justified. With so many women being transported to Auschwitz daily from the occupied territories, the SS realised that a percentage would be pregnant. Those who couldn't hide their condition were routinely sent to the gas chambers, but as the war dragged on and healthy young women were needed for work, there was the problem of those who didn't show yet. So the Nazis set up a primitive abortion clinic in Birkenau run by prisoner-doctors. Many of the women forced to have abortions in such hostile and unhygienic conditions lost their lives anyway. The few who were able to hide their pregnancies and even conceal their births usually lost their babies due to malnutrition. Those allowed to go to full term were often denied access to their infants, who either starved to death or were given to Dr Mengele for experimentation. In his special block, referred to as 'The Zoo', the SS captain and his team of medical staff carried out unspeakable operations on twins, babies, dwarves and adults that ranged from sterilisation and castration to electric shock treatment and amputation – sometimes without anaesthetic. Some mothers were encouraged by the prisoner-doctors to murder their infants in order to save their own lives.

Then, in an apparent change of policy, the SS announced that all abortions would be stopped and extra rations issued to pregnant women, who would be exempt from the innumerable *Appelle*. The order was revoked soon afterwards and any Aryan child of non-Jewish were taken away for 'Germanisation' before being passed off as the offspring of childless Germans. Almost three hundred pregnant women in the special birthing block were sent to the gas chambers. Those babies not sent away died of hunger, thirst or disease. Others were gassed or fed to the ovens. Some were administered injections to the heart. An untold number were drowned in a bucket.

Rachel could have known none of this, but she did know that the business of Auschwitz was death. Still shattered by the news of her family's annihilation, she and her sisters then had to take in the additional information from their fellow *Häftlinge* that the gas chambers in the camp were disguised as showers. 'Sooner or later, we will all join our loved ones in the chimney,' they were told coldly. So, a few hours later, when the prisoners were nudged awake in the dawn and commanded by the SS to shower, they broke down. Sobs racking their bodies, they followed each other blindly to the slaughterhouse, one hand on the other's shoulder, no longer caring about their nakedness. Many of the prisoners prayed out loud, making deals with God that if they survived they would be better Jews and devote their lives to helping others. 'They took us in a room and I saw the showers,' Sala said. 'I thought, "Well, this is the end of us. I will smell gas," but – no – water was coming out and again we were safe.'

Hope flared in them briefly as jets of icy water flushed away their fear. Water signified life. Life equalled *Arbeit*. Work could mean survival. Still wet, and sprayed with disinfectant that stung their nostrils, they were marshalled out of the showers, thrown their prison garb, handed a little bread and soap and marched smartly to the railway tracks that had brought them through the gates a little over twenty-four hours earlier. Stunned into silent obedience once again, the sisters managed to remain close enough in the confusion to be pushed up a wooden ramp into the same freight wagon before the doors were slammed shut and bolted from the outside with a horrible clang.

Inside that nauseating atmosphere, stacked together in the half-light, the sisters almost suffocated on the sweat, fear and urine of the previous wretches who'd recently arrived from the world beyond the fences, no doubt to be sent straight up the smokestack. Their eyes growing accustomed to the darkness, the eighty or so women had no idea where they were going or what would happen to them when they reached their destination. They would likely not see the sky for days or be able to move their limbs as they were pressed against one another with no room to sit, rest or breathe.

None of them would sleep. All would suffer. Some might die.

But all they cared about was that they had somehow been saved from the hell of swallowing human remains. Although they'd wondered about the possibility of an 'afterwards' which had seemed beyond all imagining, they'd hardly dared hope there really might be a time *after* Auschwitz; the place they'd expected to inhale their loved ones in a final, fatal gasp.

With a shudder and a jolt that sent them crashing into each other with a cry, their train pulled away from the labyrinth of barbed wire as they held their collective breath. Sala elbowed her way to the small window of the wagon as they were slowly dragged back across the threshold of that cruellest of places.

As the train gathered pace, she peered out at the land beyond the camp in the grey morning light. Having passed through a portal into another world, she saw orchards full of apples and vast fields with

Railway tracks to Auschwitz II

people toiling in them or tending to pumpkins and cabbages as if it was just another day. The countryside that unfurled before her eyes comprised thousands of acres of farmland worked by prisoners and German settlers who'd been imported as part of an agricultural experiment. While those within Auschwitz-Birkenau starved to death, these fertile pastures just beyond the high-tension fences swelled with fresh produce.

All of a sudden, Sala spotted something that made her heart leap with hope. There was a woman working in the fields who looked exactly like their mother, Fajga. Her relief that their blessed Mama might still be alive sent her into hysterics. 'I started screaming "Mother! Mother!" She looked up at me like I was crazy but I will never forget her face – she looked just like my mother.'

Rachel, standing close by, grabbed her younger sister by the shoulders and slapped her hard across the face. The two women fell against each other as the engine gathered speed and pulled them away from the wraiths of all those they'd ever loved.

## Anka

When Anka and her friend Mitzka arrived in Auschwitz II-Birkenau in the third-class passenger carriages from Terezín, they were in very poor condition, physically and mentally. For the two days it had taken them to get there they'd been crammed together with insufficient air and no chance to move. The space they were forced to share with so many others reeked of unwashed bodies, or worse, and they were forbidden to lift the blinds or open the windows. With no food or water to drink, Anka said, 'The worst experience of all was the thirst.'

Long before the snaking train began to slow, those who defied the orders to peer under the blinds spotted the chimneys spouting fire. 'We did not know then what it meant but the impression was gruesome ... The smell was of things I had never smelled before and which you couldn't place ... I will never forget that smell

but ... the look of the chimneys was so frightening that even without knowing what was going on, you drew back.'

As soon as the train stopped and the doors were thrown ajar they
half-jumped, half-fell from the carriages as if drunk. There was
immediate pandemonium, and shouts of 'Raus! Schnell! Laufen!'
(Out! Hurry! Run!) Panic-stricken, they were surrounded by what
looked like 'demented' men in striped pyjamas who told them to
drop the luggage carefully painted with their names, assuring them
they'd be reunited with it later. They never were.

'There were dogs barking and people screaming. It was bedlam. No
one knowing where to go ... millions of people milling about ... at
least a thousand people. I don't remember if it was night or day,' Anka
said. 'The SS were shouting and hitting everybody who came their
way. It was like the apocalypse. You felt something eerie but you didn't
know.' The Kapos quickly separated men from women but the prisoners who'd been used to being segregated in Terezín didn't fear that
so much at first. 'I was in the same wagon with a male friend who was
about my age. We'd known each other all our lives and he said, "Well,
we had better say goodbye because I must go with the men and you
with the girls, so see you after the war." I never saw him again.'

Men and women then had to line up in front of a high-ranking
officer – the infamous Dr Mengele – who directed some to one side
and some to the other. 'I was young and healthy and so I went right.
And all the women with children and people older than forty ...
went left ... It seemed quite senseless at the time. It wasn't, though.'

Anka and the other Häftlinge, including her Terezín girlfriends,
were then jostled into rows of five and marched away without a
moment to catch their breath. 'We had to run in that mud ... with
that smell and those flames. It was frightful. No one could imagine ...
how terrible that place was. It's indescribable.' Driven like geese to the
remote Sauna building and into what they were told was an 'undressing chamber' they found women in various states of nudity. They too
were commanded to take off all their clothes and underwear and leave
them in a heap. The order was accompanied by the warning that if

they resisted they would be shot. Like all those before them, they had their jewellery torn from their hands, necks and wrists.

In all her years at Terezín, Anka had somehow managed to hold on to her plain wedding band and the amethyst and silver engagement ring Bernd had given her, secreting it under her tongue or holding it in her fist. Somehow, in spite of the beady eyes of the Birkenau *Kapos* and guards, she managed to hang onto it again.

Pushed into the next room, the women were forced to sit naked while men and women wielding razors that snagged the skin roughly shaved their heads. Anka tried not to cry as she watched her once-silken tresses drop to her knees and then onto the floor. These locks were then swept by a birch broom into a kaleidoscopic cloud of hair – much of it still adorned with pins, ribbons or combs. Like shaven animals, the young women felt utterly barbarised and no longer human. Anka described it as one of the worst things that happened. 'You feel more than naked; you feel degraded . . . like a cockroach you can step on. It didn't hurt but . . . the humiliation . . . if you don't do it of your own free will . . . you can't imagine what you look and feel like without hair.'

Hair clipped from women's heads in Auschwitz

When they were ordered back into line, Mitzka, who'd been separated from her friend for only a few minutes, shouted frantically,
'Anka! Anka, where are you?'

Anka replied, 'If you are Mitzka, then I am standing right next to
you.'

She recalled, 'We were running around naked with the men looking at us and it was so awful. We were frightened but we still didn't
know of what.'

Pushed outside into the wind and rain for another *Appell* and her
next 'Mengele test', Anka passed muster once again as she covered
her breasts and prayed for some dignity. On seeing that everyone
was being searched for any last valuables, she retrieved her rings and
allowed them to slip from her fingers. Tears pricking her eyes, she
ground the rings deep into the soft clay with her bare foot. 'I took
my two rings and I threw them in the mud and said, "No Germans
will have them." It broke my heart but it was my choice, not
theirs ... Perhaps somebody found them but that was the most precious thing I had at that moment.' She knew that she'd lost her love
tokens from Bernd for ever, but it felt like an important act of defiance. It was a path she was set to continue.

Shuffled inside from the parade ground, they were told that they
would have to take a shower – an experience they welcomed
because they had no idea what 'going to the showers' might otherwise have meant. The water that hissed out instead of gas was
cold, intermittent and foul, and there was nothing with which to
lather away their sweat. Still wet, they were thrown odd, shapeless
clothes in rough material that immediately irritated their skin. 'We
were given some dreadful rags to wear and somebody was lucky
enough to get shoes or not so lucky. I got wooden clogs.' Then they
were driven towards the serried rows of huts that constituted the
prison blocks. As they ran, their nostrils became clogged with the
strange sickly smell that lingered constantly and appeared to
emanate from the belching chimneys.

One of the women turned to Anka and asked, 'Why are they

roasting meat here?' She looked at the strange wreaths of black smoke but couldn't answer. 'By then we were so frightened and confused and everything became a ghastly nightmare, which unfortunately was true.'

Their block was like an enormous chicken coop, with a dirt floor and no windows but narrow openings in the roof. Inside were wooden partitions each filled with three-tiered shelves that had no mattresses or coverings. The building was already perilously overcrowded. There must have been a thousand women in it with up to twelve in each bunk. The new arrivals were met with groans and the warm, malodorous stink of the unwashed. The women didn't know where they were supposed to sit or sleep or what they were meant to do.

One of Anka's friends who'd been transported from Terezín with her family desperately looked around for a familiar face but could find none. Eventually she asked one of the other women, 'What happens here? When will I see my parents again?' The rest of the *Häftlinge* laughed so hysterically that Anka thought they must have lost their minds. Was this where they'd been sent – to a lunatic asylum? Would they too go mad in this pit of despair? An older woman howled, 'You will see, and *what* you will see!' Another, with a crazy grin, cackled, 'You stupid cow! They are in the chimney by now. We will all go up in smoke, and then you'll see them!'

Anka was convinced then that the women were indeed insane. 'But we quickly came to realise that they were right and we were wrong . . . In that moment we knew what was happening there . . . they were burning people in the chimneys.'

The women from Terezín squeezed into bunks wherever they could, trying to stay together as a group. Anka and Mitzka pushed their way between two stinking bodies in a space that would scarcely fit a child. As they lay on the unyielding planks they gradually tried to take in all that had happened since they'd left what they now appreciated was the luxury of their ghetto. Some began to weep but most remained silent, overcome with exhaustion, or paralysed with fear as prisoner-guards patrolled the block.

'The *Kapos* were internees like us, only they had been there for some time and got this better job. Some of them were all right but some were worse than the Germans. They dropped a word here and a word there. We put two and two together and suddenly we knew. The people who were sent to the other side had been gassed within minutes of our arrival. My parents, sisters, Peter, and everybody who preceded us here ended in the gas chamber.'

As she was trying to take in the impossible, a woman named Hannelore who'd travelled with them broke into a popular German song. Before the rise of Hitler, she'd been a professional singer and she sang that night to try to lift their spirits. Anka said it did quite the opposite, however, and the women went crazy telling her to stop. 'That was apocalyptic,' she said, 'because you felt like listening to a song like you felt like going to the gas chamber.'

A few hours after they had arrived, the *Kapos* brought them some oily water they called soup, ladled from a dirty metal kettle. They were given an unwashed plate to share between four people and no spoons. 'We were so stunned by all these goings on – so frightened and so half-mad – that nobody was hungry, for the time being anyway.' Not yet comprehending how little they would be offered to eat, the new inmates spurned their only meal for days. The Polish women rushed forward to eagerly snatch their share, lapping it from their bowls like animals.

Lisa Miková, a Czech prisoner who'd arrived on the same transport as Anka, explained, 'The Polish women couldn't believe it and said, "You don't want to eat?" We told them, "No, it's horrible, and the bowls aren't washed." How they laughed. "Can we have it?" they asked. We saw how hungry they were then and how they licked even the smell from the plate. The next day the same soup came again and we hesitated again. The Poles told us, "We are also used to eating with forks and knives and spoons – that was normal. This place is not normal. If you don't eat then you will lose weight and then you will lose interest and then you will die." We could well imagine it, looking around us. And so we started to eat, even though it was so disgusting.'

Few slept those first nights and if they did manage to drift off they were rudely awoken for the dawn *Appell*, where they were chased out of their block by guards brandishing sticks. Then they were ordered to strip and stand in line for hours in the cold and the dark to be checked and double-checked, for no apparent reason other than to torment them. Some were beaten and called '*Saujud!*' (dirty Jew!) Others were slapped or spat at. Many were pulled out and marched away. 'Before you got there you had to wade through acres of mud and all the time above you the towering chimneys spilling flames. A real inferno ... Slowly, we started to understand what was going on.'

While Anka awaited her turn to live or die, she appreciated the importance of having shoes, however painful or ill-fitting they might have been. Those without footwear were shivering and desperate. Nobody could possibly survive without something to keep their feet from the cold, wet mud that lay thick and deadly on the ground. Her own life-support systems almost frozen, she vowed to keep her clogs with her at all times. She also learned other tricks of survival – chiefly the art of becoming invisible, keeping her head down, blending in without attracting unwanted attention. There were distinct factions among the prisoners that generally equated to East versus West, with Germans, Austrians and Czechs on one side, and Poles, Romanians and Hungarians on the other. Shoes, food and clothes were often stolen while people slept. With nerves strained to breaking point, fights broke out and it was easy to get caught in the middle.

'The more you were in the camp, the more you knew how to cope and how to survive,' Anka said. 'Everybody was trying to do their utmost not to offend the Germans ... to be like an ant crawling somewhere, [something] that doesn't matter. To get through the day somehow without being attacked.' It was helpful that she understood the German commands and could respond faster than those who didn't, and that she had a sixth sense about keeping away from those who might be duplicitous or dangerous. Whip-smart, she was able to close her mind to what the next hour might bring and focus only on getting through this one.

'The fear was overpowering but you had to cope with whatever came,' she said. 'I thought again of Scarlett O'Hara in *Gone with the Wind* saying, "I'll think about it tomorrow," so that's what I did.'

Anka spent the next ten days in what she called 'that living hell' in which she daily breathed in the dead. In a place where all concept of time was lost, it felt to her like a hundred years. She lived from hour to hour, never knowing what would happen to her. 'You were afraid all the time, twenty-four hours a day,' she said. There was nothing to fill their bellies but stale dry bread plus the insipid coffee-flavoured concoction in the morning or salt-flavoured water at night. There wasn't even a blade of grass to eat. Untold thousands in Auschwitz died of starvation or disease. What they were given brought on stomach spasms and diarrhoea, yet for the first time in their lives they couldn't just go to the toilet when they wanted to. She said that practically everybody had dysentery. 'I leave it to your imagination what it looked like and how it smelled ... you were in a dreadful state with no possibility of washing or anything. I got through that with difficulty. Being pregnant kept me going.'

With only limited access to the communal concrete holes, they were beaten or prodded with long poles or hay forks by SS officers shouting, '*Schneller! Scheisse!*' Anka said she would never forget the humiliating 'sport' the Nazis made of it, in the mud and the suffocating stench, poking women in the backside as they defecated. 'Just for fun, not even letting you do your business in peace ... a group of them said we will make fun of the Jews when they do whatever they do ... it was so degrading.'

*Appell*, announced by a bell, was at dawn and dusk with fresh *Selektionen* in between. In the complex arithmetic of death, there were so many to be counted and then entered into ledgers that the naked roll calls often lasted for up to three hours. Paraded in front of a team of medical staff smoking cigarettes, the women were mortified. 'It was just dreadful – clothes on or no clothes ... hungry and frightened and going through there and then left or right – by then we knew what it meant . . . at four o'clock in the morning . . . you stood in the rain and the wind . . . You were always frightened [that] next time it will be my turn and if they had known that I was pregnant, there was no other way.'

Anka went through at least twelve of these selections. 'I don't think they looked at us as human beings. The only criterion was, "Is she healthy enough to work?"' In her constant inner dialogue she asked, 'Will I make it? Will I get through this time?' She added, 'It becomes all about me, me, me . . . but if it's life or death you choose life . . . you don't do anything for or against it but you are relieved that you go this way and everybody else goes that way. It has nothing to do with the other people, but you have been chosen to live.'

If someone was unaccounted for – through sickness or death – the prisoners were forced to stand for hours, swaying with tiredness, until the numbers tallied. Exhausted and weak from subsisting on a few hundred calories per day, the pregnant, naked Anka tried not to faint as so many did during those interminable twice-daily *Appelle*. 'If someone fainted or became ill they were sent straight to the gas chamber. I fainted because I was pregnant and frightened and cold and hungry but my friends picked me up and stood me up and held me up and I was saved . . . everybody was very kind to me . . . because you mustn't be ill in Auschwitz – you either go to a hospital, are shot, or you walked to the gas chambers.'

And so she lived to see another day.

Just as Priska had longed to see Tibor, so Anka ached to be back in the arms of Bernd. Hope was all she had left. Hope that tomorrow would be better. Hope that she wouldn't get sick or lose her baby. Hope that she would make it out of there alive. Had Bernd, too, gone through this shocking phase of acclimatisation when he'd arrived in Auschwitz a week earlier? Was he in a bunk somewhere on the other side of the camp, his mind in equal turmoil, worrying about her the same way she was worrying about him?

Like Priska, however, Anka quickly learned that the women were kept far from the men and separated by cement posts three metres high and kilometre upon kilometre of coiled barbed wire. Nor could she find any information about the other members of her family – her parents and grandparents, aunts and uncles. Even if it was true about the gas chambers and the chimneys, surely the younger, healthier ones like her might have been saved?

What Anka didn't know was that she was in the minority. Of the approximately 1.3 million people deported to Auschwitz, 1.1 million were to perish, including most of her family, some of whom – she discovered later – had first been tricked into believing that they would stay together in a *Familienlager* (family camp). This was a section set up by the SS at Birkenau in the summer of 1943 when they expected the International Red Cross to demand a formal inspection of Auschwitz after they'd been allowed to visit Terezín. As part of the Nazis' global propaganda

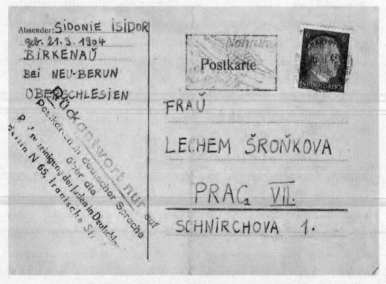

Postcard from Anka's sister Zdena from Birkenau
with Lechem for bread

campaign, from then on all new arrivals from Terezín were put in the family camp where they were allowed to keep their belongings, their hair and their clothes.

The new Czech inmates were then forced to write postcards to relatives at home and in Terezín to allay the growing fears that none of those transported ever contacted their loved ones again. In one such postcard received by their cousin Olga at her apartment in Schnirchova Street, Prague, dated October 1943, Anka's sister Zdena wrote – in German, as prescribed: *My dear ones, I am here with my husband and sister and my nephew. All are well and in good health ... Greetings and kisses, Yours Zdena Isidor.* At the risk of death, she slipped the Hebrew word *lechem* (bread) instead of 'Olga' into the first line of the address in the hope that her cousin would realise they were starving. Olga understood and immediately sent a food parcel, but Zdena and her family were unlikely ever to have received it.

Dr Rossel of the International Red Cross did pay an unannounced visit to Auschwitz that year but he was prevented from seeing any of the barracks or the infirmary. Instead, he chatted about winter sports with a young SS officer and promised to send medicines and cigarettes before he left. When his organisation didn't make the expected demand to see more, the SS liquidated the *Familienlager.* Having been protected for so long in what was called a 'harbour in an ocean of horror', the trusting parents, grandparents and children of Terezín were once again cast adrift. On the night of 8 March, in its largest mass murder of Czech citizens at the camp, some 3,700 Jews were among almost 5,000 who met their fate in the gas chambers, including most of Anka's family. Many were heard singing the Czech national anthem as they were marched to their deaths.

After more than a week in Birkenau, Anka lost all sense of time. She no longer had the strength to ponder the fate of her relatives; she couldn't even bring herself to think about the baby growing inside her, whose presence only placed her in the gravest danger. All she could think of was how to survive the next selection, all the while trying to avoid breathing in the flakes of ash that drifted ominously around the camp. On the morning of 10 October 1944, Anka overheard Dr Mengele tell his subordinates, '*Diesmal sehr gutes Material*' (This time, very good material), as he continued to make his personal choices, spinning women around to examine them front and back. Once again, her pregnancy went undetected and she was selected to live. 'We felt like cattle being sent to the slaughterhouse.'

That morning, still naked and holding onto her clothes, she and a group of women were not returned to their squalid barracks but were marched instead towards a large, low, sinister-looking building. Any who faltered in fear had blows rained on them by the *Kapos*. Anka thought, 'Is this it? Is this the gas chamber they've told us about? I thought we'd been selected for *Arbeit*.' Although she knew that all that really meant was that they would be worked to death instead of being murdered immediately.

Inside the unfamiliar building, they were ordered to take a shower. Praying, hoping, they were swept into the shower room en masse, sharing each other's sense of helplessness. They could hardly believe it when freezing cold water – not gas – sputtered through the showerheads. 'Water! Life!' some cried. Cleaner than they'd been in days, they were flung some more second-hand clothing before being given a little bread and salami, and then they were pushed to the railway ramp at a gruelling pace. Loaded into goods wagons, some five hundred of them were locked inside before their train pulled them away from the fire and brimstone, sour stink and cloying taste of Auschwitz.

Peering through a crack in the wall of her cattle car at those fat-fuelled flames blazing orange-red, Anka had no idea where she was being sent, but for the first time in weeks she dared herself to breathe normally again. 'We were sent away and we were thrilled because we knew it couldn't be worse ... The feeling that we were leaving Auschwitz alive – you just can't imagine! It was heaven.'

Losing sight of the hell of Birkenau was, she always said, one of the greatest moments of her life – just as it had been for Rachel and Priska. What none of them appreciated was that they had yet to face the greatest threats to themselves and their unborn babies – hunger, exhaustion and cold.

# 5

# Freiberg

The Freiberg factory where the women were enslaved

It was at the newly designated munitions factory in medieval Freiberg, a town in Saxony thirty-five kilometres southwest of Dresden, that the three expectant mothers were officially entered into the Nazis' slave labour ledgers for the first time.

Rachel Friedman, twenty-five, listed as Polish Jew 'Rachaela Fried-mann' (*Häftling* no. 53485), was the first of the three women to be sent to Freiberg on a train that left Auschwitz on 31 August 1944. One of 249 primarily Polish Jews, she was accompanied by her sisters Sala, Bala and Ester, still in shock after losing the rest of their family so soon after they reached Auschwitz from Łódź.

Priska Löwenbeinová, aged twenty-eight (no. 54194) and designated 'SJ' for Slovak Jew, arrived at KZ Freiberg on 12 October 1944. The train that brought her also carried five hundred Czech, German, Slovak, Dutch, Polish, Hungarian, Russian, American and a few 'stateless' women. Priska's new friend Edita, who'd assured Tibor that she would take care of his wife, was still loyally at her side. Although they didn't know each other, Priska was on the same transport as twenty-seven-year-old Anka (no. 54243), listed as Czech Jew 'Hanna' Nathan, who was accompanied by her friend Mitzka and several Terezín companions.

Another transport of 251 mostly Polish Jews had left Birkenau on 22 September. All three transports were assigned consecutive prisoner numbers, which indicated meticulous coordination between the authorities at Auschwitz and those at Flossenbürg in Bavaria – the main concentration camp for the region and the one under whose control KZ Freiberg fell. Although nameless and faceless as far as the Nazis were concerned, none of the 1,001 women and teenagers aged between fourteen and fifty-five who were sent to the abandoned porcelain factory in the heart of Freiberg town underwent the ordeal of having serial numbers tattooed on their forearms. Auschwitz was the only camp in the entire Nazi system that tattooed its inmates, a practice it had begun in 1941. Those destined for the gas chambers were never registered or tattooed, which worried any who were unmarked.

'We saw that everybody else was tattooed,' said Anka, 'but I never had any logical explanation [why we weren't], unless they knew that either we would die there or all go out to work in Germany or somewhere and it wasn't worthwhile.'

The train journey from Auschwitz took two nights and three days in closed goods wagons with little food or water. The only way they knew if it was day or night was via the chink of light through the grille of the tiny window. Leaning against each other or crouched in a corner, their legs drawn up tightly beneath them, they took turns to use the bucket with shared humiliation. Depending on which train they were on, some were fed coffee, bread and soup from a mess kitchen attached to the wagons. Others, like Anka, received nothing.

Her train finally rolled into the busy freight depot in Freiberg and disgorged its gasping cargo before its cars were hosed out and shunted back for its next payload. 'We left our wagons half-dead, half-starved and terribly thirsty but nevertheless alive,' Anka said. 'We were demented with thirst. It is unimaginable . . . You know, the worst of the lot – choosing between hunger, cold and thirst – is thirst. All the rest is bearable but with thirst you dry out and your mouth feels like mud and the longer it lasts the worse it gets . . . It is indescribably awful . . . you would give anything for a gulp of water . . . And then we stopped at the station in Germany . . . and they gave us something to drink and that was like ambrosia – marvellous. We weren't in Auschwitz but a civilised country.'

Dirty, dishevelled and frightened nevertheless, the women stared in hope at a clear sky free of chimneys or billowing plumes of

Priska's record at Freiberg

smoke. In wonderment, they were marched up the hill along Bahnhofstrasse through the medieval town. One survivor, fourteen-year-old Gerty Taussig from Vienna, said, 'It was so peaceful there. No one was in the street. Somehow we had the feeling that things were going to be better. We were wrong.' Priska said, 'When we smelled the trees and saw the greenery in a park we passed, we were dazed.'

Situated at the foot of the Erzgebirge (Ore Mountains) between Saxony and Bohemia, Freiberg had numerous ore and silver mines and an eighteenth-century university dedicated to mining and metallurgy. The only Jews left in the town were those married to Aryans, and the majority of its Gentiles worked in the mines or the optical industry. Several trains transporting *Häftlinge* to and from ghettos, concentration and labour camps had passed through Freiberg during the course of the war. Some came from Auschwitz, en route to nearby labour camps at Oederan and Hainichen, both in Saxony. Many had stopped in Freiberg to unload their human cargo, destined to slave in the mines and other industries.

Only a handful of the 35,000-strong population tried to help the unfortunate prisoners in their midst, and none of them did anything to assist the women from Auschwitz as they were herded in a ragged line through their town, a walk that took a little over thirty minutes. Rachel's sister Sala said she almost understood why. 'If they saw us from far away people would have thought we were from a crazy house for whores, murderers or prisoners. They were scared to look at us ... we didn't look like normal people – barefoot or in wooden shoes with strange dresses.' Priska concurred. 'People looked at us as if we were circus animals.'

The decision to manufacture aeroplane parts in an empty factory in the heart of Freiberg had been made in late 1943 by the Nazi government in collaboration with the armaments industry and the SS. Aside from all the planes they'd lost, many of Germany's largest aircraft assembly plants had been bombed in a massive strategic attack known as the 'Big Week' at the end of February 1944.

Thousands of Allied bombs were dropped on German cities in 3,500 sorties and the massive loss of aircraft and pilots meant that air superiority over Europe passed irrevocably into Allied hands. What was left of Nazi war manufacture had to be moved to underground bunkers or to places not previously associated with warfare.

Up until that point Freiberg had never come under military attack. Then on 7 October 1944, five hundred American bombers on a mission to destroy oil refineries in the Czech industrial region of Most were hampered by low cloud and looked around for an alternative target. Spotting Freiberg with its busy railway line and sprawling factories, they dropped sixty tons of bombs that killed almost two hundred people and destroyed hundreds of homes. In less than a week, and using slave labour already incarcerated in the town, the debris was swept away and the track repaired so that the latest transport from Auschwitz could deliver Anka, Priska and almost a thousand others to their new home.

Remains of factory and living quarters

The vast stucco-fronted Freiberger Porzellanfabrik in Frauen-steinerstrasse on a hill overlooking the town was built in 1906 to manufacture electrical isolators and clay industrial pipes. Owned by a company called Kahla AG, it closed in 1930 due to the economic depression and its Jewish owner Dr Werner Hofmann committed suicide after *Kristallnacht*. Having lain empty for more than a decade, the building was initially used for military storage and as temporary barracks for German soldiers. When it was decided to manufacture aeroplane parts there, the men were moved out and the women moved in.

The Arado-Flugzeugwerke company from Potsdam agreed a deal with the Reich Ministry for Armaments and War Production to pro-duce tailfins, wheels, wings and other parts for its Arado aircraft. More specifically, components were needed for its Ar 234 plane, the world's first jet-powered bomber, which had the reputation of being so fast and aerobatic that it was almost impossible to inter-cept. This plane was vital to the Nazis' *Jägerprogramm* (Hunter Programme) to try to regain control of the skies. Under the code name Freia GmbH, Arado agreed to pay the SS four Reichsmarks per day for every 'worker' it supplied, minus seventy *Pfennigs* a day for their 'catering needs'. For the 'loan' of labour at this one factory alone, the SS could earn up to 100,000 Reichsmarks per month, the equivalent of about £30,000 today.

Most of the prisoners worked in the main factory run by Freia, but some were transferred to the nearby Hildebrand munitions fac-tory where they made ammunition as well as precision optical parts for planes and U-boats. All were supervised by a handful of skilled German workers, as well as twenty-seven male SS guards and twenty-eight female SS-*Aufseherinnen* or prison warders. SS *Unterscharführer* (Junior Squad Leader) Richard Beck was placed in overall command of the camp and soon became known in camp code as 'Šára' by the prisoners.

The newest inmates and the first females were among 3,000 labourers including Italian POWs as well as forced workers from

Russia, Poland, Belgium, France and Ukraine who were employed in Freiberg's many factories or mines. The Italians were there as a punishment for their country's 'treacherous betrayal' of the Reich. The so-called *Ostarbeiter* (Eastern workers), forcibly recruited from the occupied territories, were dubbed *Untermenschen* (sub-humans) by the Nazis, who treated them accordingly. There were also some *Volksdeutsche*, ethnic Germans brought back to the 'Fatherland' who were told they could return to their homes once their contracts ended.

Even though the war looked to be coming to a critical point as US troops reached the Siegfried Line and the Soviets gained strength, purpose-built wooden barracks were still planned for the Jewish women a kilometre and a half from the factory near the shaft of a silver mine. Until these accommodation blocks were completed, the women were billeted on the recently vacated top floor of the six-storey redbrick factory.

When Rachel arrived on the first transport the place was far from ready. There was no machinery, nor any materials to work with, so she and the other prisoners were locked into their crowded quarters and given nothing to fill the hours. Their only chance to stretch their legs was during the interminable *Appelle* that the Nazis still

Rachel's record at Freiberg

insisted on, morning and night, where they stood in the foulest weather, waiting to be counted. Still, they reminded themselves, it was better than Auschwitz.

The sleeping arrangements were far better too; here they were two to a bunk in three tiers with up to ninety women to each room. They even had a pillow and a coverlet of sorts. There was a wash-room with (infrequent) cold water and a latrine without lavatory paper. Instead they used the linings of their clothes, discarded cardboard or old newspaper – anything they could find. They were especially happy to use newsprint if it featured a photograph of Hitler.

The prisoners were told that once they started work, they would be sharing twelve- to fourteen-hour shifts so that when one group left their bunks, the next would come back to take their places. Before they could start though, an outbreak of scarlet fever meant they were quarantined for a week and the Germans established a temporary sickbay manned by forty-two-year-old Russian prisoner-doctor Alexandra Ladiejschtschikowa (a Gentile), and thirty-two-year-old Jewish Czech paediatrician Edita Mautnerová, who was later to play a significant role in the women's lives.

Once the quarantine period was over, they were finally put to work. It was two weeks since they'd left Auschwitz. The early shift was woken at 3 a.m., roll call was at 4.30 a.m., and work began at 6.30 with a short break at noon. The work wasn't so hard in the beginning as the heavy machinery hadn't been delivered yet. The women mostly filed down or smoothed out small components. But the days were long and tedious and morale began to plummet. 'Everybody was depressed and we had to help each other ... The worst part was no sitting down for the whole fourteen hours and not even talking.'

By the time the later transports arrived, the production line was better organised, so the new arrivals were put straight to work. 'We were marched to a huge factory at the top of the hill where we started working forthwith ... ' said Anka, who was shown how to rivet tailfins. The machinery was heavy and difficult to hold but the factory was dry and warm, for which they were immensely grateful. 'I hadn't seen a riveting machine ever in my life before, and my friend neither, so you can imagine that the workmanship was beyond description ... We worked fourteen hours a day, the SS kept bothering us, but there was not a gas chamber in sight and that was all that mattered.'

| 1 | . | Munk | Edith | 25.12.24 | . | 12-10-44 |
|---|---|---|---|---|---|---|
| 2 | Stal. jüd. | Nathan | Hilda | 24.1.15 | ʍ | 12-10-44 |
| 3 | Tsch. jüd. | Nathan | Hanna | 20.4.17 | . | 12-10-44 |
| 4 | Ro. jüd. | Nadbath | Ingeborg | 15.2.24 | ʍ | 12-10-44 |
| 5 | Tsch. jüd. | Nagler | Helena | 23.11.14 | . | 12-10-44 |
| 6 | " | Nassau | Grete | 11.8.98 | ʍ | 12-10-44 |

Anka's record at Freiberg

Sala said, 'We got a job and started making aeroplanes, and that's why [the Germans] didn't win the war because we made those planes!' According to Priska, so many mistakes were made, 'You couldn't trust one plane that left that factory!'

The women were teamed up in pairs in the unheated work halls on the ground and first floors. Standing in ill-fitting or shredded shoes on cold concrete, they took turns to hold the pneumatic drills to use on wings that rested on metal trestles or were supported by scaffolding. Some were tasked with welding, rasping, polishing applying lacquer, while others sorted components or filed down the edges of aluminium sheets. For these largely educated professional women who'd never done manual labour in their lives, the repetitive work was physically and mentally demanding and put insufferable strain on arms, shoulders and hands, which ached day and night. In the intolerable din of pneumatic machines and drills, the air was thick with the dust from metal filings and the atmosphere toxic.

Rachel and her sister Bala were sent to work at the nearby Hildebrand factory, which ran a twenty-four-hour operation manufacturing propellers and small parts for planes. They were, she said, 'watched like hawks' and warned of the dire consequences of any sabotage. 'They told us that if anything left the factory wrong, then the person working on that machine would be hung from the machine for all of us to see,' said Rachel.

In the Freia factory there was a male SS officer in overall charge of each floor, assisted by a team of SS women some of whom were mean and some indifferent. Punishments were meted out daily and the *Häftlinge* were hit repeatedly. One guard slapped Priska hard across the cheek once for a minor matter but otherwise she was lucky. Anka, too, was hit by an SS guard who looked little older than a teenager. 'I was pregnant and in rags with no hair, looking like nothing on earth and ... she just came to me and smacked my face. It didn't hurt. It was just totally out of context.' Anka wanted to cry 'very much' at the 'sheer injustice' of being slapped for no offence and also for being unable to retaliate, but refused to give the guard the satisfaction. 'It hurt me mentally more than anything I can remember of that kind.'

The civilian *Meister* or foremen who worked alongside the prisoners rarely communicated with them other than to give orders. When they did speak, many of them did so in a Saxonian dialect that was not understood even by those who spoke German. Some of these men had been in the Wehrmacht and were either too old to fight or had been sent home injured. All were keen to hang onto their comfortable jobs for the duration of the war rather than be sent to the front. 'I don't think they could figure out who we were and not one of them ever spoke to me or did something good for me,' said Anka, who was paired up with her friend Mitzka. 'No one asked ... where we were from or what had happened to us. No one had any understanding at all. No one ever gave me a piece of bread or anything and they saw what we looked like and how we were treated.'

Survivor Lisa Miková had a friend who was a trained pharmacist. Her *Meister* was a man named Rausch who used sign language to communicate. One day, when she misunderstood him, the pharmacist accidentally brought him the wrong item. 'He took it and threw it across the room and it hit the wall. Then he hit her. She had enough and said in perfect German, "If you tell me what you want then I can bring it for you."'

Rausch looked at her in amazement. 'You speak German?'

'Of course,' she said. 'What do you think about us? We are doctors and teachers and intelligent people.'

'We were told that you are all whores and criminals from different cities, which is why they shaved your heads.'

'No. We are just Jews.'

'But the Jews are black!' cried the foreman, an opinion born of some of the wilder Nazi propaganda of the time.

After that, Rausch treated her with more respect. Not everyone else did. Some of the guards who'd heard that the prisoners weren't whores or criminals refused to believe it. With necks that bulged over the collars of their uniforms and buttons straining not to burst, they openly mocked such claims. One 'hunchback' named Loffman who had graduated from Gestapo school with honours and often threw hammers at those in his charge told one woman, 'You, a teacher? You're a piece of dirt!' Other guards were even more sadistic, administering beatings variously with tools, fists, belts or the end of ropes. The grumpy *Unterscharführer* known as Šára would get angry at the slightest thing and frequently struck women who annoyed him.

The female guards were often the cruellest. They not only hit the prisoners or gave them lashes but also devised punishments they knew would affect them as women. This might include forbidding them to use the toilet or commanding their friends to shave off what hair they had left, or create a stripe down the centre of their heads. One especially brutal SS officer fired her pistol to frighten the women and accidentally shot one of them in the leg, which later became infected with gangrene and began to smell.

Working their alternate shifts, the prisoners did one week of nights and then one of days, seven days a week. They had a few Sundays off which gave them a chance to rest and wash and dry their ragged clothing. Once a month, the few select prisoners who worked in the offices and therefore in closer proximity to the Germans were marched in groups to the seventeenth-century *Arbeitshaus*, a workhouse for the poor in the centre of the old town. There, they were allowed the luxury of a shower.

For all of the women, though, the work was usually so demanding and they were provided with such little nourishment that their physical decline was rapid and severe. Many fainted, which caused an unwelcome slowdown in production as a result of which they were usually beaten or kicked until they rallied. Survivor Klara Löffová said that there were two important rules: 'You don't admit that you are sick or that you don't know what to do.' Nor did they panic when the air-raid sirens went off. 'The danger of being killed or harmed by a bomb seemed to us smaller than to be supervised by SS with guns.' Privately, they cheered every Allied plane and scorned the ear-splitting flak from anti-aircraft weapons positioned on nearby roofs. If ever they saw a British or American plane being shot down morale would slip and 'the rest of the day was good for nothing'.

In spite of being paid to feed their workforce, the SS gave them only the poorest-quality food and the barest minimum required for survival. One described the provisions as 'a hot piece of dirt'. The only benefit was that they were each given a mug, bowl and spoon, which meant they no longer had to eat with hands deeply ingrained with grime. The rations were exactly the same as in Auschwitz, though – bitter black water in the morning with a piece of bread, then some suspicious-smelling soup made of beets, root vegetables or pumpkin, all of which they ate sitting on the floor or wherever they could find a space. Klara Löffová said, 'A so-called kitchen shelled out soup; sometimes thick, sometimes watery. On long tables, no sitting down, our German *Lagerführer*, an SS man, walked in his high boots up and down on top of the table, his belt with his SS buckle in his hand, ready to swing. The girls soon learned not to steal from someone else.' They also learned to shield their eyes, for the loss of an eye would mean a return to Auschwitz and certain death.

In the evenings they were given 400 grams of bread and some coffee. Occasionally, they were allowed extra *Nachschub* (supplies) such as a small stick of margarine, a dollop of marmalade or a thin slice of salami. Often, they didn't know whether to eat the margarine or use it on their dry, flaking skin. Anka said some of the women were disciplined and divided their food into portions, which they ate at intervals throughout the day. 'I ate mine all at once and then I was hungry for twenty-four hours,' she said.

Priska had a pregnancy craving for raw onion and would often try to exchange her entire bread ration for a segment. She was more fortunate than most because her protector Edita, who'd somehow managed to secrete some valuables, bribed one of the older Wehrmacht guards to smuggle in food. The man known as 'Uncle Willi, The Brave' was the only one under whose uniform there seemed to beat a human heart. He repeatedly risked his job or even his life by doing small favours for those in his charge. With his help, Edita continued to whisper, 'Open mouth,' to her pregnant friend and feed her a few extra morsels.

Gerty Taussig said, 'We knew exactly who'd smuggled gold or diamonds in their private parts, because those women looked better than the majority of prisoners. But not one of us would have given their secret away.' Even with such rare extras, the craving for food weighed heavily on the pregnant women and became their all-consuming concern. Hunger was their constant companion, along with their growing babies.

Anka never once allowed herself to consider that she wouldn't survive, though. 'I have been blessed with a very optimistic state of mind, which helped enormously ... I always looked up and not down ... I knew that I would make it, which was totally stupid and irrational, but I lived with this idea ... even though I was almost dying of hunger.'

Rachel, who also craved food, said, 'We came home very tired and whoever could save a piece of bread would share it.' One day, she found a slice of raw potato and sucked on it like a boiled sweet until there was nothing left. Another time she came across a mouldy cabbage half-buried in wet mud and, although she knew she could have been shot if she'd been seen picking it up, she was so hungry that she risked it. Although the cabbage stank and was so decomposed that her fingers went straight through it, she ate it whole and claimed nothing had ever tasted so good in her whole life.

In almost every spare moment the women continued to talk about food. 'And such food!' said Anka. 'Not one egg or two, but ten eggs in cakes with four kilos of butter and a kilo of chocolate. It was the only way we could cope. The richer the cakes the better. It gave us some sort of satisfaction. And we devised other delights such as bananas wrapped in chocolate and then jam. It was a fantasy that helped us even though we were starving. Actually I don't know if it helped or not, but you can't help thinking about it because you are so hungry.' In fact, instead of creamy cakes they had only 'loathsome' liquids to live on with a little bread. 'In the end we liked everything they gave us to eat and everything was wonderful and not enough.'

When their shift ended they were finally allowed to rest on the upper floors of the factory. It was then that the women were most relieved to be working in a solid brick building instead of a draughty hut, although when they first opened the doors to the sleeping quarters they immediately smelled *Bettwanzen* – bedbugs. The SS accused the women of bringing the bugs with them but the previous inmates must have left them there. 'The little beetles have a certain smell – sort of sweet,' said Anka. 'It is horrible and there were thousands of them ... so many that they kept dropping from the ceiling into our mugs so whatever we ate, we ate bedbugs first.

We didn't mind so much at first because bedbugs only live in a warm place, but if you squash them – they have a particular smell and it is dreadful.'

Without access to any news, or even to clocks, the women barely knew what day it was, and had no inkling of the dramatic events happening in the outside world. In that unventilated factory where they never saw the light of day or took in a breath of fresh air, no one bothered to enlighten them. Even the older Wehrmacht soldiers who showed occasional kindness told them little. They had no idea that the *Sonderkommando* in Auschwitz II-Birkenau had blown up Crematorium IV in October 1944, rendering it useless, but they did hear from some of the German workers that the Battle of the Bulge was raging in the Ardennes.

Their daily routine continued with no variation. Filthy and smelly, with aching muscles, painful feet and teeth, most women spent their days and nights fighting their own mental battles and trying to stay alive. A few couldn't stand their gruelling existence and they lost their minds, only to be sent away. 'We worked like crazy, on our feet for hours with hardly any hair or clothes. We ate, we kept quiet, and we minded our own business,' said one prisoner. 'Whatever we had on we washed and put it on wet again. No one had time for anything else.' Rotting from the inside, their gums bled, their parchment skin broke down, and any minor sore became potentially lethal. None of the women had periods as their bodies shut down and felt dead inside, and they didn't have the energy for thoughts of resistance or rebellion. 'At Freiberg we didn't sabotage anything. We were afraid of our own shadow,' said another prisoner. 'We didn't know how to fight back. If you said, "Where are you taking me and why?" you got hit over the head or they shot you. So everyone became too afraid to say anything.'

With educated but unskilled prisoners as a workforce, progress at the factory was painfully slow. So when Klara Löffová's shift finished its first aeroplane wing at Christmas, a big fuss was made. The prisoners were promised – but never received – bonuses of soap powder, bread or cheese if they completed a job. 'The German workers celebrated, attached the wing to ropes from the ceiling and were ready for a good time. Suddenly, the rope tore, the wing fell down and was badly damaged,' she said. 'Now it was our turn to celebrate.' Some of the women did receive small bonuses at Christmas – a slightly larger ration and the chance to 'buy' some celery salt – but for most it was work as normal.

On New Year's Eve 1944, six months pregnant and still concealing her condition under her baggy dress, Anka tripped carrying a heavy metal workbench which fell on her leg, cutting it badly but fortunately not breaking the bone. 'My immediate thought was, "My child! What will happen to my baby?" I was sent to a makeshift hospital and had my leg dressed and spent some time there. It was warm and I didn't have to work. There was not much food but I could save my energy to heal my leg.'

Lying in the small sickbay trying to make herself look well enough not to be sent back to Auschwitz, Anka knew that being ill was not an option in a place where the only alternative to labour was death. Some of the women weren't even aware that there was a sickbay. Others knew about it but feared it was merely a stepping-stone to execution, so they avoided it and treated their own cuts, sores and illnesses in whichever way they could. Gerty Taussig said, 'When you were sick, you worked or you died. Many people cured their skin problems with urine, which is all we had. That also helped my best friend who had impetigo and the pus was just dripping from her arm. Another time, my bunk collapsed and I fell onto my back and was paralysed for a while. No doctor came but I survived.'

Never having had time to really consider the baby growing inside her, Anka was able to focus on it in the infirmary for the first time. She couldn't feel it kicking as she had with baby Dan, but somehow she sensed that it was still alive. Recalling her romantic nights with Bernd in their Terezín hayloft she worked out that their second child would be due at the end of April. She also began to wonder what would happen if she – and it – survived. Unable to hide her pregnancy from Dr Mautnerová, the Czech paediatrician who cared for her, Anka began to confide her fears. 'I had idiotic conversations with her. I said, "What will happen if the war isn't over and my baby is born, and the Germans take it away from me to be brought up in a German family? Where will I find it?" It never occurred to me that they would kill it, or me. I discussed it often with her and she didn't let on and was kind to me and assured me I would find it.'

Anka eventually returned to work but was put on so-called 'easy' duties, which involved sweeping the floors of the factory from top to bottom, including the stairs, fourteen hours a day. Although it was monotonous, she claimed it was the best possible exercise a pregnant woman could have. Still, her guards didn't seem to notice that she was with child, or they would have almost certainly sent her back to the gas chambers.

Rachel, too, was lucky in that her boss was Czech and kind to her. 'When he saw my belly growing he had me sitting, not standing, and checking that the rivets on the wings were OK,' she said. 'I lost weight but had no morning sickness ... so I very much wanted to save the child. There was nothing more important.'

By January the new barracks for the Jewish workers were finally completed almost two kilometres away, on a street named Schachtweg in an area known as Hammerberg. As the mercury dropped, the women were turfed out of their warm, bug-infested beds and forced into the freezing new barracks. Arriving in the middle of a blizzard, they found their quarters on a snow-covered building site surrounded by high fences. The barracks, which smelled of unseasoned wood and cement, were unheated. Water dripped from the ceilings and down the walls, soaking the straw of the rank mattresses they were commanded to fill. Due to the lower ceilings there were only two tiers of bunks instead of the usual three, but none knew which were worse – the wet upper bunks or the damp lower ones.

The *Waschraum* was in a separate building and not operational at first, so the women could only wash themselves at an outside tap that repeatedly froze solid. They had small stoves and even a little coal to begin with, but the *Kapos* stole it to fuel the fires in their rooms, so thick ice frosted the inside of the windows every night. Other barracks for Russian, Ukrainian, Italian, Polish, French and Belgian prisoners-of-war were built in the same area and the women could occasionally spot some of these inmates at a distance through the coils of barbed wire that segregated them. A few of the men also worked in the factory as electricians and mechanics, so they were familiar faces to those whose jobs brought them into contact.

At a risk to all their lives, messages were occasionally passed via notes wrapped around stones and hurled across fences. Snatches of news about the progress of the war were swapped and even a few relationships sparked. Multilingual Priska was asked by a prisoner to translate a *billet-doux* from French into Slovak, a 'crime' punishable by she knew not what penalty. She undertook it gladly, though, thinking back to the love letters she and Tibor had written to each other and the wondrous moment when she'd spotted him through the wire at Auschwitz.

One day in the barracks an SS guard spotted her scribbling something onto a scrap of paper with the stub of a pencil. It was a reply for a woman who'd fallen for a Belgian. Seeing the guard bearing down on her, Priska simply screwed up the evidence and swallowed it. She received a beating for her trouble, followed by a long interrogation, but still she told them nothing.

The private German company that relied on its slave workforce to stay alive at least until the end of the war issued the prisoners with winter clothing that included stockings and black wooden clogs in which to clatter noisily to and from the factory. There weren't enough to go round, though, so many women had to make do with the thin-soled and inappropriate shoes they'd been thrown in Auschwitz. Nor was getting clogs always the best option, as they were usually too big or too small and caused painful blisters that never healed and became infected. Without any grip to their soles, the clogs were also treacherous on ice. And with no backs to them, they filled with water or snow and never dried out.

The wooden shoes had the additional disadvantage of resounding loudly against the granite cobblestones whenever the women marched, jarring already aching bones. To add to the dissonance, the well-shod SS guards in highly polished boots marched alongside them, urging them to keep pace as they shouted, '*Links! Zwei! Drei! Vier . . .*!' (Left, two, three, four . . .). Klara Löffová said, 'The people living along the street we walked to and from work were not too happy, even sending complaints to the factory about the noise at five in the morning. Imagine, five hundred people in wooden shoes marching on the street. It was blackout time constantly. They were not allowed to switch the lights on. Then at six o'clock the other group coming back from the night shift and noise again. And the morning hours were the only time they dared to go to bed – the RAF by that time were back on their way to England. We didn't care, we didn't sleep either.'

Even with new shoes, the women still wore the skimpy, peculiar items of clothing they'd been given, which by then were falling apart and were often held together by clips and string. They were mostly also without underwear or socks. If they were lucky enough to find a rag they'd wrap it around their shorn heads as a headscarf to protect them from the howling winds during their twice-daily march. Later they would use the same rag as a makeshift vest, to pad tight shoes, or to wrap around frostbitten toes. More often than not, though, the guards would snatch the scraps away.

And so the trek to and from the factory in the dark became a new torture, especially with painful feet and limbs stiff from immobility and cold. Anka said, 'It was a long walk through the town where they kept spitting at us and calling us God knows what. And we had to walk all that without coats . . . or stockings or something ... It was awful.' Survivor Chavna Livni said: 'Every day the march through the dark town – before daylight, in total darkness – hardly anybody on the street – by and by I know each stone, every corner where the wind is especially cruel – And our way back again, again in darkness, into the ice-cold huts where there are stoves, but they are unlit.'

Once winter gripped, rain turned to snow and the frozen, starving prisoners limped exhausted through trenches of slush as fresh snowfalls coated them thickly. Alongside them their guards wore multiple layers of clothing topped with knee-length military greatcoats or capes, their rifles slung over their shoulders as they thrust gloved hands deep into their pockets.

One kind German with whom Rachel worked secretly gave her some pieces of soft white cotton cloth torn from material used to polish the aircraft wings; the corners were stamped 'Freiberg KZ'. Someone else managed to get hold of a needle and thread, so Rachel borrowed it to fashion bras for herself and Bala. The same kind supervisor also slipped them a few extra morsels and it was he who found them some wooden shoes, as they hadn't been issued with any. 'His excuse was that we would cut our feet on the iron filings from the machines and they'd get infected, but we always thought it was so it would be easier for us to walk to work when it was cold and raining.'

Leopoldine Wagner, an Austrian who'd been hired as an interpreter for the Italian POWs, was another employee at the factory who risked her life to help the prisoners. She said: 'It broke your heart to see [the women] so thin, shaved, at eighteen degrees below zero without warm clothes, without socks, just in clogs ... with bloody feet.' She felt ashamed to be married to a German in the face of such misery and to see people 'so tormented' and 'dog miserable' with pus and blood oozing from their feet. After she found out that all they had to eat was 'horrible' turnip soup, she tried to slip a piece of bread or other food into a prisoner's mouth whenever they came into her office to scrub the floor. One day, she gave a bra-cum-vest to a woman who had nothing to warm her back or support her breasts.

The next day, an SS officer returned the vest to her and asked if it was hers. She nodded sheepishly. 'If you have something to give then give it to a German,' she was told coldly. 'Otherwise your name will not be Frau Wagner any longer, but number one thousand and something.'

ID card of Leopoldine Wagner

Faced with such a threat, Leopoldine Wagner was almost too scared to risk helping the prisoners any more. 'Naturally I was afraid. If a man didn't howl with the wolf then he had one foot in the concentration camp.' However, one day she came into contact with a teenage Hungarian Jew named Ilona, who she learned had been a pianist before the war. Bravely, she decided to try to help Ilona escape. 'I repeatedly recited the address of my sister in Austria so that she would remember it,' she said. 'My idea was that she would be able to disappear into a convent.' With the help of the local

Catholic priest, she hid a nun's habit in the confessional of the Johanniskirche church in the centre of the old town and told Ilona to try to slip away from her guards and run there the next time she was sent for a shower at the nearby *Arbeitshaus*. 'What became of her, I do not know. But the habit disappeared.'

Other locals such as Christa Stölzel, then aged seventeen, who worked in the factory office, also took pity on the prisoners and hid bread and cake from her lunch box in the wastepaper baskets for those who cleaned the offices to find at night. It was a crime for which there was a high penalty, but she did it repeatedly in the hope of helping the prisoners. Others too performed acts of kindness – like the foreman who would leave dressings for sores – or, on special occasions, a small bag of sweets – hidden between the struts of the aircraft wings.

The majority of the townspeople, however, did nothing – out of fear or ignorance. Frau Wagner said that the camp was 'simply hushed up'. She added, 'Most only knew that there were barracks on Hammerberg, but who was suffering in there, they didn't want to know.' With little outside intervention, the women's hardship only deepened along with the winter. Even though they chose to sleep three or more to a bunk under a thin blanket, they were frozen, their feet and hands like icicles. Intense cold was hunger's friend and the more calories they burned to keep warm, the more their bellies ached. Gradually, their bodies began to disintegrate, along with their morale.

What dispirited the women still further as they were marched through the streets each day was the sight of the Freibergers going about their ordinary business. They watched children making snowmen or leaving for school in winter coats, hats and scarves. They saw men setting off to work as their *Frauen* waved from the windows. Lisa Miková said, 'We saw people looking at us from inside their nice warm houses. There were SS all around – about twenty of them – and it would have been impossible to communicate with us or give us food – but no one even tried. There was no interest.'

Fourteen-year-old Gerty Taussig knew by then that her parents and sister had been gassed in Auschwitz. 'It broke your heart to see families sitting around happily in the warmth of their homes, eating and laughing and leading normal lives,' she said. 'No one showed us any kindness. Not a soul. We were just ghosts. None of us thought that we'd ever survive and do anything normal like that again.'

One day twenty-two-year-old German prisoner Hannelore Cohn spotted something on a morning march that made her stop in her tracks and almost trip everyone else up. Her mother, a blonde Gentile from Berlin, was standing on a street corner watching her daughter march past. One of the German *Meister* had secretly written to her family at her request to let them know that she was alive. 'Her mother moved to Freiberg just to see Hannelore walking to the factory and back,' said survivor Esther Bauer, who knew Hannelore for much of her life. 'Her mother stood every morning at the gate when we came to work. They couldn't speak to each other but at least Hannelore knew she was there,' she said. 'We all did.'

Gerty Taussig remembered the sight too, and added, 'What a tragedy to stand in the street to see her emaciated daughter walking by and not even able to wave.' Still, the mother stood on that corner every day for weeks and all those who noticed her drew comfort from her presence.

Once inside the shelter of the factory, the prisoners were able to dry out and warm up a little, although their hands throbbed painfully as they thawed. If rain or sleet was falling when they made their return march or during evening *Appell* they had nowhere to dry their clothes and no choice but to lie in them all night, shivering and wet. It was often so cold that the water froze in the tap above the trough in their communal washroom. There was one towel to share and a small piece of soap if they were lucky. They had no toothbrushes or combs and as their hair began to grow out unevenly, it itched and matted. For some, the hair grew back pure white.

As the days passed with no respite, each *Häftling* retreated into the half-life that Fate had allotted them and struggled to get through each day. Living in separate barracks, working separate shifts often in separate buildings, Priska, Rachel and Anka still knew nothing of each other. Nor were they aware of the few others also hiding their pregnancies and wondering similarly how long it would be before they were found out. A Czech friend of Lisa Miková who'd managed to hide her pregnancy unexpectedly went into labour one night. 'She delivered her own baby in Freiberg in the barracks in February, and then the SS murdered the child,' Lisa said. 'The guards took the baby away and she heard later that it had been killed.' Two more women, suspected of being pregnant also, were sent back to Auschwitz.

Their fate is unknown but their condition is unlikely to have pleased Dr Mengele, according to Czech survivor Ruth Huppert who'd been living in the Terezín ghetto with her husband around the same time as Anka. When she fell pregnant during a new round of transports at the end of 1943, she pleaded for an abortion, but the Nazis had banned the prisoner-doctors from carrying out abortions by then. Just like the three mothers in Freiberg, she was sent to Auschwitz pregnant but managed to hide it during selections. She then persuaded a *Kapo* to put her name on the list of those chosen to be sent away for slave labour.

When she had almost reached full term and was working in a German oil refinery, her pregnancy was detected and she was returned to Auschwitz in August 1944. Mengele, who demanded to know how she'd gone unnoticed, told her, 'First you will deliver your baby, and then we'll see.' Within hours of her daughter being born, the 'Angel of Death' announced that he wanted to see how long a baby could survive without food. He commanded that the mother's breasts be tightly bandaged to stop her feeding her child. For eight days, feverish and with her breasts swollen with milk, she and her baby lay helplessly together as Mengele visited daily. Only when the little girl was half-dead did her mother inject her with morphine given to her by a prisoner-doctor. Her child's death saved her life and she was sent to another labour camp, eventually to survive.

The three mothers and their babies in Freiberg might well have endured a similar fate if their pregnancies had been discovered and they'd been returned to Dr Mengele. Not that there was any guarantee they would even survive Freiberg when, in the coming months, death began to claim their fellow prisoners. First, a Slovak woman in her twenties fell sick and died of sepsis after less than a month in the factory. She was buried the same day as a thirty-year-old German woman who'd died of scarlet fever. Their deaths were quickly followed by at least seven more – women and girls aged between sixteen and thirty who succumbed to pneumonia, lung, heart or other diseases. All were cremated and buried in a mass grave in the local Donat cemetery.

The memorial to the dead of KZ Freiberg

Priska, as tired and hungry as the rest of the inmates, stubbornly refused to allow thoughts of death to enter her mind. Still pinning her hopes on Tibor being alive somewhere, urging her to think only of beautiful things, she gazed intently at the intricate frost patterns on the windows of their barracks. One of the few who lifted her head each time they plodded to and from the factory, she would kick at the powdered snow to watch it sparkle or marvel at the hoarfrost that coated the trees like sugar on foggy mornings. She'd promised Tibor that she and their baby would survive, and he'd told her that was all he was living for. 'I was just focused on my husband and baby. I didn't try to get close to anyone ... ' she said. 'I was hoping that [Tibor] would be there when I came home.'

Morale dipped lower with an even greater drop in temperatures, however, and the women couldn't help but feel increasingly desperate and abandoned. They were painfully aware that the long harsh winter would only make conditions more unbearable. Deprived of the most basic needs while slaving for the Nazis, the ghostlike figures lost even more weight. Their clothes and spirits threadbare, they developed festering sores from lice, bedbugs and their own inner decay. There was no space in their heads to think of anything but food and surviving another day. 'I don't even remember having dreams,' Anka said. 'It took so much to stay alive that there was no time for anything else.'

For Anka and Rachel, who'd already endured years of privation in the ghettos, their pitiful existence beyond all human reach seemed interminable. Whatever would happen to them and their unborn babies? What about Bernd and Monik? Were they even alive? Anka had Mitzka to share her burden and whisper to in the night, although she was afraid that even her knowledge of the pregnancy might be dangerous. Rachel, who worked with Bala every day and shared her bunk, hadn't even told her or her other two sisters that she was expecting for fear that the information might put them at risk too.

Sala and Ester had been fortunate enough to be given secretarial jobs in the factory office, which meant better food and clothing and relative comfort. 'We started off building aeroplanes but an SS officer came over to me when I was filing metal and asked me in German, "Where's your sister?" I was always with her but I looked at him in shock because I didn't even know that he knew we were sisters.' He told them to follow him and they walked to the far end of the factory. 'He kept on talking to me in German and asking me, "Do you know how to read and write?" He put the two of us in an office where all the plans were kept for how to make the aircraft, and we were safe for eight months! We were so lucky. We didn't have to work hard; we had Sundays off and they even took us to the bunkers whenever there was a raid. It was cold in that part of the factory, though, and we used newspaper to wrap ourselves in and keep ourselves warm.'

After their day in the office Sala and Ester joined the rest of the women for the long march back to the barracks, where they were reunited with their sisters Rachel and Bala and tried to encourage each other to keep going. 'It helped to share our troubles,' Sala said. 'We all did, especially when somebody was at the point of giving up. We would tell them that things would be better tomorrow. Always tomorrow.'

Even though the women were so terribly hungry all the time, they continued to invent imaginary feasts and recite recipes. A common game was to 'invite' friends for an elaborate meal and then talk them through the preparation and eating of the various dishes until their fanciful bellies were full. Another was to endlessly discuss the first thing they would like to eat when the war was over – the magical, mythical event simply known as 'Afterwards', which none could be sure would ever come. A thick slice of fresh bread smeared with butter was a firm favourite, although the younger girls often longed for something sweeter. Quality potatoes cooked in every possible way (especially fried) usually gained the highest number of votes.

Those who'd been cooked for all their lives by mothers or servants claimed that it was in Freiberg that they first learned how to prepare food, even though to hear the lists of ingredients for such extravagant meals drove them to distraction. Often it became a kind of self-defeating torture, reminding them too much of mothers and grandmothers and their comfortable lives 'Before', with all the scents and family rituals: the mouth-watering smell of freshly baked bread, the aroma of fresh coffee, or the smell and feel of lavender soap in their hands as they washed before each meal. When they looked down at the state of their begrimed fingers, they almost laughed.

'All of a sudden we'd say, "Stop! We won't speak about it!" Then half an hour later, we'd start again,' said Lisa Miková. 'Food was at the centre of our thinking – always. It dominated our lives. We longed for meat and dumplings and normal things like ham and bread. I used to say if I could just have potatoes and bread, I would not want for anything ever again.'

Gerty Taussig managed to find an entire raw potato one day, which she shared with her best friend. 'We sliced it up very thin and ate it and it was the best thing I ever tasted. I told myself, "If I survive, this is all I shall eat." It was finished far too soon.'

Aside from massive weight loss, the women's extreme malnutrition caused all sorts of medical problems for which they received no treatment or sympathy. One day, Klara Löffová developed a painful tooth infection. 'At first, nobody cared but a few days later one half of my face got so swollen and hard that I couldn't see. Our *Lagerkommandant* took me to a dentist in town. I had to march ahead of him, he had a rifle with a bayonet; people looking at us thought that he'd just captured the biggest spy in the world.' The dentist was told that as Klara was a prisoner he was only to do 'necessary work' and not 'waste' any anaesthetic on her. The SS officer wanted to watch but the dentist shooed him out, saying there wasn't enough room for him to work. 'I walked in, it was warm, clean and he was polite,' said Klara. 'Tears came to my eyes and, when he asked me if it hurt that much, I truthfully said, "No, the tears are because it has been a long time since I was treated as a human being." He worked using [the painkiller] Novocaine and told me, if asked by the *Scharführer*, to tell him that it was very painful. I understood. He let me sit down for over an hour. I enjoyed every minute and gladly came back after a week for an unnecessary check-up.'

Such compassion was rare and most lived with the daily expectation of death. Having thought that nothing could be worse than Auschwitz, they began to realise that their time in KZ Freiberg would also be a fight for survival. 'We were supposed to die,' several of the women declared. 'And we had so wanted to live!' As the days passed without rescue, it wasn't a question of if but when they would die. If not of starvation or at the hands of the guards, the increasing numbers of Allied bombs would surely kill them.

There was a full shift of women in the factory, including all three mothers, when British planes from Bomber Command attacked Dresden, forty kilometres from Freiberg. Air Marshal Arthur Harris ordered a series of raids between 13 and 15 February 1945. Most Dresdeners believed that their city would never be targeted because of its historic and cultural status. Many were unaware that in the sixth winter of the war, the Nazis had chosen it as a key location in a planned 'Elbe Line' of defence running from Prague to Hamburg, which placed it squarely in the Allies' crosshairs.

It had been six years since Hitler ordered the strategic bombing of Polish cities such as Wieluń and Warsaw, followed by devastating raids on Holland, and four years since his *Blitzkrieg* of London claimed 20,000 lives between September 1940 and May 1941. The 'Blitz' on the British capital lasted for seventy-six consecutive nights and damaged more than a million homes. Almost simultaneously, the port of Liverpool and its surrounding areas were attacked in a series of bombing raids between August 1940 and May 1941, killing almost 4,000 people. The city of Coventry was targeted in the eighteen raids of *Operation Mondscheinsonate* (Moonlight Sonata), the most damaging of which occurred on 14 November 1940.

Some five hundred German bombers attacked the city that night with five hundred tonnes of high-explosive bombs and incendiary devices, intent on destroying its factories. More than 4,000 homes were lost and two-thirds of the city destroyed. Hundreds of people lost their lives and over a thousand were injured, adding to those from previous raids. In the coming years, fresh raids on the city would result in further losses, bringing the death toll there to 1,236.

These attacks and others were matched by numerous Allied raids on Germany and occupied Poland, including Hamburg and Berlin as well as cities such as Pforzheim, Swinoujscie and Darmstadt, many with equally devastating results. Dresden, however – known as the 'Jewel Box' for the ornate rococo and baroque style of its architecture – was to become one of their most controversial targets. As the first waves of British Lancaster bombers homed in on the city after a five-hour flight from Lincolnshire at around 10 p.m. on 13 February 1945, sirens began to wail to warn the citizens of Freiberg of a possible air raid. The SS locked most of the prisoners – including Priska, Rachel and Anka – into the top floor of the factory, which could well have been an RAF target. They then fled to their basement shelters with the foremen and civilian staff.

The women were instructed to turn off the lights and draw blackout curtains so as not to attract attention but they immediately disobeyed, eager to see the seven hundred or so heavy bombers swooping in low above them. On several occasions they watched as aircraft slowly circled their factory as if on a dummy run and wondered if the next bomb-load might be for them. Anka said, 'We willed the RAF to drop a bomb on us . . . so that the factory wouldn't work on this war project . . . but they didn't.'

Rachel too recalled that on the nights Dresden was bombed they shouted at the sky: 'Come here! Come and bomb us! We're going to die anyway!' She added, 'We were absolutely certain that none of us would survive. It was just a question of living as long as we could. It was only when Dresden was bombed that the realisation finally dawned on us that we might be saved.'

A handful of German guards who'd been posted outside their door in case the women tried to escape complained bitterly about having to put themselves at risk. 'They told us not to look out of the windows and not to make any signals to the pilots with lights,' said Lisa Miková. 'We were cheering and they were furious that we were so happy.'

Although the capital of Saxony was some distance away, the night sky was lit up by the incendiary devices and high explosives that decimated it. An estimated 25,000 inhabitants of Dresden were killed and the subsequent firestorm painted the sky red, destroying more than six square kilometres of the city. 'That was the most magnificent theatre I ever saw in my life because we watched all those firebombs and their colour in the sky and we wished them all the worst things in the world. It was ... fabulous ... there was such satisfaction,' said Anka. 'After the war everyone spoke badly of "Bomber" Harris but he was a saint to me.'

The bombing of Dresden

One of the foremen came back from the devastated city the next day and reported that 'not a stone was left' in the old part, nor a family untouched. Gerty Taussig said they didn't care about anyone who'd voted for Hitler, only the wonderful artworks that must have been burned. Rachel said, 'One of the women guards told us how upset they all were. She said, "This is our town! Our people!" She said that if anyone showed any joy about the firebombing or even looked in the direction of the window, she'd be shot.' Rachel quickly spread the word in order to try to restrain the prisoners' exuberance.

The first raid on Dresden had taken place during the night shift. The next day the planes came again – dropping seven hundred tonnes of bombs during daylight. On the third day, they attacked the suburbs and a nearby oil refinery. 'You could read from the light of the fire. It burned terribly,' said Lisa Miková. 'I must say that we had no pity. We said, "What about our parents and our husbands? Who started this?" We were cool about it even though we knew there must be women and children and thousands dead. The next day the guards were furious and they did their worst, giving slaps to everyone and not letting anyone use the toilet.'

The sudden appearance in Freiberg of melancholy lines of refugees fleeing Dresden with their belongings allowed hope to flare once again in the factory. With so many hundreds of Allied planes overhead, the prisoners dared to believe that salvation might be close at hand. They didn't even mind when they were sent out onto the streets to help clear the rubble from associated raids. It was a pleasure to see what the Allies had done. Rachel's only disappointment was that the British didn't target the railway. 'Why didn't they bomb the tracks or the trains?' she asked. 'Then no one could ever be sent to a concentration camp again!'

By 31 March 1945, further Allied raids had severed the Freiberg factory's supply lines and raw materials had run out. There was no more fuel to run the machines and the electricity supply was patchy. All production was stopped. Eager not to lose their jobs, the guards told the prisoners to 'keep busy', so they fashioned things from discarded scraps of metal, including little knives with which to cut and eat what they called 'the finest meal in the world' – grass. Now that the snow was melting they could surreptitiously reach down and grab clumps of it on their way to and from the factory. Other prisoners made themselves little aluminium combs. Even though some had been shaved again since Auschwitz, bristly tufts of hair were growing back on most of the women's heads and these precious styling accessories reminded them of a time when they'd been more civilised.

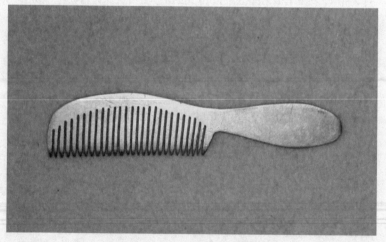

A comb made from aircraft metal at Freiberg

Gerty Taussig had a friend who was thrilled to have such a comb and kept it tightly gripped in her hand for fear someone might steal it. During an *Appell*, an SS guard spotted it and grabbed it from her. 'What do you need this for?' he snapped.

'To comb my beautiful hair,' the woman replied, running her hands across the fuzz that barely covered her scalp. Even the guard joined in the laughter, but still he didn't give the comb back.

At one of the usual early morning *Appelle* that were always carried out with a needless sense of urgency, Priska – nine months pregnant and terribly weak – was late to appear in line. Able to move only slowly, with swollen ankles and throbbing feet, she was confronted by one of the guards who rounded on her and demanded, 'Why are you late?'

Priska smiled thinly. 'My being late is hardly going to destroy the Reich.'

The guard raised his fist and beat her so badly for her insolence that she fell to the ground and curled into a ball to protect her belly. The beating could easily have killed her and her baby. When he finally stopped, she was helped up by the women either side of her. Tasting blood in her mouth, she told them, 'It's OK. I'm OK.' Attempting a laugh, she said, 'It's better than being shot!' Drawing once again on her faith, she silently told the child inside her, 'I knew you would survive.'

Spring gradually warmed the winter air and through the windows the women could hear birds singing and see the treetops budding into leaf. As a new season began, heralding their sixth year of life under the Nazi boot, the prisoners pondered what the coming weeks and months might bring. Many of their *Meisters* had been sent to the front, and when they were instructed to start dismantling the aircraft machinery to take to another factory, they didn't know whether to be relieved or afraid. Wild rumours began to fly around the place. Would they be 'liquidated'? Shot in their barracks before the SS fled? Or would they be taken away along with the machinery of war? Their greatest fear was that they might be transported back to Auschwitz. They were completely unaware that the Soviets had liberated the camp in January, along with some of the worst extermination camps such as Treblinka, Bełżec and Sobibór.

With the order to put down their tools and with nothing else to do but wait, the inmates were largely confined to their bunks. A few were instructed to do pointless groundwork such as moving rocks from one place to another just to look busy. As they were no longer working productively for the Reich, their rations were reduced. They were given less than 200 grams of bread a day each and half-portions of the rank, saltless soup they gulped down. 'They said if you don't work you don't need to eat so much,' said Lisa Miková. 'After that we got bread every day but soup only every second day. That was very cruel. We felt sure we would be killed.'

Aside from the weight they'd already shed, the women began to lose whatever muscle they had left, and with it almost all their energy. Their grey skin, which was scaly and stretched tightly across the contours of their bones, peeled and blistered. They panted shallowly, with foul breath; their legs and feet swelled so that many found it difficult to walk. Their body temperature dropped, leaving them shivering and highly vulnerable to infection. As they had throughout their time as prisoners, though, the women stuck together and tried to keep each other going. Priska had Edita and friends including Magda Gregorová, who was married to the famous Slovak actor Martin Gregor. Rachel had her sisters, and Anka had Mitzka and friends from Prague, including Klara Löffová and Lisa Miková. 'When we'd worked and stood together for hours and hours we'd talked much more and remembered poems and other things until the SS screamed, "Don't talk!" We tried that in the barracks then, telling stories and remembering films and books,' said Lisa Miková. 'Sometimes it helped and sometimes it didn't, so people would cry, "Please shut up because it reminds us of home." It was terrible, to be reminded of home then.'

And so they waited, as the Germans spent the next few days 'running around' trying to decide what to do. The women still had no contact with the outside world and were unaware that the all-important battle for the Ruhr region was about to be won by the Allies, or that Cologne and Danzig had recently fallen. They were also completely ignorant of the propaganda spread by the Allies in radio broadcasts and leaflet drops over Germany and Austria that Hitler was about to lose the war. All the women knew was that they were desperately hungry and frightened. And as they anxiously awaited their fate, squabbles broke out and tensions in the barracks ran high.

During one morning's cold-water wash in early April 1945, a Czech prisoner spotted that Priska was pregnant under her voluminous coat dress, and became hysterical. The woman had kept her family's diamonds hidden throughout the war and was terrified that they would all be searched – or worse – if the guards found out. 'You'll get us all killed!!' she screamed. 'Our deaths will be on your conscience!' She became so overwrought that the guards came running and demanded to know what the commotion was about. 'She's pregnant! She's pregnant!' the woman shrieked, pointing and groaning.

Priska froze, her heart pounding.

'Is it true?' one of the female SS guards asked incredulously, staring at Priska who was dangerously undernourished and weighed around seventy pounds. 'Are you pregnant?'

'Yes,' Priska admitted finally in a whisper, expecting to be shot on the spot.

The guards looked at each other and shook their heads in disbelief. There was a long pause as Priska held her breath. Then one of the guards asked, 'When are you due?'

'Soon. Very soon.'

The guards went away to confer as Priska slumped back on her bunk. News of her condition quickly spread among her fellow shift workers, who tried to reassure her that nothing terrible would happen. Days passed without incident and everyone went back to their own routines, such as they were. Then one day a guard approached Priska quietly and asked her, 'What do you need?'

By that stage Priska's feet had become her worst torment. They were swollen, caked in blood and oozing pus. She barely faltered. 'I would love a warm bath for my feet.' To her amazement, a bowl of hot water was brought to her. As other prisoners looked on in shock and envy, she sat in her grubby clothes, full of lice and other creatures, soaking her toes in the improvised foot spa 'like a queen'. The water was, she said, 'very hot' and such a luxury – 'Bliss!'

She added, 'People were nice to me because they were sorry for me and no one believed that I would have a living child or that it would be normal.' She knew that the sudden change of heart among the guards was almost certainly self-serving but still she welcomed it. 'My husband and I had a very good relationship and I desperately wanted to have his child.'

Anka's pregnancy too had been exposed by then, not by the Czech paediatrician she'd confided in but by others who spotted her distended belly in profile. 'I was getting thinner and thinner but my stomach was getting bigger and bigger,' she said. 'Some of the guards knew it. If they'd found out before 18 January, I would have been sent back to Auschwitz, but Auschwitz didn't exist any more ... so they couldn't send me anywhere. I didn't know that, though. I couldn't have ... I had to admit my pregnancy after they asked me. I couldn't not admit it, but they couldn't send me away.'

Although she was painfully thin, Anka's breasts had become still larger and heavier as they filled with milk and caused her much discomfort under her rough clothes, especially during the hurried marches to and from work. Her friend Mitzka borrowed needle and thread and fashioned a bra for Anka from a piece of cloth. It was an amateur attempt with unusually pointed cups but Anka was so grateful for the support that she wore it for the remainder of the war.

Rachel, who'd hidden her condition from her sisters for nine months, was also exposed around this time by some of the prisoners, one of whom found her sisters and asked them, 'Do you know Rachel is pregnant?'

'No! Are you crazy?' Bala was incredulous. 'I sleep with her in the same place!'

'She can't be!' Ester and Sala cried in unison. Although they were on separate shifts and the pair worked somewhere else, they still saw Rachel whenever she returned to the barracks and hadn't noticed a thing. Once the sisters realised it was true they were shocked and afraid, especially because Rachel had grown so weak that she could hardly walk and had been largely confined to the sickbay. Sala said, 'We couldn't believe it and were very, very sad for her if it was true. I mean, how awful to be pregnant in that place!'

Rachel said, 'There was no extra food for me and they couldn't help me.' She tried not to think about what might happen to her and her unborn child.

A few days later one of the Germans who worked with Sala secretly gave her an orange. 'They were scared to help us but still he gave me that beautiful, vibrant piece of fruit. I hadn't seen or smelled anything so lovely for as long as I could remember. I longed to keep it for myself, but I hid it in my dress and was able to get it to Rachel for her and the baby. They needed it more than me.'

By then the women hardly worked at all and were mostly confined to barracks, torpid with the kind of chronic hunger that few ever know. They could hear shelling and knew that the Allies must be near, but still they didn't know if this meant that the SS might panic and kill them all. Some no longer cared.

One day after her footbath, on the morning of Thursday, 12 April 1945 – the very day she had estimated that her baby was due – Priska Löwenbeinová went into labour. Crying out as the first contraction doubled her in two, she was taken to the sickbay in a small room at the factory and helped onto a wooden plank laid across a table. As she struggled with the waves of pain bringing on the first baby she'd carried to full term, she was assisted by Dr Mautnerová, who did what she could without drugs or any remotely sterile equipment.

Every time Priska sat up red-faced to brave the next spasm, she came face to face with some thirty or so onlookers who had crowded around the doorway to watch. They included SS guards, factory foremen and the *Lagerälteste* (camp elder). Some of the spectators placed bets on whether the baby would be a boy or a girl. 'They said that if it was a girl the war would be over, and if it was a boy then it would go on for even longer.'

While they bickered over the gender of her baby, Priska was experiencing pain the like of which she had never felt before. After several hours of labour and with a final excruciating push, at exactly 3.50 p.m. (according to a guard's watch), Priska was delivered of a daughter. Anaemic and dangerously malnourished as she was, the amount of blood that the mother lost in the process almost finished her off.

'It's a girl! It's a girl!' the Germans cried happily. 'The war will soon be over!' As the baby emerged fully, though, one of the guards yelled, 'It's a devil!'

The child that by all odds should never have survived nine months in Priska's impoverished womb came out with her little blood-smeared hands screwed up into fists held up around her ears. For a moment, even to Priska, they looked like horns. Some of the onlookers became hysterical and Priska, too, was overcome. Although incredibly relieved to have given birth to a live child after so many dead babies, she'd secretly feared that it might be abnormal or deformed. The baby did seem to have a disproportionately large head but that was mainly because – at three-and-a-half pounds – her body was so very small. Once Priska realised that the child had no defects after all, she was overwhelmed that Tibor wasn't able to share her joy, and then petrified of what might happen to her.

Up until that moment her baby had been hidden away, relatively safe inside her belly. Now suddenly she was out – a needy, naked, vulnerable child – in a world run by Nazis. Her little girl was too weak to cry and could barely move her puny limbs. Once the doctor tied off the umbilical cord and wiped her down as best she could with a cloth, Priska was able to hold her daughter in her arms for the first time. The scraggy little infant had hardly any fat or muscle on her body and excess skin rolled down her legs like stockings. Her wizened face was so shrivelled that it was, she said, 'ugly as sin', but she had her father's big blue eyes.

'*Moja* my Hanka,' Priska said, damp-eyed, recalling her whispered conversation with Tibor in the cattle truck on their nightmarish journey to Auschwitz – *Hanka for a girl, Miško for a boy*. She looked down at the child with a 'nicely shaped' round head and smallish nose and felt her mouth crease into a smile.

'Think only of beautiful things,' Tibor had told her just before they were separated on the ramp in Auschwitz II-Birkenau. His message was engraved on her heart. In Freiberg, Priska had secretly decided that if she looked only at pretty children on the way to and from the factory then her baby would not only live, but be beautiful too. While the other prisoners clutched each other, heads down, her eyes had deliberately sought out the face of every blonde-haired, blue-eyed Aryan child she could find. Praying that she would give birth to a similar-looking son or daughter with a 'turned-up nose', she didn't want her baby to look as Jewish as she did and hoped it would more closely resemble her father with his pale Polish colouring.

It had worked. Hanka had arrived, and to her mother she seemed almost perfect. Conceived with love in an apartment in Bratislava by an adoring couple who'd lost so much, the tiny little thing in her arms had survived Nazi occupation, the rigours of Auschwitz, the bitterest of winters, and six months' noise, violence, starvation and hard labour to push her way into war-torn Europe. With her birth, she'd dared those on both sides of the conflict to hope for something better. 'It was the most beautiful child I had ever seen,' Priska said of the little bag of bones covered with skin. 'We had been through so much and yet here we were, alive!' She knew that they would never have survived without the kindness of the stranger Edita who had helped her through the whole ordeal, so she decided to call her baby Hana Edith Löwenbein, known as 'Hana' or 'Hanka'.

The pain of her labour and the loss of blood took what little strength Priska had left, however, and she sank back onto the table barely conscious. Her baby was so underweight and lacking in insulating layers of body fat that she was dangerously susceptible to hypothermia. Unable to offer either much sustenance or any kind of medical after-care, Dr Mautnerová couldn't be certain that either mother or child would survive. Priska was hardly aware of the next twenty-four hours, other than that she and her child slept deeply. Whenever she woke she cradled her baby contentedly, but she couldn't help but lift the tip of Hana's nose with a finger to try to encourage even more of a *retroussé* profile.

As the end of the war seemed closer than ever and with the apparent relaxation of the previous rules, a few of her friends were allowed to visit her, including Edita, who wept at the news that the baby had been part named after her. The women had pooled their precious supply of marmalade and mixed it with a little water to make syrup for the baby, which they gave to Priska in the cleanest mug they could find. They'd also found some of the soft white cotton with *KZ Freiberg* stamped on it and stitched Hana a smock with an embroidered Peter Pan collar, as well as a bonnet complete with blue chain-stitch edging and tiny red flowers. These were items Priska would always treasure.

Hana's baby outfit made from KZ Freiberg cloth

Her visitors told her the news that Franklin D. Roosevelt had died of a massive cerebral haemorrhage on the day she'd given birth. The American president, who'd come to power the same year as Hitler, had been sixty-three years old. A prisoner overheard an SS officer shouting the 'good news' to his colleagues. The women prayed his death wouldn't prolong the war still further.

On her second day of life, malnourished Hana 'jumped' onto her mother's breast. 'She sucked out all the milk, which was really only water,' Priska said. 'She was a very good child. She drank and she went to sleep crying.' Whatever nutrition Priska had to offer she gladly gave her child, but the giving of it depleted her still further, and even after feeding Hana remained pale and floppy, whimpering piteously.

Priska was aware of little more until 14 April, thirty-six hours after she'd given birth, when the second-in-command to the *Unterscharführer* shook her awake just after midnight and told that the camp was being evacuated. '*In einer Stunde muss alles marschbereit sein!*' he cried. (All must be ready to march within one hour!) That included her and her baby, and she hoped that not being shot in her bed or left to die in the sickbay might mean that she and baby Hana still had a chance. 'The Soviets were coming to town so they were running away and they were taking us with them,' she said.

Since December 1944, the Nazis had evacuated camp after camp all across occupied Europe in a race against time. Realising that they were almost certain to lose the military offensive, many were determined not to lose their war against the Jews and continued to annihilate them. Thousands were gassed or shot before the camps were evacuated, but some were allotted a different fate. The Nazi high command clung to the belief that, whatever happened, they would still need slave labour to rebuild the Reich. Hitler and Himmler planned an *Alpenfestung*, or 'alpine fortress', to which the German high command and its elite forces could retreat. It was an area intended to stretch from southern Bavaria across western Austria to northern Italy.

As prisoners would be needed to help defend the region, the decision was made to move any *Häftlinge* who'd survived incarceration in the south deeper into Reich territory. For speed and efficiency, those chosen to survive until the Nazis were done with them were transported by train, but where no rolling stock was available, or where the tracks and stations had been bombed, they were forced to evacuate on foot. These 'death marches' during one of the harshest winters in living memory were a fresh form of torture and killed off the weakest while leaving only the strongest alive.

In the final six months of the war, an estimated 300,000 of the 700,000 concentration camp and death camp prisoners who'd so far defied the odds to survive were to perish. At Auschwitz that January 60,000 surviving inmates were marched forty kilometres to a railway station where they were herded onto trains and sent deeper into Germany. Approximately 15,000 died en route of exhaustion, exposure or starvation as their cattle cars became abattoirs. Many more died elsewhere and the SS guards had orders to shoot any too feeble to continue.

The women of KZ Freiberg had no choice but to obey the orders to evacuate – even Priska, who should never have been moved so soon and had no support for a baby that would normally have been placed in an incubator.

Rachel, in a similarly poor state, still rose from her bed to warn her sisters as soon as she learned that the camp was being evacuated. 'I was too weak. I couldn't do anything or even give birth. But then that night I heard they were taking us away. I knew I had to do something so I went to my sisters and said, "Make yourselves ready. We are leaving tonight."' The Germans were, she said, 'organised and disciplined to the last minute' as they ordered the prisoners to destroy any evidence and clean everything up. Then they marched them through the town for the last time, five abreast and at a punishing pace. 'They didn't know where they were sending us to. They were just told to get us away as the Russians were close.'

Lisa Miková was surprised at the speed of the evacuation as the barracks were cleared one by one. 'There was a sudden departure in the night – always in the night,' she said. 'They came and said take everything – your bowl and spoon and your coverlet . . . We had no warning before we were marched to the station in the dark and sent away. We didn't know that Auschwitz no longer existed and we were so afraid to go back there – that would be the worst.' Even though it was the dead of night, it felt as if the whole town of Freiberg had been mobilised as Allied aircraft manoeuvred menacingly overhead. As well as the increasing numbers of refugees fleeing south, entire families packed up their most precious things and took to the roads or hurried to the station. The imminent arrival of the soldiers of the Red Army frightened them far more than the planes of the RAF.

Priska with her baby and thirty-five other sick women were among the last to leave KZ Freiberg. Initially they were ordered to march in the rain with the others, but they only made it a few hundred metres before it became clear that they couldn't go any further. The guards conferred and then told the rest of the women to move on, leaving those who'd fallen by the side of the road. 'The other women were convinced that they were going to execute us then,' Priska said. 'They were saying goodbye and crying with us.'

But instead of being gunned down in the middle of the town for all to see, the women were loaded into a sealed military truck. Once they were inside, the doors slammed shut behind them and they were driven off by the SS. Baby Hana was so lethargic she hardly cried or moved, even though her skin had started to blister. Trying to keep her warm, Priska pressed her daughter against her heart under her baggy dress. The women in the van had no idea where they were going and as they bumped along, many feared they would be driven to a remote location and shot. Others, having heard rumours of Chełmno and elsewhere, felt sure that they were to be gassed by exhaust fumes. Priska kissed Hana's head and prayed. 'I am a believer so I told myself it is all in the hands of God and his power. He knew where I gave birth, so that's why he helped me.'

With the Red Army approaching Freiberg from one side and the Americans from the other, there was little time to spare, so – whatever the initial intention – the van stopped for an agonising period for no apparent reason before starting up again. When it eventually pulled to a halt and Priska and the others were helped off at the station, their arrival was cheered by the women who never thought they'd see them again.

Virtually every train across occupied Europe had been deployed to ferry troops or munitions to and from the advancing fronts, and any remaining passenger carriages were reserved for fleeing citizens of the Reich. The only wagons available to the Nazi-run rail network for the transport of the 990 Jewish women and some male prisoners from the adjacent barracks were fifteen open-topped or 'semi-wagons' and a handful of closed cattle cars. Some of the wagons had been utilised for transporting anthracite and were ankle-deep in soot. Others had been used to ferry animals or human cargo, while the rest had carried dry goods including slaked lime that would burn feet already in a pitiful condition.

The spring weather had turned wet and cold and as the women were herded into the open cars, sixty to eighty at a time, the rain turned to sleet. With nothing but their thin blankets to protect them from the elements, they were pressed against each other once more as the bolts were slid shut behind them. If they stood on tiptoe or lifted one another up they could just see out. Much to their mutual dismay, a German *Aufseher* (overseer) was placed in most of the wagons to stop the prisoners looking out or trying to escape. Panic-stricken, they began to speculate where they were being sent. One claimed to have heard that they would be taken to an underground munitions factory and buried alive. Others feared they would be transported to the main Flossenbürg concentration camp in Bavaria (the destination of many death marches) to be exterminated like vermin. What possible use would the SS have for so many half-starved women incapable of doing hard labour in a granite quarry?

Priska simply focused on trying to get through the next few hours. Squashed into one of the open wagons, she struggled to protect her newborn from the crush and slid to the blackened floor, pulling her baby's little bonnet over her eyes.

Somewhere a few wagons further along was Rachel – almost to full term and so fragile that she'd been placed with the dying. The only consolation was that the car wasn't quite so packed as the others and she could at least find a small space in which to lie alongside the rest, 'like herrings in a tin'. None but her sisters and a handful of other women, loaded onto separate open wagons further along the train, knew that Rachel was with child. Neither were any of them aware of Hana's birth. Struggling to stay alive, they had more pressing concerns.

Anka, nine months pregnant and a 'walking skeleton in rags', was squeezed into an open-topped coal truck with Mitzka, but she was in no better condition than her fellow mother-to-be. As frightened as the rest of them and praying fervently that they weren't on their way back to Auschwitz, Anka gripped the side of the wagon with both hands to keep her balance as it shunted forwards with a lurch just after daybreak.

Belching black smoke, the hulking locomotive began to drag its wretched cargo away from a beleaguered Germany to they knew not where.

# 6

# The Train

Prisoners transported in open wagons, winter 1944

Anyone standing on the platform of Freiberg station that damp morning in April 1945 probably wouldn't have taken much notice of the freight train slowly pulling out on a westerly track. As with any departure, a signalman would have swung a lantern in the half-light, the stationmaster would have blown a whistle or waved his flag to indicate that the 'special' was about to pull out, and the driver would have opened up the steam regulator as his crew fed coal to the firebox.

The only indication that this wasn't just another war-time locomotive delivering supplies or munitions to the front would have been the scruffy heads of the tallest prisoners, just visible over the top of the sturdy goods wagons. Even then, few of the frightened Germans swarming around the station looking for an escape route would have suspected that somewhere in amongst those broken, decrepit creatures was a two-day-old baby, with two more babies about to be born. Nor were they likely to have much cared.

Under the direction of the *Deutsche Reichsbahn* (DR), assisted by various government ministries and their associated railway companies, the Third Reich's vast 100,000-kilometre cross-Europe rail network had some 12,000 locomotives at its disposal, carrying both freight and passenger wagons. Aside from their primary function of mobilising troops and supplying the fuel and machinery necessary to maintain a war, the captured trains of occupied Europe became a fundamental instrument in Hitler's ultimate goal or *Endlösung*. Between them, they transported a sizeable percentage of the millions destined for death by extermination or labour.

Crammed to capacity to maintain quotas for the rapacious gas chambers, the large wooden boxcars accessed via a heavy sliding door became the favoured method of transportation for the 'freight extras' – one of many terms the Nazis used for the deportees as part of their elaborate web of deceit. The beauty of the sealed 'sardine tins' was that they kept the prisoners out of sight and there was no escaping from them, unless as a corpse. The standard wagons, ten metres long, had also proved themselves to be the most efficient in terms of maximising revenue in what became an entirely self-financing operation. Coupled together these trains could easily carry the minimum 1,000 *Stücke* ('pieces') to qualify for the bulk travel discount offered for freight transportation.

The German railway operators charged the SS only a third-class fare if transporting more than four hundred passengers, which worked out at one *Pfennig* per kilometre for every person their trains hurried to the camps. In a chillingly calculated system, these fares were sometimes charged directly to the prisoners, who were forced to pay in cash or valuables or have the amount deducted from their 'wages'. Children under four were transported to their deaths without charge, and those under ten went half-price. Each 'piece' was only ever issued with a one-way ticket.

Transported in conditions designed to inflict the maximum suffering, millions of *Häftlinge* were sent on journeys that could take a few hours or many days. The longest known shipment was from

Continental boxcar with elevated compartment
used for transporting prisoners

Corfu in Greece in June 1944 and took eighteen days. When the doors were slid open in Auschwitz, hundreds of the train's 2,000 occupants had expired. The rest, most of them dying, were immediately gassed.

The DR also charged the guards who escorted the prisoners, although they were issued with return tickets. Once each transport had been loaded, these men and women often climbed into the special elevated compartments built for the brakemen, an addition common on continental trains, or travelled in adjacent cars with comfortable seating. Sometimes they rode in passenger carriages coupled to the end of the trains. Only rarely did they remain with their charges inside the stinking boxcars.

Even so, not all the guards or rail staff were happy to accompany such transports. After one twelve-hour journey from Terezín to Auschwitz, some soldiers were reported to have broken down and declared that they'd 'rather go to the front'.

A Czech train chief named Adolf Filipik who was ordered to shepherd a transport of *Häftlinge* is reported to have had a nervous breakdown and was unable to continue working after handing over his cargo. In Kolín, fifty kilometres from Prague, train drivers and their chief collapsed under similar strain and were no longer able to take up their 'unusual service'. Their replacements only made it as far as the town of Český Brod, before they too had to be hospitalised. In such cases, SS officers were then brought in as engine drivers.

In spite of these few unwelcome interruptions to what was a highly efficient service run with bloodless proficiency, the freight wagons were used again and again; cleaned out after each delivery before being sent back for their next consignment. Some of the cattle cars were fitted with ropes and metal rings for tethering animals, apparatus that was put to deadly use by those prisoners who chose suicide over uncertainty. Had livestock been transported in the same wagons then they would have been treated far more compassionately, with straw spread across the boards, and basic humanitarian measures would have been adhered to in order to minimise the animals' suffering. No such allowances were made for the enemies of the Reich.

The powerful Class 52 *Kriegslocomotiven*, the so-called 'war trains', that became a symbol of Nazi domination were those that made the most frequent journeys to and from the camps. In effect, they made Hitler's 'Final Solution' possible. The workers from each occupied nation who – under Nazi supervision – drove, fuelled, fumigated or waved the trains through also played their part. These employees, who were repeatedly warned that if they helped any of those on the transports they would be shot, not only contributed to the efficiency of the planned annihilation (often profiting from it) but became often unwitting accomplices to industrialised murder.

Some authorities alerted to the true purpose of the trains were so horrified about the 'special freight' being transported through their districts – especially towards the end of the war – that they refused them passage. Sadly, that often only meant that the prisoners were sent back to the hell of their camps or 'terminated' where their journeys were interrupted. The majority of transports, however, were allowed through.

Over the noise of the engines the railwaymen may not have been able to hear the wails of distress, the desperate cries for water from those whom they ferried, but they couldn't have failed to hear them each time the trains stopped for an air raid, curfew or blackout, or when they had to pull into sidings to let preferential trains pass. During these numerous halts, SS guards and rail staff alike were reported to have baited those in the wagons, demanding jewels, clothing or cash in return for the water they craved – often snatching the prized item before cruelly refusing to give the donor refreshment.

Any maintenance staff working on or near the trains would have had to hold their breath against the eye-watering stench of the urine and excrement dripping from the wagons. They would have witnessed the corpses of those who didn't make it being thrown off at various stops. Some drivers were allegedly paid in vodka to numb their senses or help them ignore what they had become a part of. Others accepted the work for monetary gain or because they were too afraid to refuse. The trains also passed hundreds of civilians every day as they plied their way across Europe – ordinary citizens who saw, heard and smelled the trains rumble past and then watched them come back empty. Most did nothing, but there were a few who took enormous risks by alerting those further up the line so that they could be waiting to throw food, water containers, clothes or blankets into the wagons.

Others helped the many small resistance groups who were determined to stop all enemy traffic, including its most deadly trade. Despite the constant threat of torture and execution, tracks were blown up, signals, brakes and engines sabotaged, water cocks opened, coal stolen, and drivers persuaded to slow down by ambushes and derailments. Brave resistance members and partisans did much to disrupt the Nazi killing machine.

For the sick and starving women of KZ Freiberg, though, there was no such help. In snowstorms and temperatures that were to drop well below zero, they huddled together in the few centimetres of space each was allowed. 'We couldn't even sit on the floor all at the same time,' said Klara Löffová. 'There was a shortage of wagons so they crowded us in tight ... April in Europe is cold, snowy, rainy – it was hellish.' Without food or water, exposed to the weather and in pitch darkness for much of the time, they were at the mercy of the Nazis once more as their train hurtled them headlong towards what they feared was a place of no return, lurking somewhere far away in the night.

Their route south took them across the northwestern part of occupied Sudetenland and on to the Protectorate towns of Teplice-Šanov before heading for Most and Chomutov. The journey had to be constantly plotted and re-plotted by Germans directing staff from the *Böhmisch-Mährische Bahn* (Bohemian-Moravian Railway,

BMB). Along the way, points had to be hastily opened and signal-men alerted to allow the train to continue its deadly course over well-polished rails. The women were powerless in the control of those with no regard for human life, and there seemed no possible escape from an inevitable end. Tantamount to a death sentence, their lice-bitten nights turned to days then to night again, and so it went on, never coming to an end.

Map of the route from Freiberg

'We didn't know where we were going but we were so very afraid,' said Lisa Miková. 'The wagons were open and it was raining and sometimes snowing, although at least we could drink the rain or collect snow to eat ... Sometimes we travelled at night as well as daytime – it depended on the air raids. It was very cold at night and that is when people often died.'

For those who still had their wits about them, the mental torment was excruciating. After all they'd been through, the daily expectation of death was more than many could stand. Had they held out for this long only to be destroyed somewhere worse, like Flossenbürg, a camp largely run by criminals? An estimated 100,000 prisoners had passed through the Flossenbürg complex and a third of them had died, including 3,500 Jews. Brutality and sexual exploitation was rampant. They had no idea that Flossenbürg had been evacuated two days after they left Freiberg and that its 16,000 surviving prisoners were forced on a death march by foot and then by cattle car to Dachau concentration camp in Germany. Approximately half perished before they reached their destination, where the majority died of starvation and exhaustion or were gassed.

With Allied planes continually flying missions, and towns and tracks bombed behind and ahead of the slow-moving train from Freiberg, mounting confusion about their destination amongst the guards and in the rail control rooms caused further delays. As they zigzagged between the two fronts, their sodden blankets clutched around them, the women waited and prayed. Gerty Taussig said, 'We couldn't see out. We could only see up. Overhead we watched planes fighting and Allied bombers heading for their next target but we were too weak even to wave. The guards let us out occasionally to relieve ourselves but they were always watching us closely. We tried to scratch at the grass that grew between the tracks. It was all we had to eat unless they threw some bread into our wagon, and then there'd be a big fight as everybody wanted a crumb.'

More often than not, the prisoners' tongues and throats were so dry that, hungry as they were, they could barely eat or swallow the scraps they received. Instead they clasped the precious morsels tightly in their hands as the train pitched them from side to side. Lisa Miková said, 'All we knew was that our route was destroyed and so we had to go somewhere else. The train kept stopping and starting and whenever we stopped they opened the doors for us to throw out the dead. We saw other transport trains almost daily – full of prisoners in striped uniforms. Some were going in our direction and some the opposite way.'

Those who were lifted up to peer gingerly over the top of their wagons were able to report when their train had crossed the border into Bohemia and Moravia because they could see Czech station names as they passed. As in the rest of occupied Europe, each town had been given a new German moniker but the original name was often still visible or only partially erased. The Czechs on board were especially overcome at the idea of being 'home'. Survivor Hana Fischerová from Plzeň said: 'The feelings I felt while going through our country are hard to explain ... Knowing that we are home but having to go on to an unknown place from where we expect never to come home.'

Above the noise of sirens and anti-aircraft fire, they were moved to hear cries of *Nazdar!* (Hi!) or *Zůstat Naživu!* (Stay alive!) as the Czechs assured them that the war would be over soon. Their countrymen and women ran at the train to throw in food even though the guards threatened to shoot them. But their unhappy odyssey continued, which only brought fresh agony. As the train edged tentatively towards its destination, one station at a time, Anka prayed that it would turn southeast and head to Terezín. 'That place seemed like heaven to us now,' she said, 'and an attainable heaven at that ... but with no water, no food, no covering, and it was raining – it was unimaginable and terrible and I was in my ninth month!'

Many prisoners collapsed under the appalling conditions. Lice plagued them day and night and all they could do was itch and scratch. Delirious with hunger, some fainted where they stood, or lay on their sides in tight configuration just as they had in Auschwitz. They'd been told to bring their bowls and spoons but that now seemed like some sort of sick joke. Their bodies were wasting away still further beneath their horribly soiled clothes and all hope was wasting away too.

Those who died were stacked in one corner in a macabre pile of white limbs until they could be dealt with. Hungry no more, their unseeing eyes stared at those who peeled the shoes from their lifeless feet before they were rolled off in places that bore no witness. Other poor wretches had death in their eyes and wouldn't survive the next twenty-four hours. Eight women died in Gerty Taussig's wagon in the first week. 'At fourteen years old, all I could feel was gratitude that there was a little more space for the rest of us,' she said. 'There was no ceremony and not even a prayer as they were left to rot by the side of the tracks.' In one district of the Protectorate more than a hundred corpses were discovered discarded from such transports.

Rachel said that every time the train was shunted into a marshalling yard or backed somewhere into a dead-end siding, their SS *Aufsehers* went to the nearest farm or shop and either begged for food for the prisoners or simply took what they wanted for themselves – usually eggs – which they cooked on little stoves in their own special carriages. The women could smell the eggs frying but the Nazis rarely shared any of their spoils.

Plagued more by their burning thirst than by hunger, the prisoners continually begged for water – '*Wasser! Bitte! Trinken!*' – but few took any notice. To Rachel's surprise, though, one of the SS women attached to her wagon suddenly took it upon herself to spoon-feed her water and a little food. None in the wagon could believe this sudden change of heart and all were suspicious of it, but Rachel was too weak to care. 'She was feeding me and I was saying, "Leave me alone. I don't have the strength."'

And so their repugnant prison-on-wheels jerked and jolted along, moving its miserable human freight towards its inhuman destination. These once beautiful, cultured young women, many of whom had represented the cream of their societies in Europe's finest cities, had been reduced to spectres. Crawling with vermin and reeking with the foulest odours, their teeth were falling out and their flesh had broken out in sores. None had seen their own reflections for months, if not years, but whenever they looked at the other *Häftlinge* with their split lips, hollow cheeks and hair standing up like a brush, they realised how they too must have appeared and their sense of hopelessness only deepened. 'No food. No washing facilities. The coal dust caked and was sort of greasy and you felt not like a human at all. It was just dreadful,' said Anka.

Whenever they stopped in a siding, regular passenger carriages passed them, along with troop trains. As the prisoners squatted shakily to relieve themselves or clung to the wagons looking around desperately for any weeds to eat, they'd see well-fed, well-dressed men, women and children gazing out at them as if they didn't exist. To add to the cruelty, the prisoners could sometimes smell cooking from the kitchens of homes they passed – aromas of meat or bread, vegetables or fish that nearly drove them insane. They had long since abandoned the 'torture' of devising elaborate recipes or even talking about food. Mostly, each remained locked in their own private hell.

Lisa Miková said that with no end in sight, most people simply shut down and hardly spoke. Others talked too much and tried to keep up morale. 'We'd ask, "What can you see?", "Do you know something?" or "Have you heard of that place?" Each of us had terrible moments of despair but we tried to hold each other up, physically and emotionally.' Pressed against each other without mercy, they continued their relentless journey into darkness. The train made long, unnerving halts, often for no apparent reason. At every stop the women continued to clamour for water but the dead-eyed SS officers offered none. At one stop, a few women stumbled towards a dirty puddle but the bored guards shot at them to scare them off before ordering them back onto the train. Whenever there was an air raid, the train would stop and the SS fled or crawled under their carriage. Once again, the women prayed to be bombed, telling each other, 'How wonderful it would be if we were hit right now! They're right beneath us and we will crush them!'

Priska's chief concern was to try to encourage baby Hana to feed, but her breasts were flat against her chest and there was no substance to the little milk that she had. During her pregnancy, when she should have been eating at least five hundred calories a day more than her pre-war diet, she and the other mothers had been forced to exist on between 150 and 300 calories daily with no iron or protein. And that for a body that was doing heavy labour twelve to fourteen hours a day, seven days a week, in extreme temperatures.

Somewhere further along the train, Rachel – herself weighing just seventy pounds – could no longer support the weight of her distended belly, so she lay stiff-necked and squeezed between bony carcasses on the hard floor of the open wagon. Close to her time and even closer to death, in spite of the attentions of the SS officer, she couldn't even contemplate giving birth. Aside from her own discomfort she was greatly troubled by a woman with severe mental problems who insisted she needed to keep her swollen feet elevated. 'She had bad legs and the only high place ... was on my stomach, so she put her legs on my stomach!' Rachel said. 'There is no language to describe what we saw and how we lived ... I sometimes think, "How did you make it?"'

Anka, too, was struggling to stay upright and positive. 'It was raining and it was snowing and then the sun shone and we were squashed in that coal dust ... cold and hot, and hot and cold, and unwashed and hungry ... when it rained the soot stuck to us so how we must have looked. I am glad I didn't see myself ... Human spirit kept me going.'

On or about 18 April, the train pulled into a siding near Trieb-schitz, not far from the city of Most, to allow priority transports carrying munitions and wounded soldiers to pass. There the women from Freiberg remained, becalmed, for several days until it was safe to move on. In a parallel siding was a transport from the Buchen-wald forced labour and concentration camp in Germany, which had been liberated in early April. Some of the prisoners evacuated prior to liberation called out to ask for news. They even managed to throw each other some lice-infected garments before the Freiberg train moved off again towards Most.

Located between the Central Bohemian Uplands and the Ore Mountains, Most – renamed Brüx by the Germans – was heavily industrialised and had a major railway junction to service its petro-chemical and synthetic fuel plants. British and American bombers taking part in the so-called 'Oil Campaign of World War II' attacked it repeatedly. In spite of these continuing bombardments and with the Czech railway system in a shambles, the Freiberg train was directed onwards and slowly made its way towards the steel town of Chomutov. Then, in the growing confusion, it was turned around and sent back where it came from, away from the approaching American front.

Somewhere en route they stopped so that another transport car-rying approximately nine hundred prisoners from Flossenbürg and its satellite camp Venusberg could be coupled to their train. There were also prisoners from a camp that manufactured bazookas, anti-tank rocket launchers. Not that the women from the Freia factory were aware of what was happening in the next wagon, let alone at the far end of their transport. They were fighting simply to stay alive.

Forced to a halt in a vulnerable location and clearly visible from the air, their snaking train ended up caught between Most and Chomutov when the two cities came under major aerial attack on 19 April. In the middle of that night, in the midst of an air raid, Rachel's waters broke. As Allied pilots dropped their deadly cargo and bombs shook the earth far around, she went into labour. Sprawled on the faeces-covered floor of the wagon in which lay several women who'd recently died, Rachel shivered in her water-logged blanket. Feeling the contractions ripple through her belly for the first time, she knew that the baby conceived with Monik in their little room in the Łódź ghetto what seemed like a lifetime ago was determined to push its way into the world regardless.

Panting, she tightly gripped the arm of her sister Bala as the contractions contorted her body. The guard called for help and someone found the Czech doctor Edita Mautnerová, who'd helped Priska give birth to Hana and who ran the infirmary in Freiberg. Guards held up a torch so that the doctor could see when the baby's head began to show. Word quickly spread along the train that a child was being born, so some of the other guards crawled out from under the wagons to watch and – no doubt – place bets. Rachel was indignant. 'Can you imagine lying in an open coal train giving birth to a child with women all around?'

For hours, illuminated by anti-aircraft fire as the April rain soaked her skin, she arched back against the wagon as she fought the waves of pain. Then, some time that night or early the next morning, sodden and cold, she emitted a last scream and gave bloody birth to a tiny creature. The child, who barely looked human, was so small and – someone told her – a boy. 'Another Jew for the Führer!' one of the SS guards cried, laughing.

In the darkness of her bunk at Freiberg, when she'd allowed herself to think of the baby growing inside her, Rachel had secretly decided to name him Max (later to be known as Mark). Covered in his mother's blood, his whole body was wrinkled and he had a tight, scrunched-up face. He must have weighed less than three pounds. Too weak to be happy, his mother felt numb. 'I was like, "So I have a child, or I don't have a child." We didn't know what was going to happen.' In that unspeakable squalor and with no sharp objects to hand, no one knew how to sever the umbilical cord that had connected the baby to his mother and kept him alive until then. Someone suggested Rachel bite through it. Eventually an SS guard handed the doctor a dirty razor blade. 'They also found a cardboard box used for bread and they put the baby in,' she said. 'It was raining and snowing so I was holding the baby in the box all the time.'

Incredibly, like Priska, Rachel had a little breast milk and was able to nurse her newborn. She wouldn't have known it, but the bodies of malnourished pregnant women have been known to recognise the size and vulnerability of their babies and produce milk that is surprisingly high in fat, even though the process of doing so depletes the mother dangerously. 'I was glad I had enough milk,' she said. But there was nothing with which to wash her son, and little to keep him warm or protect him from the weather.

'What date is it?' Rachel asked, determined to remember her son's birthday, whether he lived or died. Nobody could be sure, but the SS guard who'd cared for her said, 'Say that the boy was born on Hitler's birthday – April 20th. It might save him.' Rachel was even handed a small 'extra ration' of bread at that point – not because she'd just given birth but because the guards realised it was the Führer's birthday. In a moment of rare humanity, another guard gave her an old shirt to wrap around her baby. She was still wearing the 'cripple's' dress with a yoke she'd been given at Auschwitz, but after seven months of continual wear it was threadbare and torn and she was shivering with cold and shock. As she delivered the afterbirth, someone found her a coat and draped it around her shoulders.

Quite overcome, Rachel asked if she could see her other two sisters, so the guard walked the length of the train calling for Sala and Ester. When the two young women, several wagons further along, first heard their names being called they were afraid to answer, but eventually they responded. 'Your sister's had a son,' they were told.

'Can we see her?' they asked, amazed. They were even more surprised to be told they could. Helped down from their wagon for the first time in days, they staggered to the car where their nephew had been born and found him and his mother in an extremely sorry state. 'She was huddled in the corner in an overcoat. It was not a pretty picture,' Sala said. The wagon stank and there were women dead or dying near by. 'She was so ill and we were so sure that the baby wouldn't survive that we couldn't even be happy for her. Then they took us back to our wagon. We were crying because we thought we'd never see either of them again.'

With no end to their suffering in sight, their train moved off, at speed this time, past bombed Chomutov towards the town of Zatec. It was their eighth day on the transport and they stopped again and waited and waited. 'Now and then some people threw some bread into the trucks for us to eat. That was indescribable,' Anka said. Mostly, the guard who was with them grabbed the bread and refused to share it, but sometimes they were able to catch a piece and eat it quickly. Anka, encumbered by her bump, never did. Half-lying, half-sitting, and describing herself as 'the epitome of living hunger', she heard from an inmate who could see over the top of the wagon that scores of Nazi flags were flying. 'It's Hitler's birthday,' the guard explained.

'Then it is my birthday too,' Anka replied weakly, and her friends tried to cheer her by joking that the red and black flags were really for her. Trying to remember what year it was, she realised it must be 1945, which meant that she was twenty-eight years old. Hearing that it was her birthday, the guard unexpectedly tossed her some bread. This manna from heaven seemed like a small miracle after she'd received so little for so long. As she clutched the morsel to her like a prize, never before since she'd been born on 20 April 1917, to Stanislav and Ida Kauder in Třebechovice pod Orebem, had Anka been pleased to share the date of the Führer's birth.

Watching the position of the sun as the Allied planes wheeled and spun to avoid the constant flak, the women on the train specu-lated that they were heading south to Plzeň, one of the frontier cities of annexed Sudetenland. Plzeň was famous for its Pilsner beer, but what they didn't know was that it was also the place where the

Wehrmacht chose to have its feared Panzer tanks manufactured at the huge Skoda Armaments complex. As the Soviets advanced on Plzeň ahead of the Americans, the US military repeatedly bombed the city and its railways to try to prevent the manufacture and mobilisation of any more Panzers, howitzers or tank destroyers at the plant that had been taken over by the Nazis. Then the Americans drew up plans to wipe out the factory 'once and for all', rather than have one of the Reich's largest munitions factories fall into Soviet hands. Almost three hundred B-17 'Flying Fortress' bombers and some two hundred fighter aircraft from the Eighth Air Force were readied for the mission planned for Wednesday, 25 April 1945. It would be their final combat operation of the war.

With baby Max Friedman and his mother Rachel just skin and bone in one wagon, and Priska attempting to suckle sallow Hana in another, Anka held onto her swollen belly as their train approached the city, praying that she wouldn't give birth just yet.

On Saturday, 21 April, with news of an imminent attack on Plzeň having been announced in advance by General Eisenhower, their train was forced to divert along a railway line no prisoner transport had ever taken before. In heavy rain, it arrived that night in the small town of Horní Bříza (renamed Ober Birken by the Germans), where it lurched to a halt under the jurisdiction of the town's stationmaster, Antonin Pavlíček.

A silver-haired father of two who'd lived and worked in the station house since 1930, Mr Pavlíček prided himself on running a clockwork service for the railways and the almost 3,000 inhabitants of his town. He was also known for keeping meticulous records. He was responsible for the supervision of several staff and was greatly admired throughout his community as someone of the highest standing and character.

Horní Bříza, whose sole industry was a nineteenth-century kaolin factory, had managed to remain largely untouched by war. Its five Jews had been rounded up and sent away to concentration camps soon after German occupation and there had been a few minor

Antonin Pavlíček, stationmaster at Horní Bříza

disturbances between the Hitler Youth and local teenagers, but otherwise the townspeople's lives were undisturbed by Nazi rule. The West Bohemian Kaolin and Fireclay factory, established in the town in 1899, even remained in Czech control under occupation. It mined 40,000 tons of kaolin a year and produced 22,000 tons of ceramic goods, fireclay and silica, mostly for export. A few partisans who worked in the factory had caused some trouble, bringing the unwelcome attention of the Gestapo from Plzeň (who took the agitators away never to be heard of again), but aside from those few unfortunate events, life continued much as it had before the war.

With frequent air raids on Plzeň and neighbouring areas, Mr Pavlíček suddenly found himself in charge of a far busier section of railway line. On 12 April, a train full of collaborationist Soviet soldiers from the Armed Forces of the Committee for the Liberation of the

Peoples of Russia (known as 'Vlasovites' under Red Army General Andrey Vlasov) arrived at Horní Bříza, attracting Allied fire. Fleeing from their train, they abandoned it. Five days later, at dawn on 17 April, Soviet fighter planes swooped in overhead, bombing buildings and cutting the electricity supply to the town. As the air-raid sirens wailed, nine planes also attacked the abandoned Vlasovite transport and locomotives, damaging nearby warehouses. Mr Pavlíček, who refused to leave his post, kept careful notes and when the electricity was turned back on he gave an almost blow-by-blow account to his superiors in Prague, the record of which remains on file.

Vlasovite train with carriages at Horni Briza

Four days later, on the evening of 21 April, the transport from Freiberg rolled into the heavily wooded valley and drew to a halt at Horní

Bříza. Previously, any 'specials' such as this would have bypassed the town to take the faster line south. With his usual efficiency, Mr Pavlíček noted that this train was number 7548 and arrived at precisely 20.58. 'The train had forty-five wagons and consisted of three transports – one of men and two of women,' he reported. Some of the wagons contained up to one hundred prisoners each and he estimated that the total number of passengers amounted to approximately 3,000. He also noted, 'Two transports consisted of closed wagons whereas one transport of women consisted of fifteen semi-wagons.'

Because the track ahead was being repaired – a process that would take at least twenty-four hours – the train was shunted into the marshalling yard of the kaolin factory adjacent to the station. At more than half a kilometre long, many of its furthest wagons couldn't even be seen from the town as they curved around the bend.

Even under Nazi occupation, the train was officially within Mr Pavlíček's remit, so he ignored the efforts of SS guards to keep him back and insisted on walking the full length of it in the rain. That is when the full horror of its living cargo first struck him. Many of the wagon doors had been opened and he was astounded to see hundreds of cadaverous creatures sick or dying of starvation, disease, damp and cold. Repelled by their smell and appearance, he was even more shocked by the behaviour towards them of the guards – especially the female ones – which was, he said, brutal and 'rude'.

Realising that the prisoners in the open wagons were especially vulnerable in the almost constant rain and 'extremely cold weather', the stationmaster demanded to speak to the commander of the transport, to whom he made a bold suggestion. The Vlasovite train abandoned a week earlier had been pulling several closed freight wagons, so Mr Pavlíček proposed that as many as possible from the open wagons be relocated into them 'for humanitarian reasons'. Those who knew him all agreed that he took a great risk in challenging *Unterscharführer* Šára, who initially pushed him aside and could very easily have shot him for his impudence. But the kindly stationmaster was determined to do something to help the prisoners temporarily under his control, and so he persisted.

Jaroslav Lang, a ten-year-old boy in 1945, glanced out of the window of his family house just fifty metres from the tracks and was intrigued to see the unusually long freight train in the sidings. 'There had been no school that day because there were planes everywhere in the skies and it was too dangerous. My older brother Milan and I saw the train and we watched the stationmaster arguing with the SS commandant, but still we didn't know what was happening. There were several officers and many Germans with guns. They were very strict and the SS were bellowing at people to stay away. They clearly didn't want us to see anything. But it was the first time Milan and I had ever seen the SS or Germans with helmets in our town. As little boys we wanted to see everything. It was very exciting.'

Mr Pavlíček's tense negotiations continued for several hours and, after offering generous supplies of food and drink for the guards, he finally persuaded Šára to agree to move as many of the shivering women as could be accommodated in the covered wagons. 'The exchange was made after an agreement from the commander of transport,' he said later. 'The people in the wagons were hungry and no one had access to them at night. While moving the transport and delivering them to the closed wagons, I succeeded in getting some food to them, which I could only do at night-time.'

Priska was one of the lucky ones moved, as were Rachel and those closest to death, but the heavily pregnant Anka remained in an open wagon, completely unaware of what was happening further down the train.

When Mr Pavlíček saw how grateful the prisoners were for this small kindness and realised what terrible condition they were in, he had an idea. It had been by sheer chance that their train had stopped in Horní Bříza but – as a devout Catholic – he wanted to do what was morally right. At 6.30 a.m. the following morning, Sunday, 22 April, instead of going to mass he paid a visit to Josef

Zoubek, the director of the kaolin factory, and Antonín Wirth, the landlord of the *Tovární Hostinec*, the local inn, which doubled as the factory social club and was situated next to the station. He asked the two men how quickly they could prepare a large quantity of food to be given to the prisoners – 'if the commander of the transport agrees'.

As he suspected, the *Unterscharführer* was even more resistant to this latest suggestion. Intent on obeying his orders until the final days of the war, he saw no point in feeding those destined to die. He couldn't openly admit as much to the stationmaster, though. After protracted negotiation, an agreement was eventually struck that a canteen would be made available at the town's expense to serve one hot meal to the half-starved *Häftlinge* while they were in Mr Pavlíček's jurisdiction.

Word of the prisoners' plight quickly spread around the citizens of Horní Bříza, who gathered whatever they could spare and hurried to the three-storey social club carrying baskets of bread, eggs, fruit, meats and cheeses. Ten-year-old Jaroslav Lang said, 'To begin with we didn't even know there were prisoners on the train, but when we saw people carrying food to the station we followed them and realised what was happening. That's when we ran home to our mother and asked for some bread to give them. She was very afraid but still she gave us a little something. Everyone was living on coupons at the time because of the shortages, but they gave up their own rations for those on the train.'

Sensing the urgency of the situation and his townspeople's eagerness to help, Mr Pavlíček enlisted the local schoolteacher, Jan Rajšl, to coordinate the supplies of food that began to flood in. Rajšl was perfect for the job – 'strict but fair'. He lived in the teacher's house, played the violin, and rode a bicycle to school. The miller, Jan Kovář, and the butcher, Mr Kočandrie, also volunteered their services and delivered flour, pastry and sausages. Many other people from surrounding areas rushed to help, although all were kept well away from the prisoners by the guards who formed a cordon along the length of the train, standing at fifty-metre intervals with their rifles raised.

Throughout that Sunday, the kitchens at the inn went into overdrive, with staff hurrying from their homes on their day off and everyone offering their services. Between them they baked 5,000 loaves and prepared huge platters of pastries and pots of coffee. Bags of soft buns and baskets of hard-boiled eggs were brought for the sick.

Meanwhile, Mr Pavlíček continued to patrol his domain and check on the prisoners, hoping to speak to a few of them privately. He discovered that they were mostly Czech although many nationalities were represented, including Greeks. He later described their condition as 'very bad'. When he told them that he was coordinating the distribution of some food for them all, they repeatedly urged him to hand it to them personally and not to the guards, who would steal it and not feed them a thing. The concept appalled him.

He was further shocked to find in one of the wagons a fellow stationmaster, a Mr Šiška from a neighbouring town, as well as Ilsa Fischerová, the widow of Plzeň dentist Dr Otto Fischer who'd been beaten to death during a camp evacuation. Mrs Fischerová, thirtynine, and her seventeen-year-old daughter Hanka had been in Auschwitz and Freiberg with the rest of the women and they begged Mr Pavlíček to send a message to their loved ones that they were still alive. Their snatched conversation was brusquely interrupted when the *Unterscharführer* spotted the dentist's wife talking to the stationmaster and mercilessly beat her to the ground. Prevented from intervening, Mr Pavlíček had no choice but to walk away, but he did rush back to the station to transmit the message to the woman's family as he'd been asked.

Survivor Liška Rudolf also managed to speak to the stationmaster through the tiny window of her closed freight wagon. 'On the morning of the 22nd I met Mr Pavlíček,' she said. 'He saw in my eyes that I was hungry and he told me, "I will send you some food." ... Later the leader of the transport asked me why I spoke to a civilian in an enemy area. He told me, "You'd better not be near the window again or I will have you eliminated."' Later still, with the doors to her wagon slightly open, two slices of bread and jam were thrown in and she managed to grab them as the other *Häftlinge* gave her murderous stares. 'The whole wagon envied me,' she said. 'In the afternoon I received two buns and two eggs the same way.'

The stationmaster continued to feed whomever he could while promising to send messages to prisoners' loved ones, at continual risk to himself. As he passed one wagon, he heard a baby cry. Horrified, he demanded to know how many children were on the train. Šára did not want to tell him and certainly didn't want others to know. When he finally admitted that there were 'two or three' infants on board, the stationmaster insisted on seeing them; he was stunned to discover undernourished newborns with few or no clothes to wear.

News of the 'babies on the death train' spread through Horní Bříza like a bushfire. Some, like Hana and Mark, had come from Freiberg, while others belonged to the women from Venusberg (none of whose babies are known to have survived). Still, amidst the chaos and confusion of so many thousands of people, not one of the mothers was aware of the others. Mr Pavlíček immediately summoned the local doctor so that he could check the babies over and medically examine their mothers. 'I told the commander that the local doctor, Dr Jan Roth, was available to help the sick.' His request was brusquely denied. 'I was told that they had their own doctor, who was one of the prisoners.'

Upset that he couldn't help, Dr Roth went home and told his wife, who was pregnant with their first child. Mrs Rothová had a layette of baby clothes prepared for her new arrival, but when she heard about the babies on the train she delivered the tiny hand-stitched clothes to Mr Pavlíček and asked him to ensure the newborns were each given something to wear. Two other mothers, Mrs Benesová and Mrs Krahulíková, likewise donated items and Mr Pavlíček did as he was asked. 'They thanked me with tears in their eyes . . . For these mothers special food was prepared,' he said.

Priska was one of the lucky women who received food for herself and clothing for Hana, as well as nappies, swaddling clothes and a blanket. 'There was a complete set of clothes. There were even cosmetic items such as talc and soap and all the hygienic things one needs for the correct care of a baby.' When she looked at the beautiful embroidered garments, she was ashamed to even touch them with her soot-blackened hands. She was even more reluctant to dress Hana in them, for her baby's skin had broken out in running sores. Pressing the tiny dresses to her face, Priska smelled starch and fresh linen – aromas that reminded her of a time when to be clean had been the norm. Putting them carefully to one side, she resolved to keep them for when she and Hana reached their destination and could – she prayed – have a long-awaited wash.

Breaking open a bread roll she'd been given, Priska found a note inside which read in Czech: *Hold on! Be strong! It will not last much longer!* She allowed herself a fleeting moment of happiness. Others, finding similar messages of support in the rolls and sandwiches they were given, were equally moved.

Further down the train, Rachel and her son received nothing that night. Like Priska, she'd been grateful to be moved to the warmer freight cars, but with the women in such close proximity to each other and only one small window for ventilation, the air inside quickly became unendurable, and there was no longer any rainwater to drink.

Anka, at the far end of the train, wasn't even aware that clothes were being handed out or food prepared. Losing her grip on reality and on life, she was simply grateful that the train had halted for a while and that, with the door of her wagon open, she had a brief respite from being crushed. By then, she said, 'It wasn't even a question of surviving one day at a time. It was a question of surviving each new hour.' Supervised by guards, she stood in the doorway covered in sores, her skin blackened with soot. Sustained by nothing but hope, she inhaled the forest air and thought of the times she'd strolled through woods with friends or family. Such nostalgia was mental torture, so she once again summoned her literary hero-ine, Scarlett O'Hara, to remind herself, 'I'll think about it tomorrow.'

She added, 'It is just my luck that I was born like that with that sort of nature which helped me enormously all through my life . . . It is sheer stupid optimism, nothing else. Whatever happened, I said, "I'll think about it tomorrow," and tomorrow it was already changed somehow . . . I was so lucky that I didn't die, which I could have done every minute of the day.'

Hearing voices, Anka looked up and saw a group of people hurrying past, presumably on their way to deliver food. 'They didn't expect what they saw,' she said. 'One of them was a farmer and he stopped in his tracks. I will never forget the look on his face when he stared at this pregnant corpse, weighing maybe sixty-five pounds and most of it belly . . . a scarcely living skeleton without hair and dirty as you can imagine.' She said that as the colour drained from his face, he must have thought that he'd stumbled into some sort of apocalypse. 'You would think people knew what to expect but they really had no idea there.' Standing nearby was the SS commandant, armed with a gun and a whip, and he glared at the farmer until he staggered away in shock. Five minutes later, though, he returned with a glass of milk and, boldly approaching the wagon, held it out to Anka.

She stared at him incredulously. 'I hate milk . . . never in my life before did I touch milk and never after, but I took it.' As she did so, the *Unterscharfuhrer* raised his whip above shoulder height as if to beat her with it. 'The farmer was so stunned he almost fell to the floor and died. He didn't say anything but I could see it in his face. His expression spoke volumes when he saw what was about to happen. I do not know why, but the commander lowered his whip then and I drank that milk, which was like an elixir of life. I enjoyed it like nothing on earth . . . it was like nectar . . . I think at the time it may have saved my life. After that glass I was as strong as an ox . . . That glass of milk brought my humanity back.'

She wiped her mouth with the back of her hand and passed the glass back to her stunned Samaritan. Then she thanked him in her native Czech before retreating back into her coke-caked prison cell.

Priska was the luckiest of all the mothers. As well as the layette, she was personally fed bread and jam by Mr Pavlíček – 'the best thing I ever tasted!' She said people were 'lined up' to help, and when some of the guards from Freiberg saw what was happening they asked what news there was of the mother and baby born in the factory.

'She lives! She lives!' someone cried, incredulously.

Not everyone did. Nineteen men and nineteen women died on the train at Horní Bříza that day and their weightless corpses were thrown onto the tracks. Mr Pavlíček saw them being discarded like rubbish and insisted that they be given a proper burial. 'I asked the commander to tell me the names or numbers of the dead because they had died on railway land,' he said. 'I was denied, with a note that these people "meant nothing to the world".'

Appalled by the commandant's attitude, he alerted the local police, who sent uniformed officer Josef Šefl to investigate. The sergeant issued the transport commander with an official document from the town hall to confirm that the corpses of thirty-eight prisoners had been removed from the train. He and Mr Pavlíček were then able to achieve a little dignity for the dead when later that night, under cover of darkness, the Germans dug graves and laid them to rest in the forest.

As the light faded, the commandant finally agreed that the large quantities of food prepared so lovingly by the people of the town could be brought from the inn. The plan was to give every prisoner a bowl of traditional Czech potato soup, a loaf of real white bread, some coffee, pastry and fruit. The *Unterscharführer* was said to be 'furious' when the stationmaster insisted that he and his people be the ones to serve it to the prisoners on the station platform, rather than giving it to the guards. After further strained

Memorial to the dead from the train in Horní Bříza cemetery

argument and with the hot food at risk of being rejected or spoiled, the commandant eventually agreed, but he decreed that only Mr Pavlíček and Mr Wirth would be allowed to serve the meal, or to see any of the prisoners at close quarters. Everyone else was to be kept well away.

The Plzeň dentist's daughter, Hana Fischerová, and her mother were among those fed. 'The railway inspector and all the staff tried to do everything they could for us. The people behaved so nicely. They cooked the soup in the canteen and I'm sure there will not be better food in my life than that soup.' Other prisoners concurred.

One said, 'I will never forget that bread and that potato soup which we ate with tears falling. I think none of us will. It is one of the little things that stayed with me – a beautiful memory.' Another said she could barely grasp that white bread still existed and couldn't stop crying over this 'greeting from another world'. Isolated for so long, the prisoners thought they'd been abandoned until the station-master and his neighbours risked their lives to help them. Light briefly pierced their darkness.

Liška Rudolf remembered, 'In the evening almost the whole transport received soup and bread. Everybody was crying with happiness and saying, "We came through Ukraine, Poland, Hungary, Austria, Germany, France and nowhere did anyone see us! Only in Czechoslovakia the people have heart ... We will never forget Horní Bříza."' Klara Löffová said, 'The whole village came with soup and bread ... It seemed like a miracle. We thought this was home; these were our people and we were theirs.'

Jaroslav Lang and his brother Milan hid in the forest to watch the prisoners being fed, wagon by wagon. He said, 'We were kept quite a distance away and we couldn't see very well but we could tell that the prisoners being brought forward for food were sad and exhausted. They had to hold onto each other just to walk. A lot of them were wearing uniforms and caps and they kept thanking everyone.' The boys couldn't tell if the inmates were male or female. 'They were taken out of their wagons in lines with guards on either side so that they couldn't escape. They had no bowls and so they had to eat one by one; some ate with their hands. It took a very long time and not everyone on the train was fed.'

In spite of Mr Pavlíček's intentions, many received nothing. Although the prisoners had been fed separately, the SS stole much of the food on the pretence of handing it out to speed things up, while some of the furthest wagons were completely overlooked. Lisa Miková said, 'In the place we stopped they asked to bring us some food. The SS commandant said we will give it to them and distribute it but they took most of it and gave us a few potatoes.'

Jaroslav Lang, still watching the train from the woods with his brother, said, 'We saw one of the prisoners ask for food and a German went to whip him, but he was too quick and he ducked out of the way. When we saw that we were very afraid. Then the rain started again and it grew dark and we could see tracer fire and hear aeroplanes. The Germans started shouting and there was a lot of shooting so we ran away. The next day we heard that some prisoners escaped from their lines or from the wagons.' It was, he added quietly, 'an experience to be remembered your whole life'.

Hana Selzarová, twenty-three and from Prague, who weighed seventy-seven pounds, was one of the women who escaped from the train that night in the rain. In her rags, she slipped away from an SS guard standing on duty in a waterproof cape, and stumbled into the forest. As shots rang out, she saw a light in the distance and ran towards it to discover it was the police station. But when she went inside she was told, 'Oh my God! Go away. We would have to arrest you!' They directed her to some local houses where they promised she would get help. 'There they gave me other clothes and a scarf because I didn't have much hair. They gave me something to eat and even money for the trip and told me where to catch the train.' She stayed overnight and then left the next morning for Prague, where a friend took her in.

Vaclav Stepanek from Horní Bříza was seventeen years old when two women who'd slipped away from their guards knocked on the door of his parents' house in the woods three hundred metres from the station. The women – one of whom may have been Hana Selzarová –said they were from Plzeň and Prague and wanted to know how far it was to Plzeň. 'They were in prison clothing and very hungry,' Vaclav said. 'My parents gave them food and something to wear. Everyone knew about the transport by then and was very sorry for them.'

His father, a woodsman, agreed to let the women hide in his barn. 'They weren't the first people my parents had hidden in the barn,' said Vaclav. 'My mother was very frightened but we hoped that if they were found we could just claim we didn't know they were there. They left early the next morning and from that day on, we never heard a word from them. I always wondered what happened to them.'

Having fed as many prisoners as possible, including Priska and Rachel, Mr Pavlíček could do little more. The remainder of the food was given to the commandant, who lied to him that it would be divided amongst the prisoners later. When the stationmaster received word from Plzeň that the railway line ahead had finally been cleared, he knew he had no further excuse to delay the train. Speaking to the commandant one last time, he tried to persuade him to leave the prisoners in the siding and make his escape with his guards, but the *Unterscharführer* was 'beyond persuasion' and determined to do his duty right until the end. He even asked Mr Pavlíček which was the best route to Bavaria, refusing to listen when he warned him he was unlikely to get that far alive.

'We heard his conversation with the stationmaster who was trying to convince him to leave us here,' said Czech survivor Helga Weiss, who was fourteen at the time. 'They would take care of us, he said – food, everything . . . [he] wouldn't hear of it. He wants to leave here at any cost.'

There was nothing more Mr Pavlíček or the townspeople could do to keep the prisoners from death. At 6.21 p.m. on Monday, 23 April, with a newly designated number – 90124 – the transport from Freiberg left the sanctuary of Horní Bříza to head south in a cloud of steam. Full of despair, the stationmaster watched the final wagon disappear around the bend and prayed that the war would end in time to save its cargo of hapless souls.

Leaving all kindness behind, those on board train 90124 crawled through Plzeň, a city dearly familiar to many of them. 'It was an unforgettable and horrible moment,' said one woman from the city. 'To see our home and then go past it.' Two days later, the Škoda Panzer factory they had passed was reduced to rubble. Seventy per cent of it was obliterated with incendiary and fragmentation bombs.

The train lines were also decimated. The *Häftlinge* had just missed the air raids that might have either killed or saved them. There would be many more frustrations and delays as the Nazis' plans were repeatedly confounded by bombs and the increasing danger posed by the two approaching fronts. The Red Army was closing in, and the Germans were more afraid of them than they were of the Americans.

Still not sure where to go, or which concentration camp would agree to take almost 3,000 prisoners, the DR directed the train further and further along the narrow line south. Every station passed was noted with increasing anxiety through the slits of windows or over the tops of wagons. Each name was repeated out loud for all to hear – 'Plana! – Tachov! –Bor! – Domažlice! – Nýrsko!' – as those women strong enough to speak cried, 'That's my home town!' or 'My family live there!' Those who could see out fell into a nostalgic silence as they watched the achingly beautiful countryside roll by, with well-fed animals in the fields and citizens free to do as they pleased.

The latest German order to the train driver and his SS guards was to proceed to Železná Ruda, but then the authorities heard that General Patton's Third Army was already there, so they had no choice but to turn it back to Nýrsko. On or about 27 April, the transport reached the town of Běšiny, where fifty male prisoners strong enough to walk were enlisted to help repair the bombed railway track to Klatovy so that the train could carry on. Those left behind were allowed out briefly to relieve themselves, swill out the soot, urine and excrement, and throw off their dead. Some tore up reeds to eat or fell onto a rivulet to quench parched throats, while the guards gobbled up the leftover pastries from Horní Bříza.

When the rail repair detail returned, Liška Rudolf said that the men told them the people of Klatovy had wept when they saw them and tried to give them food but had been pushed aside by the SS. 'In the evening the people from Běšiny and other areas came carrying boxes full of bread, buns, salami, soup. But everything had to be taken to the kitchen of the SS men. We were watching through the window and singing Czech songs. It went well – we got just a few lashes of the whip. From all the gifts, though, nothing was shared.'

After more waiting, the Nazis heard that it was possible to send the Freiberg train southwest through Horaždovice and Strakonice to the Dachau concentration camp in Bavaria. But the German high command was in total disorder and Nazi control over Europe was almost at an end. The Soviets had reached Berlin, Mussolini had been captured and would soon be hanged, and the German forces in the Ruhr had surrendered. On 28 April, after more delays, they were stopped in a siding near České Budějovice, a town full of fleeing Germans. The following day, the US Seventh Army liberated Dachau, saving the women of Freiberg from their latest potential destination. Opened by Himmler and hailed as the prototype for all later camps, Dachau had set itself up as a 'school of violence' for the SS who attended a training college within its grounds. An estimated 200,000 people had been imprisoned there, of whom more than 40,000 perished.

During one remote overnight stop, as the night sky filled with the noise of flak and tracer fire, some of the women were surprised to hear a loud wrenching noise in their wagon. They were even more shocked when the face of a Czech partisan appeared through a gap he'd created in the planking to allow prisoners to escape. Ironically, most were too weak, sick or scared to try, although several did flee – including the paediatrician Edita Mautnerová, who'd helped pregnant Anka when she'd hurt her leg and had delivered Priska's and Rachel's babies. She took her chance to live and survived the war. Once the escape was discovered, the SS, demanding to know who'd helped them and where they'd gone, beat the remaining women in the wagon. Most were past caring. Barely conscious, many simply lay down and died. Others were unravelling mentally.

Liška Rudolf said, 'The prisoners were howling with hunger ... some were going crazy because of hunger, the eyes shining as beasts in the dark night.' For many, the moment their locomotive gathered speed in the night at České Budějovice to head south on the venerable *Summerauer bahn* line from Czechoslovakia to Austria was one of the worst of their entire incarceration. The long dark nights on the train had always been something to dread, but that night – their last and darkest night, lying numbly in their rocking train – was surely the longest of all.

Lisa Miková said, 'When we changed direction we said, "My God, they will take us to somewhere terrible!" That really shook us. We were very afraid. Everybody thought her own thoughts – there were no more stories; no more talk. Like everyone else I didn't want to believe it but I knew my family was dead. I thought if we have to go to the gas chambers too, so be it. We were all too tired to fight.' This emotional surrender after so many years of survival rippled throughout the wagons once it was realised that the only possible route left to their train was across the border into Austria and the city of Linz. For the only camp near Linz was one that many of the prisoners feared almost as much as Auschwitz.

'When we headed out of there, there was only one way to go. There was nowhere else left,' said Anka. 'We were going to Mauthausen ...'

All seemed lost.

Many knew what that name meant to the 'enemies of the Reich' and they blanched at the thought. As a Nazi concentration camp, Mauthausen had been notorious even in the ghettos. While Anka was in Terezín, news had spread that the famous Czech singer-songwriter Karel Hašler had been murdered in Mauthausen. The information may even have come from two prisoners who'd escaped from Auschwitz and hidden in Terezín for a time. Hašler, a Gentile married to a German, had been arrested by the Gestapo for his patriotic songs and sent to the camp in the Austrian hills where, in December 1941 – having been tortured – he was turned into an 'ice statue': taken outside, he was stripped naked, repeatedly doused in icy-cold water and left to freeze solid.

Shocking as that was, the camp was most feared for the means by which most prisoners were worked to death. 'The business of Mauthausen was death – via a quarry,' Anka said. 'Everyone in Terezín knew that . . . People were forced to cut stone there and then climb one hundred and fifty steps or so or be killed. It would be the most dreadful end for us all.'

After all the women had been through – their years under Nazi tyranny, their survival in the ghettos, escaping Mengele and Zyklon B, avoiding death by starvation, disease, exhaustion or Allied bombs, and finally clinging to life on that train – suddenly they were frighteningly close to the end.

Mauthausen. One night away.

Not far from Linz, the huge granite camp was just a short train ride along the Danube valley. Salvation would come too late, it seemed. They and their babies – born and not yet born – were about to be delivered by train to one of the most notorious terminals in the entire Nazi genocide network.

It was the end of the line.

# 7

# Mauthausen

Picturesque Mauthausen, on the banks of the Danube

In spite of its fearsome reputation, KZ Mauthausen had perhaps the most picturesque location of any Nazi camp. With commanding views over much of Upper Austria as far south as Salzburg, it sat at the top of a hill in a region admired for its enchanting scenery.

Close to the borders with Germany and the Czech Protectorate, the town of Mauthausen on the River Danube enjoyed direct access to the continent's second-longest river as well as to an efficient road and rail network. Vienna was less than two hundred kilometres east and Linz twenty kilometres west. Adolf Hitler had grown up in Linz and it was the place he considered home. He reserved some of his grandest plans for the city he decreed 'the most German in all Austria', earmarking it as one of his five so-called 'Führer cities' along with Berlin, Munich, Nuremberg and Hamburg.

The showcase building was to be the *Führermuseum*, a grand gallery designed by Hitler's Minister of Armaments, Albert Speer, to rival the Uffizi or the Louvre. With a 150-metre façade of Roman-style columns, it was to be filled with fine art looted or con-fiscated from museums and private collections, much of it owned by Jews. The finest-quality golden granite needed to build this enduring monument to Hitler's glory, as well as his planned opera house and theatre, would come from the *Wiener Graben* (Vienna Ditch) quarry at Mauthausen, blasted out and chiselled into blocks by the most expendable enemies of the Reich.

The quarry had been owned by the city of Vienna for decades and its stone already paved the boulevards of the Austrian capital. After the *Anschluss* in 1938, the quarry was leased to the SS-owned German Earth and Stoneworks Company, which not only adver-tised its wares widely in glossy brochures right up until 1945 but also exported its products across Europe for use in monuments, construction projects, industrial complexes and *Autobahnen*. Career criminals imprisoned in Dachau built the concentration camp, designed to house the quarry's slave labour force, from the ground up on an adjacent hilltop. This monolith to the superiority of the Nazis, complete with gatehouse and watchtowers ringed by an impregnable granite wall, opened in 1939 and was visible for kilo-metres around.

Many of the earliest inmates were political and ideological pris-oners and members of the intelligentsia, including university professors – all sentenced to extermination through hard labour. Among them were *Häftlinge* from every creed and occupied nation, including Jehovah's Witnesses, priests and Spanish Republicans. Even after Auschwitz and other camps were evacuated in early 1945, Jews were in the minority at Mauthausen and there were few women in the camp (apart from those forced to work as prostitutes in the brothel) until 1945. The Soviet POWs were treated most brutally of all and less than two hundred out of 4,000 survived. They were not only worked to death in the quarry, they were given half rations and made to sleep naked in windowless huts. By the time they'd completed the building of their own 'Russian camp', their number had decreased so radically that the barracks were instead used as an infirmary camp, although it retained its original name.

One of only two 'Class III' punishment camps, and known within the Reich by its nickname of *Knochenmühle* ('bone-grinder'), KZ Mauthausen quickly gained a reputation as one of the camps with the harshest conditions and the highest death rates. One senior Nazi official is reported to have declared in 1941, 'No one leaves Mauthausen alive,' and many of the prisoners' files were marked RU, standing for *Rückkehr Unerwünscht* (Return Undesirable). Designed to turn a massive profit for the SS, Mauthausen and its more than forty satellite camps, including nearby Gusen (the other Class III camp), had access to an unlimited supply of prisoners. By 1944, this complex proved to be one of the most profitable camps in the Nazi empire, making more than eleven million Reichsmarks a year.

Work in the quarry was especially harsh and involved the digging, blasting and shaping of huge blocks of granite, often by hand or with pickaxes. Then each block – with an average weight of ninety pounds – had to be carried on prisoners' backs up a steep shale cliff which frequently subsided beneath bleeding feet, sending them sliding to their deaths. Later, 186 steps were rough-hewn and dubbed the 'Stairway of Death'. Armed guards frequently

waited at the edge of the steps to harry, beat and jostle those struggling with their load or trying to step over those who'd perished
before them.

The Stairway of Death at Mauthausen quarry

Inmates also faced the daily threat of being forced off the sheer
edge of the quarry in a spot the Nazis called The Parachutists' Wall.
As the guards laughed and shouted, '*Achtung! Fallschirmspringer!*'
prisoners were shoved over the edge to be dashed on the rocks or

drowned in the stagnant pool at the foot of the cliffs. Those not killed immediately were left to die, a process that could take days. Many jumped voluntarily rather than face the gruelling twelve-hour shifts on starvation rations in extreme temperatures, with brutal treatment meted out daily. Aside from being worked to death, there were more than sixty methods of murder catalogued in Mauthausen including beatings, shootings, hangings, medical experiments, injection with petrol, and various forms of torture. The final death toll in the camp complex is unknown, as many prisoners were killed in a mobile van or sent to a nearby castle to be gassed. That was, until the inmates were commanded to build their own gas chamber in 1941. Estimates vary as to how many died in total, but it is thought to be approximately 100,000, of whom more than 30,000 were Jews.

To begin with, the corpses were transported by truck to the town of Steyr or to Linz to be disposed of, but doing so openly was considered too great a risk, so a crematorium was commissioned to take care of them. The ashes were scattered in the forest behind the camp or in the waters of the Danube. As late as autumn 1944, when plans were being made to evacuate Auschwitz II-Birkenau, ten large 'waste incinerators' were dismantled there with the intention of rebuilding them at Mauthausen – a plan that was never carried out even though a local company was awarded the contract in February 1945.

This genocide took place within a few kilometres of the pretty riverside town after which the camp was named. Many of its 1,800 mainly Catholic residents watched new inmates march through their midst from the station, never to return. They witnessed those who collapsed being put against a wall and shot, and afterwards they washed away the blood. They heard prisoners being brutalised or murdered in the quarry and they gathered by the ferry to stare at the strange-looking men in striped uniforms being transported downriver to satellite camps. That was, until the SS threatened to shoot 'curious onlookers' and moved them on.

Despite the announcement by the Reich in 1938 that the creation of a concentration camp at Mauthausen was a 'special distinction' for the district, few can have welcomed it. The presence of its four hundred or so SS guards, however, ensured that the town was kept well supplied and soon became a vital lifeline to the local economy. Its bars, shops and restaurants did especially well from the brisk trade, and the inn nearest the camp became the most popular haunt of the SS. Many other locals profited from the money the guards spent freely on everything from cider and bacon to fish. There was also a thriving black market in soap, food, clothes and jewellery stolen from the camp, and several local women struck up relationships with the guards, sometimes even marrying them. Civilian workers and stonemasons were well paid as supervisors at the quarry, while slave labour from the camp was 'loaned out' for domestic and civil projects for the town, including decorating, gardening, farming and building. In 1943, Polish artist Stanislav Krzykowski, a prisoner at nearby Gusen, was commissioned to create a statue of a deer in repose for the garden of the chief of the SS.

The Nazi guards frequently joined local hunters for game shooting and they created their own football team, which played on a pitch the prisoners built for them overlooking the Russian camp. Sited just outside the main walls, it even had stands cut into a grassy slope. Once the Mauthausen 1 team was promoted to the regional league, all home games were played at the ground and the team were cheered on by local supporters who must have seen, smelled and heard some of what was going on. The games were reported by the press, who casually commented on the sight of prisoners sitting on the rooftop of the infirmary to watch games.

Close to the football pitch, a deep concrete reservoir constructed by the prisoners in case of fire in the camp was later used as a swimming pool for the SS. Selected locals were invited to swim there and to visit the camp cinema, although not on days when the crematorium was in full production. There was also a walled vegetable garden and orchard where prisoners were forced to tend to produce they would never be allowed to eat.

The townspeople were under no illusion as to the deadly intent of the uniformed men who guarded the camp up on the hill. There were warnings posted throughout the town that anyone found trying to help the prisoners would be shot, and civilian workers were arrested and imprisoned if they were overheard speaking about conditions inside the camp. One stonemason sacked for complaining about the inhumanity was later sent to Buchenwald, so people quickly learned to stay quiet and keep their heads down.

Historians have found a few instances where the townspeople did complain or try to help. A woman named Anna Pointner, who was a member of the Austrian resistance, hid documents and photos of the camp taken secretly by Spanish prisoners. Another young *Frau*, Anna Strasser, who worked in the accounts office of a warehouse opposite the railway station, watched transport after transport arrive. The condition of the prisoners horrified her and robbed her of sleep, so every day at midday she went for a walk during her lunch break and, through a small slit cut in the bottom of her pocket, deliberately dropped pieces of bread, sachets of salt and sugar, needles, thread and buttons in the hope that the next transport might discover them. She also found identity cards and desperate notes wedged between the planking of the wagons with messages pleading for someone to 'warn my family'. She stopped her humanitarian efforts only when her boss – a married Austrian with a family – was arrested after a guard saw him throwing bread to some prisoners. He was later sent to his death at Dachau.

Frau Strasser was reassigned to work in a tank factory where she was caught helping prisoners there too. Arrested by the Gestapo, she was sent to Ravensbrück concentration camp, where she almost died but was saved by a resistance doctor and managed to survive the war.

In February 1945 there was a mass escape of Russian prisoners from KZ Mauthausen and a few local farmers took enormous risks in hiding some of them. Many locals however took part in a so-called 'hare hunt', tracking down and shooting the fugitives, having been warned they were hardened criminals who would harm their families. Of more than four hundred Russians who escaped, many were shot or froze to death overnight. Two were hidden in the attic of the local mayor's house by his staff. Of the fifty-seven recaptured alive, only eleven survived.

A nun who worked in a local infirmary run by the Order of the Holy Cross recorded the frustrations of those in the town who wanted to intervene but felt unable to do anything. 'How much one wants to help these people, but sadly the harsh rules of the SS do not allow it and each small act of assistance put one's own life in great danger.' Other townspeople met secretly to discuss what they might be able to do to help the prisoners, but most were too afraid to act. Many were unwilling or unable to fully grasp the truth of what was happening on the hill, or lived in mortal fear of the same fate. Some complained about the smell of the camp, the smoke and ash from the crematorium that drifted into town. To appease them, the SS commanders ordered that the crematorium staff only 'put the burners on' at night. To address concerns about the possible spread of communicable diseases, they also set up a *Sonderrevier* or special sickbay (it was this which would later become known as the infirmary camp), staffed by prisoner-doctors, to try to contain the many infectious epidemics that it was feared would jeopardise the health of local residents.

The only remaining record of a formal complaint to the local political party about the mistreatment of Mauthausen's prisoners was in 1941 from a farmer's wife named Eleonore Gusenbauer, whose farmhouse overlooked the quarry and who consequently witnessed several shootings there. She wrote:

> Those who are not shot cleanly remain alive for some time and so are left to lie next to the dead for hours and even half days ... I am often an unwilling witness to such crimes ...

[which] takes such a toll on my nerves that I will not be able to endure this for long. I ask that an instruction be commissioned to cease such inhuman acts, or that it be done somewhere else where one does not see it.

It was to this town and to this camp that, after their sixteen-day journey crisscrossing Europe, the human ruins of KZ Freiberg finally arrived. Among them were Priska and her seventeen-day-old daughter Hana, Rachel and nine-day-old Mark, and Anka, heavy with child. Still none of them knew of the others, and still each was struggling to survive from moment to moment.

A few minutes after Train 90124 ended its long journey at Mauthausen railway station, experienced hands undid the bolts and the doors to their jail were pulled open. Many of the occupants had failed to survive the previous few days. Those still alive were dulled by shock and dazzled by the light that streamed into their sealed wagons. Wild-looking creatures, they emerged bug-eyed and delirious. Before they could even catch their breath, they were tugged from the wagons by SS guards and pushed into ragged columns on a purpose-built loading ramp just a few hundred metres from the sparkling waters of the Danube.

In the incongruous beauty of that place on the north bank of the river, all Anka could see on the wall opposite her were big black letters spelling out the name that translated to 'toll house' – MAUTHAUSEN. That deadly configuration of characters not only rammed home to her the truth on that bitterly cold spring evening of Sunday, 29 April 1945, it was enough to trigger her first contraction. Not even the optimism of Scarlett O'Hara could save her now. Tomorrow had come.

'As soon as I saw written that which I didn't want to see – my birth pains started,' she said. 'Even if I couldn't imagine anything else, that was that. It was a fact . . . I was so frightened that I started labour. Mauthausen was in the same category as Auschwitz. Gas chambers, selections – in short, an extermination camp.'

Lisa Miková felt the same. 'We saw the station name and knew it was something like Auschwitz. "OK," we said. "That is the same, so this is the end." We stared at each other and it was terrible how we looked – skin and bone skeletons. So dirty and full of lice. We looked dead already.'

Anka braved the first contraction that tore through her body. Paralysed with horror and pain, still she tried not to let on that she was about to give birth and gripped the wagon door for a few more seconds to catch her breath. Almost nine months earlier to the day, in the languid summer of August 1944, when all her loved ones had most likely already gone up the flue at Birkenau, she and Bernd had comforted each other in their charming cubbyhole in Terezín. Defiantly, they'd planned a child to replace little Dan whose death had almost broken them four months earlier. A few weeks after their second baby was conceived, Bernd Nathan was also sent East. Anka had no idea if he was still alive and she tried not to lose hope but, having experienced Birkenau, she feared the worst. That would mean that all she had left was this baby whose existence she'd hidden and whose tenacity in the face of hourly perils she couldn't help but admire.

She'd been petrified of the consequences of giving birth in the Freiberg factory. She had fought against going into labour in an open coal wagon. She would have been staggered and humbled to know that there were two mothers and their babies on the same train who had done just those things. Now it was her turn, and all she could think was that she was about to deliver a child that would most likely be thrown straight into a gas chamber, along with its mother.

Clutching her belly and struggling for breath, Anka somehow climbed down from her squalid wagon as brutish guards swarmed all around them. When her legs buckled she collapsed into a crumpled heap in the dirt. Dragged to one side with others too weak to move, she lay doubled up and vaguely aware of a farmer's cart being brought forward. She watched as the sick and the dying were flung up onto it in a haphazard pile of torsos and limbs, then she was thrown on top. 'Those who could walk were marched off up to the *Festung* or fortress,' she said. 'They unloaded all the people who were sick or dying and put them on a cart because the camp was on the top of the hill above Mauthausen.'

As the peasant cart moved off creakily, Anka lay feverish and disorientated amongst the sweaty bodies, staring back down the hill at the most breathtaking view. Even though she was pressed up against so many rank-smelling women dying of typhus, and even as her waters broke in all that filth and vermin, she couldn't help but gaze around her in wonder. 'I was as hungry as a wolf, weighed about thirty-five kilos, and had no idea what was waiting for me at the top ... As if I didn't have any other worries, I admired the countryside!'

It was around eight o'clock at night and the sun was setting over the valley as she half-lay, half-sat, overwhelmed by the spectacular sight after more than two weeks inside a blackened wagon deprived of any beauty. 'The sun was shining and it was cold something awful, but such a beautiful spring evening. We were going up the hill and I noticed the Danube below and the [fields] that were already beginning to turn green ... I thought I had never seen anything more beautiful in my life – maybe the last nice thing I would see on this earth.'

By the time the cart had climbed the two and a half kilometres to the top of the hill, though, her contractions had worsened and the picture-postcard scenery of Upper Austria with its churches, *Schlösser* and distant snow-covered Alps was no longer a distraction. The shocking reality of her situation helped rob her of her breath. 'The cart was smelly and muddy and I was with those creatures, without hair and in those rags. There were women dying and lice in millions, crawling all over the place. The poor women were unconscious and leaning on me and lying across my legs. I was sitting up and my baby started to come,' she said. 'I had only one fear – that the baby wouldn't survive.'

As they drew closer to KZ Mauthausen she turned to see, looming before her, the formidable stone fortress, built boulder on boulder by its unfortunate inmates. Her baby starting to push its way out between her legs, she looked up at the enormous wooden gates with their glowering granite watchtowers that gave an eagle's-eye view as far as the Alps. Within those walls, she feared there would be no possible escape.

The main gates at Mauthausen where Anka's baby was born

Knowing that she needed help, she suddenly spotted shuffling alongside the cart the Russian prisoner-doctor who had worked in the Freiberg infirmary alongside Dr Mautnerová. 'I begged her to help me but she just waved her hand, shrugged, and walked the other way. She didn't even look at me, or say, "I'm sorry. It will be all right."'

Holding onto herself and still trying to prevent the inevitable, Anka was manhandled from the cart in the shadow of the gates and inexplicably loaded into an open wooden wagon, 'like one in which you transport coal'. Squashed in with the same women, plus a few

others who appeared to have lost all control of their mental facul-
ties, she was stupefied. Her eyes squeezed shut against the pain,
Anka felt the wagon move off – away from those infernal gates – as
it made its way slowly down to the *Sanitätslager*, the infirmary, next
to the football pitch.

As her baby continued to push its way out, Anka screamed but
then stopped herself because of the proximity of the SS. There was
at least one guard accompanying the cart, and another steering it
and acting as a human brake. The one closest to her said, '*Du kannst
weiter schreien*' (You can keep on screaming), but she never knew
if he was being compassionate or sarcastic. Convulsed with pain and
convinced those were to be her final minutes on earth, she raged
freely.

Anka said, 'All the time this was going on I was thinking of my
mother Ida – not that she would be sorry for me, but how she
would say, "How dare you have a child under those circumstances!
I mean on a cart ... not having washed for three weeks?" ... She
would be so cross!' As the sun went down, and in those hellish conditions that Ida Kauderová would have so objected to, Anka finally
gave birth. Her newborn slipped from her body in a mess of blood
and mucus, a surprisingly quick delivery after her first protracted
labour with Dan, but then it was so very small. 'Suddenly my baby
was here – it was out!' The tiny infant didn't breathe and it didn't
move. 'For maybe seven to ten minutes it did not stir; it did not
cry ... I was sitting up and the women were lying across me, and the
baby was there and it was – indescribable!'

Moments later, the cart drew to a halt at the infirmary and someone summoned a prisoner-doctor who, she discovered much later,
had been the chief obstetrician of a hospital in Belgrade. 'He came
running out and he cut off the baby, smacked its bottom [to make
it cry and breathe], and everything was fine. It started to cry ... He
told me, "It's a boy." Somebody wrapped it in paper and suddenly
I was terribly happy.'

Anka had secretly wanted a little girl but she cradled her miracle baby and decided to name him Martin. She asked someone the time and date, determined to remember that her child was born at precisely 8.30 p.m. on 29 April 1945. Taken inside, she was astonished to find herself being helped to a bunk in which she was allowed to lie on her own. Even though there was a dreadful stink of excrement and the place was far from sanitary, she knew that the rest of the prisoners would have been less fortunate.

Her shrunken infant with a full head of dark hair was laid flat upon her chest, just as Dan had been the previous year. A baby so small should have been put in a heated incubator, but Anka gave her child vital skin-to-skin contact and became 'the best incubator in the world'.

'I was as happy as I could be – under those circumstances,' she said. 'I was the happiest person in the world.'

There was no such joy for Rachel and baby Mark. They were loaded onto a similar cart of the dying at the station and driven straight to the hungry gates of the camp, which were waiting for them, jaws open. Pulled from the wagon once they were over the threshold few re-crossed, they were pushed into a tattered line and told to wait in a vast elongated *Appellplatz* made by hand from square boulders filled in with tiny granite stones. All around them, the camp appeared to be in a state of high chaos. Choking smoke filled the air as documents were thrown into the incinerators to be reduced to ash, along with the corpses of those most recently gassed. German soldiers ran around waving pieces of paper as if they were preparing for something major to happen.

None of the women from Freiberg was aware that in the previous few months the size of the camp's population had doubled, thanks to the steady stream of evacuees arriving via the death marches. The situation was completely unmanageable. Food had virtually run out, disease was out of control, and even a provisional tent camp had been overrun. At this point in the war an estimated eight hundred inmates a day were dying in Mauthausen and its sub-camps and, in spite of the large number of newcomers, overall prisoner numbers would be down by 20,000 on the previous month. The German guards were eager to leave no trace of their crimes, especially after 23 April when Churchill, Stalin and Truman had ordered a massive airdrop of leaflets in every language which threatened to 'relentlessly pursue and punish' anyone guilty of mistreating prisoners. This, coupled with the fact that Red Army and American forces were almost upon them, meant that the world was close to discovering what had truly been taking place in this scenic region of Austria for the previous six years.

The women on the train were just another problem for the camp commanders. But once they finally decided what to do with the new arrivals, Rachel and her sorry group were shaken from their exhaustion and herded fifty at a time down a flight of steps, having been told that they'd be taking a shower. With baby Mark hidden under her grimy dress, Rachel was so weak that she was barely aware of what was going on, but she remembered enough from Auschwitz to know what having a shower could mean. Mauthausen's sixteen-square-metre gas chamber, disguised as a shower room, had already been used to 'euthanise' thousands of people in the camp since it was constructed, and camp records showed that 1,400 prisoners were gassed there during the final weeks. On 28 April, the day before the Freiberg train arrived, thirty-three Austrian Communists deemed 'enemies of the state' had been executed, along with five Polish prisoners, four Croatians and an Austrian with British nationality. The executions went ahead in spite of the presence in the camp of Red Cross officials negotiating to evacuate several hundred French and Benelux prisoners.

The gas chamber worked a little differently from those in Auschwitz, but it still used Zyklon B. The lethal crystals were tipped into a large metal box connected by a narrow pipe outside. A brick was heated and placed inside the box. Once the crystals reacted with the heat, the gas they emitted was blasted into the chamber by means of an electric fan.

The gas chamber at Mauthausen

Rachel knew nothing of this. She had no idea where her sisters were or even if they had survived the train journey. She had almost resigned herself to the fact that her husband Monik had been killed. She never expected to see her brave brother Moniek again and held out little hope for her parents and younger siblings at the hands of Dr Mengele and his cronies. She only knew that when she and her baby boy were pushed into a large tiled chamber with sinister-looking pipes, she believed that they were meant to die. It would have been a suitably pitiful end to the wretched existence the Nazis had forced on her and her family since the invasion of Poland six years earlier.

'They took us some place to gas us,' she said afterwards, 'but the prisoners had dismantled the gas chambers so they couldn't do it.'

It may never be known if Rachel and others from the train were really herded into the gas chamber that day, or whether they were taken to the genuine shower room at Mauthausen, closer to the

*Appellplatz.* Reports differ, and in the confusion of the last few days of the war few authentic records were kept. Several statements by prisoners, clerks and SS officers indicate that the last gassings took place on 28 April, after which they stopped because further murders would have been too difficult to cover up. Numerous prisoners from the train avow that the intention was to gas them the day they arrived, but it isn't known if this was a form of mental torture played on them by the Nazis, or if the SS officers who'd travelled with them were determined to fulfil their orders and eradicate those they'd brought so far.

Gerty Taussig, who may have been in the same group as Rachel, insisted the prisoners were meant to be gassed, not washed: 'They sent us to the "showers", fifty of us, but it was a gas chamber. The gas didn't come out, so they threw us out again. They ran out of gas, I think. They weren't dismantled – they just weren't working any more.'

Rachel said that after they emerged from the chamber, dry, fully clothed and still alive, there was even more pandemonium in the camp. 'All the Germans were running around and yelling then and one of them said, "Don't worry, we will put them in the Russian camp and the lice will eat them to death."' The women were pushed back out onto the parade ground as the sun set; rain began to fall and they were given a little soup and water, courtesy of Red Cross parcels that had been delivered to the camp. Then they were forced to sit in the cold and wait for the first batch of ragged skeletons from their train who'd been considered strong enough to stagger up the hill.

'They had to climb and it took them hours,' said Rachel. Only when they'd finally arrived were the prisoners forced to drag themselves to their feet again and lurch down the hill to the Russian camp. There, a few hundred metres from where Anka and her baby lay in the sickbay, they were pushed through a gate in a fence of barbed wire charged with 2,000 volts and locked into one of the huts.

The steep climb to fortress Mauthausen

Gerty Taussig said, 'There was nothing there but straw and bedbugs. I was sick with typhoid. I don't know how I survived. I guess I was lucky.' Other prisoners described the conditions. 'We were very sick . . . Women were dying in each other's arms . . . We had no feeling . . . We were like iron . . . We were lying half-dead in our own waste . . . We were waiting to die.'

Others, including Priska – carrying tiny Hana and her layette from the mothers of Horní Bříza – were still making the slow ascent up the hill. Priska fought for each breath in the more than two hours it took her to climb to the fortress camp. Her baby, whimpering piteously from the pain of weeping sores under her grubby smock and bonnet, lay limp against her mother's dry, depleted breasts.

In spite of their severely weakened state and visibly stricken feet, Priska and the surviving members of her group were jostled and beaten by the guards who'd accompanied them from Germany, who in turn were urged to savagery by agitated SS guards from the camp. Five abreast and barely clothed, the *Häftlinge* were prodded on through the picturesque town with its pretty window boxes and half-timbered buildings. Most of the inhabitants ignored them, but some spat at them or coldly told them they would all die when they reached the top of the hill.

Every now and again they were allowed a stop to catch their breath. Stunned, they drank in all they could of their brief glimpse of 'the free world', and especially its incredible scenery. For Priska, the view had at its heart the added poignancy of the Danube, a river that also ran through her lovely Bratislava. 'Think only of beautiful things,' Tibor had instructed her, so she tried desperately to focus not on her parching thirst or her crippling fear but on the astonishing lushness of the hedgerows, the meadows bursting with wild flowers, and the almost forgotten sound of birdsong.

The prisoners' experience of arriving at Mauthausen differed widely, depending on whether they were loaded onto carts or forced to ascend the hill in columns via one of two different routes. Those marched in plain view through the centre of the market town felt completely invisible to locals who waved and called out greetings to the guards, inviting them to social events or asking what film was showing in the cinema. Some, desperate for a drink, broke ranks when they spotted the ancient stone fountain in the square. Lisa Miková said, 'Half-starved, we dragged ourselves through the town. The thirst was so bad. There was a wonderful fountain in the centre and we all ran to it intending to drink but the locals chased us away and threw stones at us . . . There was a big row with the SS who beat us and pulled us back into line.'

The fountain in Mauthausen where the women were refused water

Those taken up a more rural back route where they would be less noticeable fell upon weeds growing at the side of the twisting lane, sucking on them through cracked lips. Some plucked cherry blossoms from the trees, gobbling them whole. Others fell onto scabby knees to lick water from a spring that trickled down the steepest part of the hill.

Priska clutched poorly Hana to her as she climbed, and in her reverie of starvation wondered if Tibor would ever know that he was a father or whether her daughter would live to see her one-month birthday on 12 May. 'I desperately wanted to save my child,' she said. 'That was so important to me. More than anything in the world.' Still in a daze, she eventually reached the fortress at dusk and breathlessly fell into line with the rest of the women, who'd been pushed together into a crumpled mass of misery. 'I could not recognise my friends after that horrible hunger,' she said, but there was an even greater surprise in store. 'In the courtyard there were packages from the Red Cross waiting for us. They gave us coffee and cake!'

Ravenous, and so thirsty they could hardly swallow, the women consumed as much as they could manage, convinced they were about to be gassed. A tall brick chimney towered over them, eclipsing hope. Made to wait for two hours after their small repast, they sensed the inevitability of what was about to happen. Too tired to fight or run, they could barely even lift their heads to look into the faces of those about to annihilate them.

Lisa Miková said, 'We stood or sat in the courtyard and waited for the end. There were some male prisoner workers there and they asked us where we came from and told us we were in luck and that the gas chamber wasn't working any more. One said, "Help isn't far away. They won't hurt you any more. They aren't interested. They are too busy trying to leave." We weren't sure we believed them. Even if help was one day away then in that one day we could be killed.'

Slumped on the paving as an Alpine wind whistled straight through her, Priska was awoken from her delirium by the 'cold' voice of an unfamiliar SS officer. In a language she understood only too well, he explained to his colleagues as she listened that they'd run out of gas and that the new arrivals could go to the *Zigeunerbaracke* (gypsy barracks), where prisoners evacuated from Ravensbrück had recently been housed. 'This transport can be put down there – for now.' With the familiar cries of '*Schnell!*' and the sudden sensation of guards and *Kapos* intimidatingly pressing around them once more, the women drew together protectively. As they prepared to be herded towards yet another unknown destination, baby Hana stirred and moaned. One of the female *Kapos* spotted the tiny bundle at Priska's breast and shrieked, '*Ein Baby! – Ein Baby!*' Another *Kapo* rushed forward, hands outstretched, to grab Hana as she cried, '*Keine Kinder hier!*' (No children here!).

With strength she didn't know she possessed, Priska fought them both off, spitting and clawing at their faces as each of them grabbed one of Hana's skinny legs and began a deadly tug-of-war. '*Nein! Nein!*' Priska screamed, fighting them like a savage. Her treasured layette fell to the ground and was trampled underfoot, lost for ever. For several minutes the tussle for Hana's life hung in the balance as the three women and the baby howled their collective indignation. Then, almost as soon as the skirmish had begun, it stopped – when an unlikely person stepped in to intervene. An older female *Kapo* placed one hand on Priska's shoulder and raised the other to her deputies, who immediately let go. Reaching out to stroke Hana's head, she said quietly, '*Ich habe nicht ein Baby in sechs Jahren gesehen*' (I haven't seen a baby in six years), adding, 'I should like to spend some time with her.'

Priska pulled a howl of protest back into her throat and stared at the camp veteran in astonishment. Without protest, the other *Kapos* backed away and Priska, her dress torn, realised that this could be her only chance to save her child. When the unknown saviour held out her hands to take Hana from her, Priska hesitated for a moment but then handed her over. 'Follow me,' the woman said, in an accent she recognised as Polish.

In a surreal sequence of events, Priska was ordered to wait outside the guards' barracks while the stranger took Hana inside. Rushing to the window with its pretty gingham curtains, the new mother watched anxiously as the stranger undressed the baby and laid her on a table. Then she stood over her smiling and cooing, seemingly oblivious to Hana's appalling condition. The *Kapo* went to a cupboard and pulled out a length of string and a bar of chocolate – a luxury Priska had almost forgotten existed. The guard broke off a cube of chocolate, tied some string around it, and dangled it tantalisingly over the baby's mouth. Enjoying her first-ever game, Hana's sore-covered legs jerked in evident delight and her little tongue hungrily shot in and out as, standing outside in the cold, Priska's breath steamed up the glass.

After almost an hour, the guard wrapped Hana in her grimy smock and bonnet once more and carried her back outside. 'Here,' she said brusquely, returning the baby to a shivering Priska. She then instructed another *Kapo* to escort mother and child to the gypsy barracks to join the others. She turned on her heel as if what was about to happen to them was none of her concern.

To reach her new quarters, a building where parts had formerly been made for Messerschmitt fighter planes (and therefore also known as the 'Messerschmitt camp'), Priska had to descend the Stairway of Death to the quarry, which had thankfully fallen silent for the night. The route down was treacherous enough in the day-time, the steps dangerously uneven – but at night, holding a small baby, her legs quivering with fatigue, she almost slipped and fell several times. When she finally made it to the bottom and stumbled past the cliff at the foot of which so many had died, she and Hana were led to the farthest of Mauthausen's thirty or so blocks, which was little more than a damp structure on the edge of the quarry. Inside a group of women who looked like prostitutes were quarrelling noisily in a corner; they didn't even look up. A few handfuls of straw and some broken pallets had been thrown on the floor of urine-soaked clay. The bodies of the exhausted women from the train lay folded where they'd collapsed.

This wasn't a place to see beauty. This was a place where people were left to rot.

Others from the Freiberg train had taken the exact same route as Priska earlier that evening while the *Kapo* was playing with Hana. They could hardly walk another step and many fell down the steps and had to be carried to the bottom. By the time they reached the barracks they simply found a place and sank down, 'too exhausted to live'. Some of the luckier women, like Lisa Miková, had been assigned slightly better quarters in the main camp at the top of the hill, where – even though they were put into bunks four at a time – they were cared for by male prisoners who risked their lives to give them their own food and water in the hope of keeping them alive. But none of those women had new-born babies to feed.

With Anka and her infant in the less than hygienic *Sanitätslager*, Rachel collapsed with Mark in the lice-infested barracks nearby, and Priska and Hana curled in exhaustion on the floor of a filthy hut, the women's interminable 'death march' had finally come to an end. They were still at the mercy of a murderous regime, however, and their war was far from over. There were countless ways to die in KZ Mauthausen, the most frequent of which were starvation, exhaustion and disease – all of which they and their infants were already suffering from. In such conditions, all three babies were dangerously prone to hypothermia, hypoglycaemia and jaundice.

None of their mothers knew what the next day might bring and all were too exhausted to think about it. As dawn crept over the Alps on Monday, 30 April 1945, the three mothers and their babies remained oblivious to the arrival of a new day, or to its significance.

For, later that afternoon – as Soviet forces closed in on the subterranean *Führerbunker* in Berlin – Adolf Hitler and his new bride Eva Braun sat sit side by side on the couch in the study of his bunker and took leave of each other. As they bit down on glass vials of cyanide, Hitler also shot himself in the right temple with his pistol. Their bodies were carried outside, soaked in petrol, and burned. In his last will and testament, written on the day Anka's baby was born, Hitler said that he had 'chosen death rather than suffer the disgrace of dismissal or capitulation'. He ordered his followers to uphold the race laws 'to the limit' and to 'resist mercilessly the poisoner of all nations, international Jewry'.

News of Hitler's suicide would have spread very quickly through the dwindling Nazi command, but it didn't reach the dying men and women under their control in those last desperate days of the war. If the prisoners were aware of anything, it was that there was shooting and shouting all day long, which only served to remind them that they were still trapped in the heart of one of the last operational camps implementing Hitler's plans to exterminate the enemies of the Reich.

'The Germans were hysterical and yelling at everyone,' said Lisa Miková, who lay in the hub of the camp up on the hill. 'Everyone was afraid to go outside in case they were shot.' She had slumped onto a stinking mattress on the floor of her barracks and when a Czech prisoner brought her some bread she thought to herself, 'Now I must live.' The bread, made from sawdust and chestnut flour, looked and smelt deeply unappetising, but it wasn't that which prevented her from eating it. 'I was so tired I couldn't eat. I was feverish and everything was like in a dream world. Then a woman came and prised open my hand to release the bread from my fingers. I watched her impassively. I was too weak to move or fight.'

Only Anka and her new baby in the infirmary camp were shown any kind of care. With few medical facilities, it was mostly a place in which inmates waited to die. Compared with the way she'd been treated on the train, though, Anka thought the Germans 'couldn't do enough' for her – although her infant stayed unwashed and wrapped in newspaper and she remained filthy and weak, sur- rounded by others dying untreated of typhus or worse. She said, 'By the time we arrived the Germans were already frightened out of their wits and they started feeding us.' She described their change of attitude as 'cloying and horrible', adding, 'I knew the day before they would have killed us and now everything was fine and we were the "chosen" people.'

She remembered from Dan's birth that she was advised a new- born shouldn't be fed for the first twelve hours of its life, so she rested and allowed baby Martin to sleep before she tried to feed him. To her surprise, when she did she had so much milk that she could have 'fed five babies'. She added, 'I don't know where it came from. If I had faith I would say it was a miracle.' Her baby, whose arms were the width of her little finger, guzzled greedily.

After weeks in which she had eaten not much more than a few mouthfuls of stale bread, Anka was given a bowl of macaroni swimming in fat. 'I was so hungry I ate it. I can't tell you how hungry I was! ... but it could have killed me on the spot. My intestines couldn't take it.' Almost immediately, she became incapacitated with diarrhoea and was extremely sick. 'I didn't have much left to give and could have contaminated the milk for the baby. But how can you resist food when you are starving?'

Somehow she managed to survive that setback, but still she didn't know if she had lived another day only to be murdered by the Nazis the next. The other prisoners tried to assure Anka from their adjacent bunks that she didn't have to worry about the gas chamber any more because it had been 'blown up', but she was afraid to trust anyone. She had no idea if what they said was true, but she certainly hoped so.

In the barracks beyond her *Sanitätslager* there was little hope for the rest of the women from the Freiberg transport. Their new quarters were alive with vermin and full of diseases. Tormented by lice, they were now even dirtier than they'd become accustomed to. It was difficult to breathe because of the smell of excrement and decomposing human flesh. The corpses of some prisoners had been dragged into the woods to form piles of flesh-covered bones. Gerty Taussig, who'd staggered from her hut to relieve herself, slumped onto a log, shocked. A male inmate sat next to her and said conspiratorially, 'I will share something with you – the best pieces of meat are from the thigh.'

For the first time in almost as long as they could remember, no one arrived to make them get up the next morning. Nor was there any coffee-water to drink. Up on the hill they could hear shooting and the mounting sounds of violence as the Germans panicked. The noise of an explosion in the distance was music to their ears. There were also the sounds of work continuing in the quarry beyond their compound, but then an eerie silence fell and the women wondered if they'd been left there to die.

In the days immediately after Hitler's suicide, the longer-term inmates of Mauthausen, who'd formed their own prisoner committees and resistance groups, noticed a distinct change in the atmosphere of the camp. There were still *Appelle* but work in the quarry virtually ceased (although the strongest were still instructed to break up and carry rocks). Then they realised that there were fewer and fewer Germans around. The 'old-timers' were suddenly able to move freely, taking food and water to the weakest, encouraging them to hang on. There was an almost constant roar of diesel engines as vehicles left the camp and the Red Cross ambulances were finally allowed through the gates to remove their agreed French and Benelux evacuees. Not that the *Häftlinge* down the hill were aware that potential rescue was so close at hand, while most of the food parcels the Red Cross brought in were taken by the fleeing Nazis.

As Anka slept soundly for the first time in months, Rachel and Priska also tried to rest and regain a little strength as their babies squeezed the last drop of milk from them. All were completely unaware of the moment when in the early hours of Thursday, 3 May, thirty-nine-year-old Frank Ziereis, the SS commandant of the camp for the previous six years, gave the order for his men to leave. The Zyklon B box that fed the gas chamber had been dismantled, and the camp was handed over to a unit of *Feuerschutzpolizei* (fire police) drafted in from Vienna, assisted by some older German soldiers. *Standartenführer* Ziereis then fled to his hunting lodge with his wife, but was later captured and killed. His SS officers scattered to the winds.

That day, a French officer released the previous week by the Red Cross managed to get a message to the Allied authorities warning them that tens of thousands of prisoners in Mauthausen and its satellite camps were likely to be killed following a letter received from Himmler ordering the destruction of anything that could be used as evidence against the Nazis. *[The officer] stated that the Germans are planning to exterminate these completely*, the secret message read. *Gas, dynamite and barges for mass drowning have been called forward and received. Massacres had started when the officer left the camp.*

Two days later, on the morning of Saturday, 5 May 1945, a reconnaissance squad from the 'Thunderbolts', the 11th Armored Division, Third US Army, was on patrol in the area checking on the safety of bridges when it was persuaded by an agitated Red Cross delegate to accompany him to Gusen and then into Mauthausen. The troops were led by platoon leader Sergeant Albert J. Kosiek, a Polish-speaking non-commissioned officer whose lieutenant had recently been killed but who turned down a promotion to remain with his men. The son of Polish immigrants to America, Sgt Kosiek was in charge of twenty-three soldiers with just six vehicles including a tank and his scout car when he first saw the fortress on the hill at Mauthausen, mistaking it for a huge factory.

Mauthausen liberator, US Sgt Albert J. Kosiek

When he began to smell the 'foul odours' emanating from the camp he discovered, to his horror, that it was a factory of sorts – a place of murder on a previously unimagined scale. Like so many of the Allied soldiers who stumbled across the Nazi killing centres in the final months of the Second World War, it was an experience that would never leave Kosiek and his men. Beyond the high stone walls and double electrified fences they came across thousands of saucer-eyed prisoners, many of them catatonic and on the verge of collapse. A huge number were unashamedly naked after years of being forced to stand in *Appell* after *Appell* without any clothes. In the final stages of the war, their rags had either fallen off or been torn from them by their stronger fellows. Exposed to the weather, their skin was covered in sores or had been eaten away by disease.

'It's a sight I'll never forget,' Sgt Kosiek said. 'Some had just blankets covering them and others were completely nude, men and women combined, making the most emaciated-looking mob I have ever had the displeasure to look upon ... They hardly resembled human beings. Some couldn't have weighed over forty pounds ... it made me wonder what kept them alive.' In spite of their appalling physical and psychological condition, some of the prisoners were rioting and even more went 'wild with joy' – screaming, yelling and crying in a discord of languages as soon as the Americans drove in through the gates.

Urging the prisoners to stay calm, Sgt Kosiek radioed his headquarters to report what he had found, but witnesses said he 'couldn't explain what the heck it was'. He and his soldiers had already come across hundreds of prisoners on the side of the road who'd been shot or had died from exhaustion on the death marches as the Nazis fled, but they were mentally unprepared for the sight of their first concentration camp. Stunned, Sgt Kosiek formally accepted the surrender of the Austrian and German guards, who put up no resistance and handed over their weapons. Not only were they relieved to give themselves up to American rather than Soviet soldiers, but the liberators realised later that when the Germans saw the distinctive red bolt of lightning on the 'Thunderbolt' insignia (similar to the jagged 'SS' symbol), they believed their unit was the equivalent.

The rest of the German guards had either fled or tried to disguise themselves in striped uniforms, but they were soon found out and many were killed in an explosion of prisoner anger. The surviving Russians, especially, wanted revenge, and killed their former German masters with their bare hands. Several were beaten, hanged and thrown onto the electric fences, where their corpses remained for days. Others were cut open and butchered. Some were stamped to death with the wooden clogs they'd issued to the prisoners.

At the Gusen sub-camp four kilometres away, Sgt Kosiek and his men had already witnessed similar scenes in which hatred of the guards led to mass lynchings of the *Kapos* and others, and more than five hundred of the 24,000 prisoners died. In Mauthausen, people also mobbed the few members of the American platoon wherever they went, and they stood powerless as prisoners went on the rampage, storming the SS *Kommandantur* and helping themselves to whatever they could carry. They watched two women hurl themselves at the electric fencing in a double suicide. They were told later that the women had been prostitutes for the Nazis and didn't want to be taken alive. There was a riot in the kitchens after hundreds broke in and raided it 'like a horde of savages'. Starving men grabbed fistfuls of flour from sacks and poured it down their throats. Skeletal prisoners were on the floor wrestling to the death for scraps. Desperate to maintain order, Sgt Kosiek fired his pistol three times in the air and spoke to the prisoners in Polish, ordering them to calm down.

In the middle of the mayhem he and his men were offered 'a guided tour' by the inmates, among them a professor who spoke perfect English. They were shown several different areas of the camp including the crematorium, where the ovens were going 'full blast' and were 'smoking hot'. The incinerator was burning five bodies at a time instead of the usual one and the floor was stacked with freshly slaughtered prisoners, many with their heads split open, leaking blood. They also found rats gnawing on corpses strewn around the camp. Most bodies were barely recognisable as human. There was talk of cannibalism and they were shown fresh piles of humans 'stacked like cordwood'. In the adjacent gas chamber they discovered the fully clothed corpses of more prisoners.

Knowing that he and his men couldn't safely remain in the camp that night, Sgt Kosiek arranged for a committee of prisoners to be put in charge to prevent further riots or retribution attacks on any remaining *Kapos* and prostitutes, and to supervise the distribution of whatever food was left. He threatened that if order wasn't maintained the Americans would pull out and leave them to the Nazis.

With the stink of Mauthausen still in their nostrils, the US platoon eventually left the camp, taking with them most of the guards (many of whom begged for their protection), and promised that the US Army would arrive in force the following day. Many inmates were terrified that they'd been abandoned or that the Nazis would come back, so those who were strong enough found weapons and organised themselves into patrols, vowing to defend themselves until death.

Klara Löffová said, 'The Americans suddenly left and we were scared again – either that there would be nobody to feed us (and you can imagine how scary that is) – or that the Germans might come back. We also didn't understand why. The explanation was that because of the closeness of the demarcation line [between the Soviets and Americans] the authorities didn't know under whose jurisdiction we should be.'

By day's end on 5 May 1945, however, they were officially free. The twenty-seven-year-old son of Polish parents, Sgt Kosiek had personally liberated some 40,000 prisoners at KZ Mauthausen and KZ Gusen, as well as accepting the surrender of 1,800 German prisoners-of-war.

In 1975 Kosiek was to return to Mauthausen with his wife Gloria to lead a procession of liberators back through the main gates of the camp to mark the thirtieth anniversary of the liberation. He remained in touch with many of his fellow liberators, and with a few survivors including Hungarian teenager Tibor Rubin, who emigrated to America and went on to win the US Medal of Honor for his bravery as an infantryman and prisoner-of-war in Korea. There were also two Polish survivors who visited Sgt Kosiek and his family years later at their home in Chicago, Illinois, to personally thank him for what he had done. He died, aged sixty-six, in 1984.

His son Larry said, 'My father found his experiences difficult to talk about his whole life, but he did give me his personal written account when I was thirteen years old and studying the war in school. He knew about the babies in the camp, which always amazed him, but he was mostly enormously proud of the accomplishments of his platoon.'

# 8

# Liberation

Survivors recovering after liberation in Mauthausen

The first Priska knew about the arrival of Americans in Mauthausen was the sound of something she hadn't heard in years – laughter, 'a most beautiful thing'. Somewhere in the distance, she thought she could also hear music being played.

Rising unsteadily from her hollow of soiled straw she peered out of her window, squinting in the noonday sun, and spotted three unfamiliar military vehicles with white stars carrying young-looking soldiers, none of whom were wearing German uniforms. So that was what Americans looked like. After dreaming so long about their Allied liberators, the sight of such beings in the flesh seemed like an illusion. Everything about them was different, from their uniforms to their helmets, even to the way they walked, talked and smelled.

While many of the prisoners were ecstatic at the Americans' arrival, crying, 'Peace! Welcome!' or 'We are free!' in a Babel of languages, others just slumped where they lay, apathetic and indifferent. Others sat overcome, tears streaming down their faces, praying that the smiling men in uniform weren't a cruel hallucination. Some of the younger women, who'd dreamed of meeting GIs all their lives, suddenly became self-conscious. Repelled by their own smell, they pinched their cheeks or tried in vain to smooth hair crawling with creatures and stiff with dirt.

One of the American soldiers was a young medic, Technician Fifth Grade LeRoy Petersohn. Just twenty-two years old, a newspaper employee from Aurora, Illinois, Petersohn was travelling with General Patton's Headquarters Combat Command B (CCB). He had a large red cross painted on his helmet and another on an armband. Pete, as he was known, had already 'patched up' numerous men in the field and had been awarded the prestigious Purple Heart for valour after being shelled and injured during the Battle of the Bulge. Once his division reached Mauthausen he spent almost two weeks tending to the sick and dying, and was initially sent down to the barracks below the main quarters to see who most urgently needed his help.

'I had seen a lot before I ever got to that camp,' he said later, 'but I was more affected by seeing the people that were starved and were just skin and bone.' When he reached a hut where men slept five to a bunk, he found a 'skeleton' with a weak pulse who died before his eyes. 'It was just a horrible mess; very strength-consuming.' The unarmed young medic had been warned not to get too close to the prisoners or to let them embrace him because of all the vermin and infectious diseases, but said they 'just swarmed' around him. As he continued to work his way through the huts examining the sick and dying, he was helpless to intervene when SS guards trying to pass themselves off as prisoners were discovered and beaten to death by those taking their revenge.

LeRoy Petersohn, the medic who saved Hana

Priska, leaning unsteadily on the window-frame of her barracks, heard the voices of the soldiers and recognised the language. The young teacher of languages who had given English lessons in her garden as a girl summoned up as many words as her fevered brain could recall and cried out for help. 'I called out to them in English to come to the barrack,' she said. 'One of these soldiers was thankfully a medic. He looked at my bundle, opened it and saw this so little baby with pus-filled furuncles [boils] caused by malnutrition.'

Pete was amazed to come across a mother and newborn baby in the infested, insanitary barracks. Both were severely malnourished and dehydrated, and the baby was suffering from a 'massive infection' and covered in lice 'bigger than her'. Having seen enough, he hurried to find his senior officer, Major Harold G. Stacy, to tell him what he'd found. The major was the division surgeon who'd been with Pete when they were shelled on their way to replace two medics killed in the Battle of the Bulge.

'I said, "Doc, would you come with me? I've got something I want to show you." So he and I went over to the barracks and sure enough this little girl, little baby girl, was just [a few] weeks old. She had been born in one of the other camps.' Pete asked what the baby was called and someone told him, 'Hana, her name is Hana.' He added, 'When they arrived at Mauthausen, they were scheduled to be killed. It just happened to be that, the day they arrived there, they had run out of gas.'

Gravely malnourished and riddled with infection as Hana was, both men knew that her chances of survival were extremely slim. They were also completely overwhelmed by the thousands of prisoners needing urgent medical attention and knew that they were facing mass epidemics of typhus and other diseases. Even so, the major and his young medic took pity on the child and decided to operate immediately.

Seeking Priska's permission to take her child away, Pete assured the anxious mother that they would do all they could to save her. It was the second time in less than a week that Priska had been asked to hand over her baby to a stranger and she was extremely reluctant to let Hana out of her sight again. Her English failing her, she begged to go with her baby until Major Stacy, who spoke German, managed to calm her down. 'The mother was trying her best to go,' said Pete. 'My officer . . . explained that we would bring her back, that we were going to make her well, and that settled her down.' Priska was too weak to argue further. Watching them disappear, she wondered if she would ever again see her beautiful little Hanička with the blue eyes and the pretty, upturned nose.

The two doctors jumped into a jeep, Major Stacy cradling Hana while Pete drove them straight to the 131st Evac (Evacuation) Hospital at nearby Gusen. It was the only place that had the necessary surgical equipment to deal with her infection. Major Stacy then sent Pete further on down the Danube to where the 81st Medical Battalion was stationed. He was instructed to collect some vital penicillin, the miraculous new 'wonder drug' that had only just been made available, and had to be kept in specialised coolers.

By the time he returned, Major Stacy was already operating on Hana in the field surgery, opening up and lancing her numerous abscesses. In a slow and complicated procedure, he tackled each pustule individually, surgically cutting away infected areas of skin where necessary. Pete followed him around her tiny body, cleaning the pus and dousing each wound with swabs of penicillin. Hana, whose face was distorted from crying, then had to have several of her sores stitched up in a process that would leave her scarred for life.

As Priska waited for news of her baby, the hours passed with no relief. When a US Army nurse eventually brought back the heavily bandaged bundle the following day, the woman had tears rolling down her cheeks. Priska, who'd been moved to a makeshift infirmary with just three to a room and each in their own bed, took one look at the nurse's face and cried out in anguish, 'Is she dead?'

'No, no! She's alive! She's healthy!' the nurse reassured her as Priska took baby Hana in her arms and vowed never to let her daughter out of her sight again.

Pete Petersohn continued to closely monitor Hana's progress and saw mother and baby regularly. His major explained that all those weeks in the coal wagon had almost killed the baby. 'He said she'd picked up an infection that had travelled throughout her body.' Both men tried to persuade Priska to evacuate to the US once she and the baby were strong enough to be moved. 'My officer tried to talk her into bringing the baby to America,' said Pete. 'He was going to make arrangements for the two of them to come ... because he felt she needed further treatment than what we could give her, but she wouldn't have it. She wanted to go back to Czechoslovakia because [of] her husband ... she had hoped that he would show up.' Resisting their kind offer, Priska carefully folded away all that she had left of her child – the little white smock and bonnet the women of Freiberg had made for her baby – and prayed she would make a speedy recovery so that she could soon take her home.

A few barracks further along, Anka's baby remained wrapped in the paper into which it was first folded for the next three weeks. There were no nappies and nothing soft to wrap it in – just more newspaper. Still no word had reached her of Priska and Hana, or of Rachel and Mark, so each mother still believed that hers was the only 'miracle baby'. The reaction of their liberators didn't disabuse them. 'When the Americans arrived, they came and started to look at us like we were one of the Seven Wonders of the World,' Anka said. 'I was filmed for newsreels. They couldn't get over it. A seventy-pound woman with a three-pound baby alive and kicking. They had never seen anything like it in such a place!'

Aside from all the attention, she said the best thing of all was the chocolate the American soldiers gave her. 'That was lovely, except that they said we could have it, but then we couldn't have it all. What torture was that?' In the end, they were allowed one tiny cube at a time. After a few days, Anka called one of the American nurses to her bedside. 'I asked if she could please give my little boy a bath as he had never been washed. She looked at me as if I had gone mad and said, "What do you mean? You have a little girl!"' ... I got hysterics – my first hysterics after all this – how can it be a "she" when they said it was a "he"? ... I didn't know what to think. I had never heard anything like that.'

Anka created such a scene that several doctors rushed to her bedside. At her request, each of them examined the child she'd called

Martin and confirmed that she'd given birth to a little girl and not a boy at all. One doctor eventually explained that it was a common mistake in sexing small or premature babies, as the genitals are often enlarged and swollen. 'I was delighted!' Anka said. 'I had always wanted a little girl! . . . She was like an angel. I kept warming her little feet with my hands.'

Cradling her daughter still closer after her first bath, Anka chose the name Eva because it couldn't be shortened or changed in any language. That felt important to her, having lived through a period when people's names and the language they spoke had taken on such sinister significance. And although she had been born on 29 April in the back of a cart below the gates of the camp, Anka decided that her child would always celebrate a second birthday – 5 May, the date when she was liberated and 'born again' as Eva Nathanová – a free citizen. It was a decision shared by the other mothers individually.

Rachel's sister Sala had been the first of the Abramczyk sisters to realise that the Americans had officially liberated Mauthausen when she heard artillery on 6 May, the day after Sgt Kosiek's acceptance of the German surrender. Then she saw walking, talking GIs in the camp. 'US Jeeps carrying soldiers came in and I started crying and everyone started screaming and people were lying on their carts clapping that the Americans were here. That is how they died – clapping and thanking them for coming. At least they knew they came but, gosh, so many people passed away then! They were too sick and too tired and they gave up.'

Sala was so excited to share the news with her oldest sister that she hurried to her barracks to see her. 'I told her, "Rachel! Rachel! The war is over!" and she gave me a slap across the face because she thought that I'd gone crazy! . . . but that was the day we were all born again, especially baby Mark. The US soldiers were so good to us. God bless America!'

Rachel eventually accepted that her younger sister was telling the truth but she was too weak to get out of bed and see the liberators for herself. In any event, by then there was bedlam in the camp. Relief at being free and the sight of a white flag hoisted over the gates brought indescribable joy to the prisoners but also incredible outrage at what had been done to them. Grown men were crying and behaving wildly. The huge wooden *Reichsadler* (imperial eagle) that had presided over the SS garage block was torn down and smashed to pieces by vengeful inmates. Any remaining guards were beaten or killed, while bands of prisoners in tattered uniforms played out-of-tune instruments or sang rousing renditions of their most patriotic songs.

One of the US soldiers at the camp that week was Captain Alexander Gotz, MD, present with the medical detachment of the 41st Armored Cavalry Reconnaissance Squadron. He described that day as the witnessing of a 'macabre and grotesque opera with the performers barely resembling human beings'. Even when things calmed down and the Americans had regained control, the surviving prisoners weren't yet out of danger. They faced a new and unexpected enemy – compassion.

The US soldiers had strict instructions not to feed survivors until medical staff could properly assess their condition. After the liberation of previous concentration camps, the Allied command had learned the hard way that feeding the starving could be fatal. But the young Americans of the 11th Armored Division hadn't any such experience before Mauthausen and they found it impossible to refuse the hungry multitudes, with tragic results. Gladly, they handed over their rations – including sweets and cartons of cigarettes – not realising the consequences. Men and women who'd been living on liquid, supplemented by bark peeled from trees or blades of grass, gobbled up the cigarettes rather than smoking them. Those who'd never seen chewing gum before swallowed it whole. Others used sharp stones to feverishly hammer their way into tins of beans and then gorged the lot, along with unhealthy quantities of bacon, cheese and Hershey bars, unable to stop themselves.

After years of extreme privation, and contaminated by decay, their bodies had broken down to the point where they could no longer digest solid food. An estimated 1,300 weakened and dehydrated prisoners died of sickness and diarrhoea due to their intolerance to the rations they were given in the days following liberation. A further 2,000 died from disease – mostly typhus and dysentery.

The three mothers and their babies were equally at risk. Rescued from their vermin-infested barracks, they were moved to better quarters where they were each given something to eat and drink. Then women started dying around them in droves. 'The Americans didn't know how to handle this,' said Rachel. 'They had never seen starving people before. They gave them everything.'

One GI offered Rachel his military ration of chocolate wrapped in brown paper. She couldn't remember the last time she'd seen chocolate and so, for several moments, she just sat and stared at it, speechless. After a while she held it to her nose, closed her eyes and inhaled. The soldier, thinking that she didn't know what it was, spoke slowly as he told her, 'You chew it and swallow it.' He even made hand gestures to show her, which only made Rachel weep. 'He asked me, "Why are you crying?" I couldn't tell him so he went away.' When he returned he asked her again.

'Because you were telling me what chocolate is,' she replied.

Mortified, he apologised, but added, 'When did you last look in the mirror?'

Rachel thought it must have been about a year before, May 1944, when she was still in the Łódź ghetto with dear Monik and her lovely family.

'When we came here we all thought you were wild people,' the soldier explained apologetically. 'We didn't realise you were normal.'

Those desolate shadows of the people they'd once been had forgotten what 'normal' was. Some of their fellow fragments of humanity were too exhausted to appreciate that they were free, even when the Nazis disappeared. One survivor said that at first their minds couldn't grasp what that could mean, even though they'd been waiting so long to be saved. They were, she said, 'too weak and too empty to feel happiness'.

Many, desperate to get away in case the Nazis came back, staggered like drunks out of the camp gates, which were suddenly swinging open. The exertion proved too much for many who dropped dead just beyond the walls. Others made it as far as the town or onto neighbouring farms where they begged for food and clothing – and were almost always given something. Some of the most disorientated prisoners simply slumped to the ground, unable to grasp the concept of freedom or the miracle of Nature.

Their struggles were far from over and the next few weeks and months would see only the fittest of them survive. Few were even aware of the Germans' unconditional surrender on 7 May 1945, in a little red schoolhouse in Reims, France. Or that VE Day was celebrated wildly around the world the following day, with millions taking to the streets. With their minds and bodies broken and their loved ones almost certainly gone, in the overcrowded bunks and barracks of Mauthausen there seemed less cause for celebration.

Within weeks of the Nazi surrender, the Allies were carving up the former German empire between them. Word flew around the camp that although the US Army had liberated Mauthausen it would be the Communist Soviets who took control of that part of Austria. The deadline for the takeover was 28 July 1945, when the Americans would withdraw south of the Danube and the Red Army would be in charge of the camp and any remaining inmates. For many Jews who feared the Russians almost as much as they'd feared the Nazis, that suddenly became their own personal deadline to escape to American-held territory.

Keen to stem the tide of infectious survivors wobbling pitifully out of the camp, the Americans closed the gates once more and assured them that they would be able to leave once they'd been declared disease-free. 'We just wanted to go home,' said Sala, who was in better shape than most, 'but they said we couldn't yet because there were still some SS in the area. Many people didn't understand or accept that, so then they explained that we were in quarantine.' Determined to do what she could to help, Sala volunteered as a nurse in the temporary infirmary set up by the Americans for some six hundred-plus patients, as well as the tented field hospital they established for more than a thousand. She helped give vitamin and other shots and took care of the sick and dying for ten days. 'I had to do something, even if it was only feeding people their last meal.'

Then she contracted typhus. 'I don't remember much about it because I was delirious and in quarantine. I remember an Italian doctor saying that I wouldn't make it. From that day on, my sister Ester kept me alive. She opened the window and she climbed in to give me food. She didn't even care if she got typhus too. I was almost dead for one week but she remained at my side because I couldn't walk or see. Once I asked her to get me some strawberries and somehow – I don't know how – she found me some, but I was feverish and I told her, "I don't want strawberries!" Poor Ester. She saved my life.'

Rachel, too, did what she could. With the help of the Red Cross and other aid workers, the Americans had set up a mess squad to cook food, check on its nutritional content, and carefully monitor portion sizes. They were soon overwhelmed by the sheer numbers of people they had to feed, and had to post armed soldiers to protect supplies. After a while, they decided it would be better to provide stoves for each hut and allocate food to be served three or four times a day. Rachel quickly took charge of her barracks and, clucking over her fellow survivors, began to prepare soup. 'I had a baby to nurse and my sisters were sick, so I found a small pot and I cooked,' she said, falling back into the maternal role she'd adopted to care for her younger siblings since their childhood in Pabianice.

Sala continued to deteriorate as typhus rampaged through her body. It was weeks before she was out of danger. 'I was so ill,' she said. 'I was running to the bathroom but everything was filled and it looked like hell ... All you saw was dead people. There were corpses everywhere.' One day a doctor came into her room and announced that June had arrived. 'He said, "Let's open the windows. Summer is here and we are all getting well." And I did get well. I made it.'

In the following weeks, as the three new mothers and their babies gradually regained their strength and even began to gain a little weight, they were kept in separate sections of the camp, which was then under official quarantine. With tens of thousands of survivors to deal with, what the Americans called 'organised chaos' reigned, only ameliorated by the fact that most were too weak to leave their beds.

Apart from Rachel, who'd heard rumours that there were other babies in the camp but had never seen any with her own eyes, each mother remained completely oblivious of the others. Where they could have supported each other and shared their experiences in Auschwitz, throughout their time in Freiberg, and on the train, each continued to believe her situation to be unique. How could another woman and her baby have possibly lived through what they had each withstood? Besides, they had too many other things to think about – chiefly regaining their stamina and trying to make themselves presentable for the day when they might be released and, hopefully, reunited with Tibor, Monik and Bernd.

'They still wouldn't let us leave the camp because they were worried we would infect the Germans, so we were there for another four weeks,' Rachel said. 'But after a few days some of the girls went down into the town and people gave them some clothes and dresses and we washed our faces and began to look like normal people again.' The seamstresses among them tore up blankets to make wraparound skirts and they adapted men's underwear and shirts, some of which had been taken from the guards' quarters or pulled from the bodies of those who'd perished. Others ripped down the brightly coloured curtains or grabbed the gingham bed-covers from the barracks of the SS guards and *Kapos*, and made skirts and blouses from them. The luckiest ones raided the homes of the senior SS women and took their pick of clothes. Survivor Esther Bauer said, 'I was given a dark green woollen suit with a fur collar. I was so happy!'

When Allied commanders arrived in the camp to see the horrors for themselves, they insisted that KZ Mauthausen be opened to public view and that the bystanders of the town be brought up the hill to see what the Nazis had perpetrated in their midst. The weeping residents pressed handkerchiefs to their noses and swore they hadn't known what was going on, in spite of the permanent stink and smoke that had hung over them like a pall. The authorities then insisted that they 'volunteer' to help care for the living. This included soaping down survivors using water pumped from the Danube, sterilising or burning their clothing and linen, and spraying them with DDT to try to eradicate the lice.

The prized one-acre *Sportsplatz*, the football pitch where Austrians had cheered on the SS team, was turned into a mass grave for almost a thousand victims. Naked, they were almost all unidentifiable and many were in a state of decomposition. Units from A Company 56th Armored Engineers were brought in with bulldozers and buckets fixed to tanks to dig trenches thirty metres long, two metres deep and three metres wide. Among them was Sergeant Ray Buch, who arrived on 10 May. 'We were working to dig these trenches ... in the soccer field where the SS had built a platform out of rocks ... It was so hard to dig with a bulldozer. We had to get somebody to dig the bigger rocks out by hand. We tried dynamiting a couple of them but granite is the hardest rock there is ... they tried to get people in head to foot ... To get more in the grave without piling them on top of each other. Five hundred in each heap. One wagonload had two hundred corpses in it. The bodies were so packed in it was hard to tell how many were in them.'

Mauthausen graves and infirmary

German prisoners-of-war, including former guards and SS officers, were forced to help lay the dead to rest with a little dignity. The civilians of Mauthausen who'd benefited from the SS presence were also summoned back to the camp in their 'Sunday best'. Weeping and crying, men and women were forced to dig more graves, load the corpses onto wagons from the barracks, and lay them side by side in rows of one hundred and fifty. The graves were backfilled with rocks and soil and the final resting place of each body was marked with either a white cross or a Star of David. Many featured the names and dates of death of those interred, but even more were marked 'Unknown'. Prayers were said for the dead and locals were summoned to attend the mass funerals with their children.

After the relief of liberation, and their disbelief at still being alive when so many had perished, the survivors continued to vent their anger on the perpetrators of their suffering. When they weren't digging graves, the German POWs were forced to clean

out the latrines, dismantle and burn the most heavily infested barracks, work in the quarry, or do the kinds of dehumanising jobs
they'd forced thousands of prisoners to do.

In spite of all attempts to keep the camp locked down, homes,
farms and shops in and around Mauthausen were frequently raided
and the people of the town – frightened, ashamed or guilty – usually handed over food, drink and clothing to those who asked, all of
whom appeared horribly wretched and sick.

As May progressed and the summer sun began to drive the chill
from the survivors' bones, the situation in the camp improved
greatly. Tinged with death and translucently pale, hundreds crawled
from their bunks to lie on the grass or wherever they could find a
space and fall asleep. The sunshine seemed to soften the harshness
of their surroundings and the sound of birds singing mellowed some
of their most painful memories. Although most were impatient to
leave the place that for many had been a living hell, even more
feared life beyond its walls. The Allies had agreed to repatriate every
survivor they'd liberated but many felt unable to return to countries
like Germany, Poland or the Soviet Union, where entire communities had been massacred and there was still widespread hatred of
the Jews. They agonised continually about what had happened to
their loved ones and longed to be reunited with any who might
have survived, but what dangers lay in wait if they went back to
claim appropriated property? Did they even have 'homes' any
more?

Old and young alike were so traumatised by their experiences
that they didn't know what they wanted. Their psychological scars
would be deep and lifelong. An untold number killed themselves
rather than face up to the gulf between what they hoped for and
the reality that awaited them. Others, incarcerated for so long, were
lightheaded at the concept of freedom and wanted to make a fresh
start. Thousands planned a mass exodus to the 'promised land',
Mandatory Palestine, which they also called 'Eretz Yisrael', or to
America, Canada or Australia – nations where they hoped to

rebuild their lives and remain safe. But there would undoubtedly be great hardships in starting again with nothing and they were painfully aware that countries with strict immigration policies would hardly welcome hordes of destitute refugees.

The indecision as to where to go and what to do caused a massive refugee crisis, which initially had to be administered by Allied military personnel. There were between eight and nine million survivors of the war to settle into Displaced Persons (DP) camps run by the army, or by voluntary agencies such as the Quaker Relief Team, the United Nations Relief and Rehabilitation Administration (UNRRA), the Red Cross and the International Refugee Organisation. Although some of the smaller DP camps were set up in schools, hotels and hospitals, the most obvious place to establish them for such large numbers of people was in former garrisons, labour camps, or the very barracks where the survivors had been imprisoned. For a few weeks until the end of July 1945, KZ Mauthausen became a kind of DP camp – one of 2,500 throughout Germany, Italy, France, Switzerland, England and Austria. Within these once-electrified fences, the dispossessed were clothed and fed, housed, registered, treated, and classified ready for repatriation. They then had to wait for a country to agree to take them or for a relative to sponsor them from abroad. For some, the process took years, and the long-term treatment of those uprooted from their homes and facing an uncertain future was often less compassionate than it might have been.

In order to speed up the procedure, the Red Cross did what it could, while the UNRRA established the Central Tracing Bureau, which helped survivors try to find their relatives by publishing lists of the living in newspapers and making daily broadcasts on the radio. Volunteers interviewed every prisoner and filled out a corresponding number of forms. They were eventually able to repatriate between six and seven million people and help 1.5 million emigrate – but it proved to be a colossal, lengthy, and often controversial undertaking.

For those entrusted with the repatriation of Mauthausen's more than 40,000 refugees of twenty-four nationalities back to places they wanted to live or had once considered home, the task was no less of a logistical nightmare. Not only were the majority physically or psychologically damaged but they had hardly any clothes, no money and no documents. Europe was a melting pot. With most of the local trains, boats and motor vehicles already requisitioned to bring in supplies or to ferry troops and machinery back home, there wasn't enough transport to handle the overwhelming numbers who wished to travel to every corner of the globe. Transportation for all those repatriated would be free, but decisions had to be made about who would fund their return – the Allies or the governments who'd arranged for their deportation in the first place. In the end, the costs were for the most part borne equally.

Another major problem was that no one could prove they were who they claimed to be. Every man, woman and child who'd survived the concentration, extermination and labour camps would require an identification document of some description, and yet most had nothing but a number tattooed on their arm or one memorised from their daily *Appelle*. Many of the Nazi records had been burned or taken away and there was no means of knowing where these people officially belonged.

Even when they were eventually issued with new papers, there was mounting uncertainty about what would be waiting for those whose entire communities had been wiped off the face of the earth. There were news stories of people being exiled or murdered when they returned to their homes. Widows and orphans were considered especially vulnerable, and many soldiers did their best to persuade them that they would be better off trying to get into America.

Survivor Klara Löffová, who was befriended by a nineteen-year-old American GI named Max, from Brooklyn, New York, was sorely tempted. Max took such a liking to her that he brought her extra food and some of the all-important American cigarettes that were to become the currency of the camp. When it was finally time for her to say goodbye, Max 'formally' introduced himself and extended his hand. She started to put out her hand but then pulled it back in shame, because she was still infested with lice and ingrained with filth. He took her hand anyway and then kissed it. She never forgot that kindness; she did, eventually, go to live in America, where the story of the kind soldier became such a part of her family's history that her grandson was named Max in his honour.

Priska, gazing nostalgically at the waters of the Danube far below the camp, was desperately homesick for Bratislava and wanted to get back there with baby Hana as soon as possible. She was convinced that Tibor would be waiting for them in their apartment, surrounded by his notebooks and pipes. It had been months since she'd last seen him – through the wire in Auschwitz – but 'thinking only beautiful things' she had never allowed herself to believe that he might not have survived.

For Rachel and her sisters – all still in their twenties – there was only one place they wanted to go. 'Our father had always said that if we were separated, then right after the war we should all come back to Pabianice and meet there again,' said Sala. 'So as soon as we were all strong enough, that was where we decided to go.' Rachel hoped that if Monik was still alive, he would find her there and finally be able to meet the son he didn't even know she'd been expecting. She had no idea if they still owned the family factories, but either way they would have to start again and try to make a new life for themselves.

Anka, with little Eva, had nowhere to go but back to Czechoslovakia, but she was in 'a daze' because she had no idea what she would find. 'I knew that my parents and my sisters were not alive – that was a matter of deduction – but I still didn't know about my husband Bernd.' Would anything be left for them in Třebechovice pod Orebem? Would her father's leather factory and her sister Ruzena's villa still belong to them, or would they have been seized or even burned down? Did she want to remain in Europe at all if there was nothing and no one left?

There felt to be so much uncertainty and confusion all around them. No country in Europe had been left untouched by the war and the Continent was in turmoil. As the Allies continued to hunt down the Nazis, they began to amass evidence of more and more atrocities. Thousands of Germans fled their homes or were forced to leave. Hundreds of SS officers and members of the high command were arrested for trial and execution but many more slipped through the net; they included the Freiberg *Unterscharführer*, Richard 'Šára' Beck, who was never brought to justice.

Heinrich Himmler, Hitler's trusted deputy and one of the people considered to bear most responsibility for the Holocaust, was captured on 23 May 1945. The *Reichsführer* of the SS, who controlled the concentration camps and had personally visited Auschwitz and Mauthausen to see for himself how well the Final Solution was being enacted, bit down on a cyanide pill hidden in his mouth and killed himself before he could be tried.

In June 1945, Dr Josef Mengele – the 'Angel of Death' – was captured by the Americans, before being mistakenly released a month later. Posing as a farmhand, he changed his name and remained on the run for the rest of his life, until his death by drowning in Brazil in 1979. His wife had divorced him and his son disowned him soon after the war. Mengele remained unrepentant until his death and always claimed he was only obeying orders. He would never have heard about Priska, Rachel and Anka and their babies, who'd slipped through his manicured hands at Auschwitz.

Luck, courage and determination had sustained the three women through the war and they would need all those qualities as they contemplated life 'Afterwards'. Everything had changed. They had nothing but questions without answers. Where were their loved ones? How would their lives be? As one prisoner said, 'Physically and emotionally, I was nothing but a question mark.'

Before they could even consider booking their places on any available transports to take them home, there was one legal formality each of the mothers had to go through – certifying the births of their babies. Each child had to be registered at Mauthausen City Hall, which was done between 14 and 17 May 1945. As soon as they were strong enough, Rachel and Anka made the journey back down the hill into the town and paid the nominal fee before filling in the relevant forms. Priska – unable to face the townspeople – asked her friend Magda Gregorová's husband, actor Martin Gregor (who'd been reunited with his wife in the camp), to do it for her.

Hana's birth certificate

Each mother then received an official Austrian *Geburtsurkunde* (birth certificate). Hana was incorrectly listed as Edith Hanna Löwenbein, born in Freiberg on 12 April 1945, with the addition '*Gefangenen-Bahntransport*' (caught a railway transport). There was no mention of her birth without medical care on a wooden plank in a German slave labour factory the day before she and her mother were forcibly evacuated by train. Tibor was listed as her father and

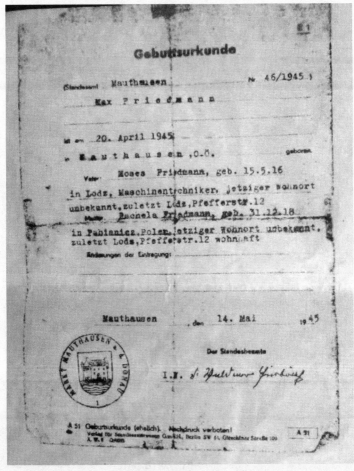

Mark's birth certificate

'Piri' as her mother, and of both it was said, '*Jetziger wohnort unbekannt*' (present address unknown), before giving their former residence in Bratislava.

Eva's birth certificate

Mark and Eva's birthplace was listed as 'Mauthausen' or 'Mauthausen *früheres Konzentrationslager*' (former concentration camp), and the dates of each delivery as 20 and 29 April respectively. They too were of no fixed abode. The registrar who signed Mark's birth certificate could never have imagined how he'd been delivered in an open coal wagon in the rain near Most. With baby Eva, who'd arrived on a filthy cart in the shadow of the camp's gates, the certificate registered the time of her birth as 8.30 p.m. but gave no indication of its gruesome circumstances.

Armed with these important pieces of paper, plus a provisional identity card that listed their names and dates of birth, and a document signed by the International Red Cross to prove that they'd been in a camp, the three women were finally declared well enough to travel. Each was further issued with a dated slip of paper, signed by a deputy of the new commanding officer of Mauthausen, stating that they were free of infectious diseases. The Red Cross handed out clothes and caps to as many survivors as possible – some of whom were still dressed in the tattered clothing they'd been thrown years before. The survivors fought over any sweaters with a coveted 'Made in the USA' label. Then, along with the rest of the refugees, they just had to wait for transport back to their chosen land to become available.

The women had been in the custody of the Nazis for between eight months and almost four years. For all of them it felt like a lifetime. Aged between twenty-six and twenty-nine, and considering themselves less Jewish than most, they were changed beyond recognition, physically and psychologically. They could barely remember the life they'd led before, with all its freedoms, or the carefree joys of being young and in love. As Rachel said, 'I was an old woman when I came out at twenty-six.'

The Russian prisoners-of-war who had somehow managed to survive such extreme cruelty in Mauthausen were the first to leave the camp – on 16 May 1945 – and were given a moving send-off. As people crowded into the *Appellplatz* to bid them farewell, the

Soviets took what they called 'The Mauthausen Oath', swearing to follow a common path to freedom, continue to fight against hatred between peoples, and strive for social and national justice. 'The gates to one of the worst and most bloody concentration camps are being opened,' they announced. 'We are about to return to our countries ... The liberated prisoners ... give thanks from the bottom of our hearts for the liberation made possible by the victorious allied nations ... Long live freedom!'

The Americans and the Red Cross handed out care packages of cigarettes, toiletries and basic food supplies to last them the journey. As the remaining survivors watched the Russians leave, they too allowed themselves to contemplate an imminent return to their homelands. Somewhere far beyond those granite walls were lives remembered from long ago. Those who had avoided being ensnared in the Nazi machine were going about their daily business, rebuilding their homes, repairing the infrastructure of their towns, raising their children and making new ones. Ordinary people would return to their ordinary jobs and attempt to forget the war – as these survivors would have to try to do.

So many of their family members and friends would never return home, but they hoped there would still be some they could rely on. Priska, at twenty-nine, wondered if her childhood friend Gizka would still be in Zlaté Moravce and whether she'd been able to keep the family valuables safe. Electrical and communication systems across Europe had been ravaged, so there was no way to telephone her – if she had even known the number. As she braced herself to leave, she vowed to keep in touch with Edita, her protector for so long, and share whatever trials they each faced when they went home.

No matter how many relatives she might have lost to the horrors of Auschwitz, Rachel knew she was blessed to still have three of her younger sisters with her. So many of those around them had lost every single member of their family and yet she, Sala, Ester and Bala still had each other.

Anka, twenty-eight, had the ever-faithful Mitzka at her side. They had lived and almost died together for four years and their bond would be lifelong. There were so many other good friends too – women who had grieved with her over the loss of baby Dan, and who had rallied around when Eva was born.

What none of the young mothers knew was the whereabouts of their husbands – Tibor, Monik and Bernd. The whip-smart journalist, the loyal factory owner and the handsome architect: three decent young men with hopes and dreams who'd swept the girls off their feet and married them just before the start of the seismic events that had since ravaged all their lives. Had they survived too? Was there a chance that each new mother and child might be reunited with their men in a fairytale ending that would trump the Nazi plan for them all? Or had their dreams been turned to dust? There was only one way to find out. And to see what was left of the countries they had been raised in, each of which had suffered a different fate.

Slovakia had been liberated by Soviet troops in April 1945. Of its 90,000 Jews, only 20,000 survived. The arrival of the Red Army was the precursor to the country's takeover by the Communist Party three years later to become part of the Eastern Bloc, a status it would have for over forty years. First, though, the Slovaks expelled all ethnic Germans and welcomed back its citizens. They sent ferries to the nearby Austrian port of Enns to bring home the Slovak prisoners of Mauthausen via the now relatively calm waters of the River Danube. In a journey that lasted less than a week, Priska would sail with Hana some two hundred and seventy kilometres east and arrive in the heart of Bratislava, the city she so loved. She would disembark at the wharf only a short walk from the apartment where she and Tibor had been arrested just after Yom Kippur in September 1944. The spinster Edita would return to a devastated Hungary and see what was left of the people she knew and loved. But the two women were never to lose contact.

Poland was changed beyond all recognition. With the largest Jewish population on the European continent, it had been at the epicentre of the Holocaust. Poland not only suffered catastrophic damage from aerial bombardment but lost millions of its citizens. Under Soviet control after the Red Army staked its claim, its minority groups were all but vanished and its German citizens forced to flee. Many Poles refused to go home and fled instead to US-controlled Germany. Rachel and her sisters considered going there too, but the promise they had made to their father was too important to break.

The Polish and Allied authorities arranged for cattle trucks to collect those who'd survived Mauthausen and wanted to go home. The wagons were cleaned out and their doors were kept unlocked so as not to remind the survivors of their terrifying journeys to the camps. Rachel, baby Mark and her three surviving siblings would be given food and water and allowed to sit comfortably on bench seats. Then they would make the eight-hundred-kilometre journey back to the country that had lost almost all of its Jews and unwitting been the host of the worst death camps.

Anka had the least distance to travel, but it was no longer a matter of simply returning to the country she'd known. Her destination was Prague, two hundred kilometres away, but the city had experienced a bloody three-day revolution that began on 5 May, the same day KZ Mauthausen was liberated. The Czech and Soviet soldiers of the Revolutionary Guard overthrew the Nazis two days before Germany's official capitulation and then called over the Czech radio waves for 'Death to all Germans!' Vengeful citizens took to the streets and hundreds of German soldiers and civilians were killed, often by brutal means. The militia turned several members of the SS and Wehrmacht into 'human torches', and mobs hounded down men, women and children, regardless of their stance during the war. Eminent professors and doctors were among those mutilated, shot or lynched.

The uprising came to an end the day before the Red Army

arrived in Prague on 9 May to claim its territory and begin the expulsion from Czechoslovakia of around three million ethnic Germans – and the murder of several thousand. Anka had married an ethnic German, which left her in limbo. As a Jew, Bernd had lost his German citizenship under the Nuremberg Laws and his new wife couldn't become a German citizen either. However, because she'd married a German she officially became German as far as the authorities were concerned. Even though she'd never renounced her mother country, this meant that she lost her Czech citizenship. As a result, after the war she was both homeless and stateless, as well as possibly being widowed and with a sickly baby in tow, an unenviable position to be in. As May came and went, all she knew was that – after four years in ghettos and camps – she desperately wanted to go home.

With the country suffering chronic fuel shortages, the Czech authorities had no trains available to send to Austria at first, so its several hundred compatriots were stranded in the camp. To speed things up, the prisoners dispatched to Prague their most prominent Czech, a law professor from Charles University by the name of Dr Vratislav Busek, who'd been imprisoned for political reasons five years earlier. Within less than a week the professor arrived back in Austria with news of a train. It was waiting for them at the station of České Budějovice, where the Czech people had dressed it with flowers and a huge banner that read *Z pekla Mauthausen – domú*, 'From the hell of Mauthausen – back home'. Anka and her baby, along with her friends from Terezín, would travel by bus or truck and then back to Prague by rail together to try to discover the fates of their husbands and families.

In shabby, mismatched clothing, the three new mothers with their tiny babies were swallowed up in the mass exodus of others preparing to leave Mauthausen throughout the summer of 1945. Grainy black and white photographs taken by American soldiers show endless snaking lines of the dispossessed like a human river spilling from the camp and down the hill towards the town.

Standing patiently in numbered columns waiting for army or Red Cross trucks to take them to the station, muster point or wharf, those who'd had such promising futures before being snatched from all they'd ever known were now penniless refugees.

Survivors leaving KZ Mauthausen

There would have been little opportunity to appreciate for one last time the glorious scenery of that place where malevolence had pervaded all. Which one of them would have looked back at the forbidding walls of their last prison and reflected on what might have been if they hadn't committed the mortal sin – in Nazi eyes – of being born to Jewish mothers? It wasn't a time to look back but a time to look forward. As one of them said, 'Now we could begin to live.'

With every breath since the day their tiny hearts started beating in syncopation with those of their mothers, they could so easily have been destroyed.

Thousands of babies born during the Second World War didn't make it.

Untold millions more never even had the chance to try.

In six years the Nazis had killed approximately two-thirds of the nine and a half million Jews living in Europe, as well as millions of non-Jews. Of almost one thousand women who had been loaded onto their train from Freiberg as well as those who'd joined their convoy, only half were definitively accounted for by the end of the war.

By a series of miracles, these three young women who'd been counted and then counted again by the Nazis over the years in *Appell* after *Appell* found themselves numbered amongst the living in the final roll call.

Thanks to courage, hope and luck, their babies were the first-ever prisoners of the camps to be given names instead of numbers. In defiance of those darkest of times, their legacy is that they are also inevitably destined to be the last-ever survivors of the Holocaust.

For them all, 1945 marked the end of something that would take years to come to terms with. But it also marked the birth of something countless generations would never experience – a new beginning and a chance to live and to love again.

# 9

# Home

*Priska*

The first passenger boat allowed on the River Danube after the war left the port of Enns and headed east on 19 May 1945, three weeks after the liberation of KZ Mauthausen. It sailed low in the water due to the numbers of refugees squeezed below decks, eager to get away. Among them was Priska Löwenbeinová.

The voyage was long, difficult and fraught with danger as the boat slowly made its way towards Vienna in the wake of a mine-sweeper that went ahead to check for unexploded bombs. The Nazis had seized control of the Danube after Hitler had declared it to be under German governance. Flotillas of warships from the Black Sea fleet patrolled Europe's main waterway, protecting vital ports and firing anti-aircraft guns at Allied planes. Towards the end of the war, hundreds of those vessels were loaded with high explosives and deliberately scuttled in horizontal rows across the width of the Danube to slow advancing Soviet forces. These unstable underwater wrecks would continue to pose huge dangers to passing ships for decades to come.

A hundred and fifty kilometres from Mauthausen, Priska's ferry was forced to stop at the historic town of Tulln, which had been heavily bombed because of its air base, refinery and railway bridge. The debris from the collapse of the bridge had made the river temporarily impassable and had to be cleared. For two days the boat, with its bedraggled cargo sleeping on straw, had to moor on the riverbank on the westerly side of Tulln. The unexpected delay further frayed survivors' nerves by detaining them in the nation of Hitler's birth. Some couldn't stand the wait and insisted on disembarking. Heading east on foot and travelling light, they stumbled into the town to catch trains to Vienna and beyond, paying for their tickets with American cigarettes which had become as valuable as gold.

With a baby in her care Priska was far less flexible, so she stayed on board and waited for the riverbed to be cleared before the boat could ferry them home. When she finally disembarked at Zimný Prístav (The Winter Harbour) in Bratislava on 22 May, she found that although the town had been bombed, its historic centre had survived largely unscathed. She longed to hurry straight to their apartment to see if Tibor was waiting, but her first priority was Hana, who once again needed urgent medical care. Her wounds had reopened on the journey, soaking her bandages in blood.

Afraid that she should have heeded Major Stacy's advice, Priska rushed her daughter straight to the Children's Hospital in Duklianska Street, where paediatrician Professor Chura took one look at the severely malnourished baby covered in open sores and announced that he would have to operate immediately. For the second time in a matter of weeks, Hana underwent emergency surgery to lance and clean out the multiple abscesses caused by a serious deficiency of vitamins. Then the doctor stitched her up again and admitted her to a specialist ward.

Priska waited anxiously for news of an improvement and prayed for Hana's survival. 'I had a good feeling because she wanted to live – she really wanted to live,' she said later. Professor Chura said the same words to Priska when he emerged from the operating theatre.

Once the surgery was declared a success and Hana was out of danger, her half-starved mother was taken to the kitchens by two of the nuns who ran the hospital. Looking around hungrily, she noticed a pot on the stove containing cooked beans in a kind of stew. Before anyone could say anything, she grabbed the pot and literally drank the whole lot down, as people watched in 'deafening silence'.

'No one stopped me or said a word,' she said. 'I was so hungry.'

Realising that Priska, too, needed their care, the nuns offered her a place to stay until Hana was well enough to be released and she'd regained her strength. She accepted gratefully and remained in their care for two weeks. After resting, and leaving Hana sleeping, she finally returned to the place she believed Tibor would head for – their old apartment at Fisherman's Gate. She was shattered to discover that it was one of the few buildings in the old town that had taken a direct hit. She found only rubble. Devastated, she kicked around in the debris and could hardly believe it when she came across one of Tibor's precious notebooks, his handwriting distinctive albeit smeared with dirt. She kept it like a talisman until her death.

Huge noticeboards had been erected in the centre of Bratislava by the Jewish community and others in order for people to leave messages for their loved ones, so Priska wrote that she and the baby had survived and gave the address of the hospital. Then she went back there to wait for Tibor and anyone else who might have made it. As the days and weeks passed, friends and family began to drift back into town, including her younger sister Anička (Little Anna) and her uncle, Dr Gejza Friedman, with whom Anna had sought refuge in the Tatra Mountains. Her grandfather had survived the Nazi purges but sadly had then died after accidentally falling from a window. Uncle Gejza suggested that they all find a place to live together. In time, Hana would come to adore her uncle 'Apu', the only father-figure in her life, and Priska thought of Gejza as a surrogate father too, especially in the absence of her own parents.

Her brother Bandi sent word from Mandatory Palestine that he was well, married, and had a stepdaughter. Amazingly, her other brother Janko soon reappeared, having fought bravely with the partisans. His hair had grown to his shoulders and the boy who'd left them returned a man. Thanks to his war record, he was afforded all kinds of privileges, including his pick of the city's accommodation, and the first thing he did was take Priska the keys to four large apartments that he and his family could choose from. These flats had almost certainly once belonged to Jewish families who were never coming home. Priska refused to inhabit 'dead man's shoes' and was determined not to move any distance from where she used to live, so that Tibor could still find her.

Weeks passed with no sign of her parents, Emanuel and Paula Rona, proud coffee shop owners from Zlaté Moravce, deported to Auschwitz in July 1942. She learned from family friends much later that her mother and father had been gassed within a month of their arrival at Birkenau. Nor did her thirty-four-year-old sister Boežka come back, the spinster whom Priska had tried to rescue from a transport that March. Years later, she learned that Boežka had been saved from the gas chambers for her talents as a seamstress and put in charge of the sewing department in Auschwitz. For three years she made and repaired uniforms and other garments for the SS. At risk to her own life, Boežka was kind to the girls who worked under her and turned a blind eye when they secretly patched what they and others had been given to wear. In one unreliable report, Priska was broken-hearted to hear that in December 1944, a month before the camp was liberated, Boežka was said to have run at the live fence and killed herself. Later though a woman who'd known her well in the camp said this wasn't true and she'd contracted typhoid, which killed her. Priska chose to believe the second version.

Weeks turned to months, but still there was no word of Tibor and no sight of him in the street, as Priska had always imagined there would be. She felt herself to be in a netherworld in which she was unable to move away or even go back to see what might be left in Zlaté Moravce in case she missed him. With a sickly baby to care for, she couldn't work and had no money. Nor did she know what would happen in her country. Although Czechoslovakia had been reconstituted and former Slovak President Monsignor Jozef Tiso hanged for his collaboration with the Nazis, eighty per cent of its Jews had been exterminated and the nation's future under the Communists was still deeply uncertain.

After a couple of weeks living in the hospital and with the little money she'd been given by the Red Cross, as well as some from her uncle, she took rooms near their old apartment so that she could walk there at least once a day to see if her husband was waiting. Their new rooms were in the second-floor servants' quarters at the back of a grand three-storey building on Hviezdoslav Square. Damp and rat-infested, they comprised a small bedroom, a living room, and a kitchen in which she set up a bathtub.

Hana and her mother Priska 1946

One day, pushing Hana along the street in her buggy to the public noticeboard to see if there were any new messages, Priska bumped into a man named Mr Szüsz whom she had known before the war. He greeted her warmly before telling her that he'd been with Tibor in the camps. From Auschwitz, he said, they had been among 1,300 men transported to the satellite slave labour camp at Gliwice (by the Germans Gleiwitz), some twenty kilometres away, where prisoners were forced into brick manufacture, construction, or freight wagon repair for the Nazi railway workshop known as the *Reichsbahnausbesserungswerk*. Then Mr Szüsz broke the news to Priska that her husband wasn't coming back. 'He didn't believe you and the baby would survive,' he told her, as her mind grappled with what he was trying to tell her. 'He stopped eating and became too weak to care for himself. He would say, "I don't want to live any more. What is life worth without my wife and child?"'

Priska, who tried to sift through his words and search for their meaning, eventually stumbled blindly away from Mr Szüsz to grieve in private. Her mind torn, she was never able to find out the precise details of Tibor's death. Eventually, through testimonies from other survivors and people who knew him, she discovered as much as she needed to know. In the bitter cold of January 1945, with temperatures down to minus twenty, the 1,300 or so half-starved prisoners of Gliwice, wearing pyjamas and wooden shoes, were forced on a death march to the huge synthetic fuels plant at Blechhammer, forty kilometres away. In close formation, they were ordered to march with the warning that all stragglers would be shot. Through snow and ice they walked, eventually joining a snaking rope of 4,000 creatures that crunched on towards Gross-Rosen, one of the last remaining concentration camps, a distance of almost two hundred kilometres. Theirs proved to be one of the most notorious of all the death marches. Hundreds of prisoners in threadbare striped uniforms whose bones could no longer carry them were shot on the spot. Their bodies were dragged from the road and thrown into ditches, out of sight.

'Tibor simply gave up,' Priska was told by one who'd survived the

march. 'He died of hunger at the end of January 1945 ... He fell by
the side of the road and that's where he remained ... He was probably shot.'

Tibor Löwenbein, the smiling, pipe-smoking, journalist, bank
clerk, husband and father, had perished in an unknown location on
the side of an icy road in Silesia, Poland, just a few months before
the end of the war at the age of twenty-nine. There was no body to
weep over or for Priska to say *kaddish* for. There would be no
funeral, no grave marker on which to lay stones, on which to light
a candle on *yahrzeit*, the anniversary of his passing. In fact, there
would be no ritual farewell at all – Jewish or otherwise.

His widow never recovered from his death. For the rest of her
days, she refused to remarry. 'I had a great marriage with my husband,' she said. 'I stayed alone because I couldn't live with anyone
else or find anyone else like him.'

Priska was comforted to have her most precious belongings
returned to her by her childhood friend Gizka, and others. Among
them were cherished photographs of her wedding, a few letters
from Tibor and images of her lost family. There were her mother's
favourite earrings and a medallion Paula Ronová used to wear on a
pretty gold chain, as well as her grandfather's fob watch and chain.

Deciding to throw herself into her studies, Priska hired a local girl
to take care of baby Hana and went back to college to study for her
master's degree in French and English Language. As she had always
planned, she became a teacher in Bratislava, at a primary school on
Karpatská Street. In 1947, she changed her surname after her
school inspector complained that he would 'break his tongue' with
the name Löwenbeinová. 'One of my female colleagues decided of
her own initiative to tell the inspector that I would change my
name to sound more "Slovak", so that is what I did.' She liked the
French word *l'homme* for a man, and thought Lom with the –ová
suffix would be a simple name. She was even more delighted with
her choice when a colleague told her that the Czech-born actor
Herbert Lom was a famous film star.

Priska raised her child as Hana Lomová and christened her in an evangelical church. Above all, she said, she was determined to give her Hanka a good education. 'I was her mother, adviser and friend,' she said. 'We lived for each other. She did not let me down.'

Hana and Priska in 1949

She remained in Bratislava for five years, by which time she finally accepted that Tibor truly wasn't coming home. Her sister Anička had married again and lived in the city until her death. Their brother Janko left in 1948 to live in Israel near his brother Bandi. In 1950, Uncle Gejza persuaded Priska to move with him to a new clinic in Prešov in the east of Czechoslovakia where he was the head of the hospital's pulmonology department. As Hana was a 'sickly child' who suffered from serious nosebleeds, adenoid and bowel problems, he felt it was better for her to live in the fresh mountain air with medical care readily available.

Priska became a professor of languages in Prešov where, after several years teaching English, German and French at local high schools, she established the department of English Literature and Language at the university and was a senior assistant in the philosophy faculty. In 1965, while Hana was away at college in Bratislava, Gezja – her adored uncle Apu – committed suicide, convinced he had lung cancer. He was sixty-five years old. It was Priska who found him in the home they shared, and the discovery almost broke her. Suddenly alone, she moved the four hundred kilometres back to Bratislava to be near her only child.

Hana had first discovered her true religious origins when she was six years old and someone called her 'a dirty Jew'. She ran home and told her mother, who said, 'Let me show you pictures of my mother and father, who were Jewish.' Hana looked at them and said, 'OK. I want to be a Jew too. Can I go and play now?' She said she had never been bothered by the issue since. Nor does she tell people that she was born in a concentration camp. 'It doesn't really come up.'

As Hana grew, Priska ensured that she knew her incredible story, and she frequently showed her daughter photographs of Tibor and shared his anecdotes and letters. She also had his notebook and his precious stamp collection, which he'd left in the safekeeping of a friend. 'I wanted her to know about her dad and what we went through, but I wanted her to have nice memories and not think about any bad stuff,' she said. 'I wanted her to be close to her father and know how life was ... I remember everything and I told her everything.'

Hana described her mother as 'a spitfire' who was 'so adamant' that she would have her child. For years Hana secretly believed that her father might have survived the camps and would peer hopefully into the face of any tall, blond, blue-eyed man with a moustache she saw. Only in her early twenties did she finally accept that he was dead.

She and her mother remained in touch with Priska's camp protector Edita, who visited them from her home in Vienna when Hana was nineteen years old. 'I couldn't stop hugging her!' Hana said. Back in 1944, as part of her *mitzvah* or moral duty, Edita had promised Tibor on the train that she would take care of his pregnant wife. She had hoped that she too might be saved and find a husband one day. Her prayers were answered and – after the war – she married a rabbi. Hana recalled of their visit, 'Her husband was very reserved and they had two young sons. All she kept saying was how brave my mother was.'

Priska also tried to find the other Edita in her life, Dr Edita Mautnerová, who'd helped her give birth in the Freiberg factory and had been one of those able to escape from the train. 'We were sorry to learn that she died after the war,' Hana said. 'So I was never able to thank her.' Priska did arrange a reunion with some of the women who'd shared her experiences, including Chava Livni and Priska's friend Magda, so that Hana could meet them. Hana also met Magda's husband Martin Gregor, the actor who'd registered her birth in Mauthausen. He told her, 'You look much better now!' And she was later to meet someone who'd worked with her father on a newspaper before the war. He said, 'You're Tibor's daughter?' and then he started to cry because he had such fond memories of him.

Priska shows Hana where the train stopped in Horní Bříza 1960

In 1960, fifteen years after Hana's birth, Priska took her back to Horní Bříza to personally thank its people for what they had done for the prisoners on the train. Mr Pavliček had passed away, but they spoke to many who remembered him fondly. They laid stones on the site near the railway tracks where thirty-eight bodies from the transport had first been buried, and visited the town graveyard where they'd been reinterred. They learned that in November 1945, the Soviets had taken several SS officers to the town and made them exhume the decomposing corpses with their bare hands. The teenage boys Jaroslav Lang and Vaclav Stepanek had watched, along with many of the townspeople. 'It was good for us to see that,' said Mr Lang quietly. 'It was retribution for what happened. The Germans had to pay.'

The bodies were then respectfully laid to rest in a well-attended ceremony at the site of an impressive new memorial that featured a large bronze sculpture of a dying man hanging from barbed wire. It was sculpted by the prominent Czech artist J. Matějů and paid for by the town. In a letter to the local authority in 1949 asking for donations, several residents wrote: *We do not know their names, not even their nationalities, we just know that they died under the rough Nazi boot so that we might live.*

Priska and Hana's visit to the town was lovingly recorded and photographed, and it features to this day in the local museum and on a special noticeboard outside the station where Mr Pavliček once lived. Afterwards, Priska wrote to the people of the town to thank them again:

At the time and even now I am sure that without the help of the brave West Bohemian people we could not have survived, and my daughter certainly not. We are so grateful to Horní Bříza ... for the unforgettable moments we spent there. We never fail to mention in interviews what the local people did for us during our sad incarceration.

Priska also took teenage Hana back to Mauthausen on a trip organised by an anti-Fascist group. But her daughter was traumatised by the experience, especially when she saw photographs of those killed in the gas chambers the day before her mother's arrival. 'It was a very raw experience for me and yet my mother seemed OK,' said Hana. 'She was talking to people and sharing experiences.' It was more than forty years before Hana felt able to return to the camp. Priska never did.

Priska and Hana on holiday in Slovakia, 1965

In 1965, Priska also wrote to the people of Freiberg, Germany, who'd invited her back as one of the guests of honour to remember the women who worked in the factory. Accepting with thanks their 'warm invitation' to attend their memorial ceremonies, she told them, 'Hana was the most beautiful child I had ever seen with ... a round head, blonde hair, and blue eyes, which I copied from the magnificent Freiberger children who amazed me daily with their big eyes on our escorted way to and from the factory.' She said they would be able to see little difference between a twenty-year-old Freiberger girl and her daughter – 'for me she is the dearest girlfriend, daughter, my whole life'. They visited the factory but were never taken to the sombre stone memorial in the town cemetery, which bore the words *KZ Freiberg* above a short tribute to the 'Sacrifices of Fascism'.

Apart from thirty or so small scars on her body from the abscesses that had almost killed her as a baby, Hana suffered no serious health problems in later life. Having been covered with lice from birth, she did develop an allergic reaction to insect bites, but the main legacy of her unusual gestation was her 'pathological aversion' to any kind of shouting or screaming, she now feels because of what she heard in the womb and in the first few weeks of her birth. 'If someone talks to me aggressively, all I want to do is run away and hide,' she said. 'Lest we forget, I was born with my hands in fists up around my ears!'

When Hana was twenty-three years old and newly married, she became pregnant with her only child. It was 1968. As her baby grew inside her, she watched anxiously as the student protesters of the 'Prague Spring' began to defy Communist rule. In August 1968, when 500,000 Warsaw Pact soldiers invaded Czechoslovakia to reinstate order, she decided to leave her country for good. 'Probably because of my beginnings, once I saw the tanks and heard the shots, there was no way that I was going to bring a child into this world there,' she said. She moved to Israel where she gave birth to her son Thomas, 'Tommy', in December. In 1972 she studied for a PhD in organic chemistry and eleven years later she emigrated to Chicago in the country of her liberators. She was married twice (to fellow Jews) and has two grandchildren, Jack and Sasha. Mark, her third husband of twenty-four years, is a Gentile physician and nephrologist and they both work in the pharmaceutical industry and live near San Francisco, California.

Hana with her son Tommy, daughter-in-law Julie
and grandchildren Sasha and Jack

Priska's chief legacies from the camps were fretting about food and a detestation of the cold. 'She would always check the refrigerator and the store cupboard and ask, "Do we have enough? Will we run out?"' said Hana. 'Fortunately, our home was small so there was only so much she could hoard.' Priska also loved the luxury of sleep; her bed and its bedding became a focus of her life, especially in her later years.

Towards the end of her life, Priska said, 'I had a beautiful life with my child after I ... gave birth to her in a concentration camp ... My daughter is very precious ... I thank dear God that he gave me this child and I wish to all mothers that they have the same feeling of love that I have for my daughter. She is a very good mother and a good daughter. She adores her son and she is a good person.' Ever the optimist, and still thinking only of beautiful things, she added, 'I survived. We are here. I brought home a baby. That is the most important thing.'

Hana said, 'My mother was always very driven and very strong. Her favourite word in Slovak was *presadit'*, which means to push forward or to make things happen. I believe that throughout her time in the camps she had a goal to make something happen and that was to survive and to keep me alive.'

Priska suffered from dementia in old age, but she lived long enough to know and love her only grandchild, Tommy. As her condition deteriorated, she repeatedly begged her daughter, 'Please forgive me,' but Hana didn't understand what she was supposed to be forgiving her for. All she knew was that the past had suddenly crowded her mother's mind again.

Following her ninetieth birthday in August 2006, Priska Löwenbeinová had to be placed in a nursing home. There she was supervised by her own carer, who gave Hana daily bulletins about her mother's health. Three weeks later Priska was hospitalised for

Priska in her eighties in Bratislava

dehydration and other medical problems. Hana flew to her side from her home in California and was with her for several weeks until she had to fly back to her demanding job. After returning to her nursing home where she mainly slept for two weeks, Priska eventually died peacefully in her sleep on 12 October 2006.

The woman who had lost three babies and her husband Tibor, along with so many members of her immediate family, in the war had devoted the rest of her life to her 'perfect' baby, born on a plank in an SS factory during the middle of an air raid. In 1996, ten years before Priska's death, her baby Hana had donated the tiny smock and bonnet stitched for her by the surviving women of Freiberg to the United States Holocaust Memorial Museum in Washington. Her mother had kept it safe for more than fifty years.

Priska's ashes are interred in a graveyard in Bratislava which bears the name Slávičie Údolie (Lark Valley). It lies on a tree-lined hill less than a kilometre from the River Danube. She is surrounded by beauty for all eternity.

Family grave where Priska's ashes are interred, Bratislava

## Rachel

In spite of the promises the Abramczyk sisters had made to their father Shaiah to go straight home to Poland after the war, they had to wait for Sala to be well enough to travel, which delayed them until mid-June. 'When it looked like I was going to make it, we decided to go home as soon as I was strong enough,' said Sala.

Although they felt pulled back by an invisible thread, the future of the four young women was still deeply uncertain. Only 300,000 of Poland's 3.3 million Jews had survived the war and an estimated 1,500 were murdered in the years after they returned home, many for anti-semitic reasons. Early hints of such atrocities would have terrified Rachel and her sisters and placed them in an even more unenviable position. Not that they had very much choice. With so many refugees seeking sanctuary abroad, the doors were closed to many alternative destinations. Britain, France and Canada took in thousands but the UK limited the numbers fleeing to Palestine, where many hoped to go. The United States eventually accepted some 400,000 refugees but denied many more access to a new life there. Unwelcome anywhere else in the world, many Polish Jews had little alternative but to return to what was by then a Soviet puppet state.

As the eldest sister at twenty-six, and back in her maternal role, it fell to Rachel to decide what was best not only for her and her baby, but for her three sisters. Sala was twenty-three, Ester twenty, and Bala nineteen when the war ended. What should have been the best six years of their young lives had been spent in ghettos and camps, and they had no life other than what might be left for them in Pabianice or Łódź. The only encouraging news they'd received was from two Polish friends they'd met up with in Mauthausen, who assured them that their father and their brother Berek had been alive the last time they'd seen them two weeks earlier. They had all been in Bergen-Belsen but then separated. If that was true, then they knew that their menfolk would also go to Pabianice as soon as they could and might even be waiting for them already.

Looking 'not very well-kept', the four young women clambered into buses and then back into a cattle truck that took them on another interminable journey, one that stopped and started numerous times along the way because of bomb damage, shortage of fuel and broken tracks. Warsaw was unrecognisable to them after the brutal suppression of the uprising, but they didn't stay long, taking another overcrowded train and eventually a tram to Pabianice.

Back in their hometown, they discovered that everything had changed. Most of the Jews they'd known all their lives had been erased from history. Their parents' once-beautiful apartment and all their cherished belongings had been stolen. A former employee was living in their flat and refused to relinquish it, claiming that it no longer belonged to them. He said he had been 'chosen' by the Communist Party to look after the property on behalf of the authorities.

Friends and neighbours they'd grown up with had helped themselves to whatever they'd wanted too, so the elegant, flower-filled home of their childhood, the one that their mother Fajga referred to as their 'castle', was nothing but a memory. There was no trace of her carefully chosen art or her fine china, and the sounds of music and laughter that had permeated their early years echoed only in their memories. All that the sisters were able to salvage were a few precious belongings that their parents had hidden with their most faithful employees, and which were kindly returned to them. Traumatised and homeless, the sisters appealed to the local authority in charge of coordinating the rehoming of returning refugees. They were assigned a small apartment where they waited, still hopeful of being reunited with their father and brother 'any day'. As the weeks passed and they were forced to sell their few belongings for money on which to exist, their hopes waned. Sala took in sewing to bring in some extra cash, but the little family unit began to realise with a sense of profound shock that they had lost almost everyone and everything from their past.

Of the 12,000 Jews deported from Pabianice during the war, there were only five hundred left. Baby Mark was the only newborn. Every time the sisters went out into the town that long ago had held so many happy memories for them, they were met only with disparaging looks. Not once were they made to feel welcome; Rachel even overheard one woman complaining, 'They burned them and they burned them, and yet still so many are alive!'

Sala said, 'Our home was not our home any more. Our whole city didn't look good to me. It was like a graveyard with no one we knew.' The pretty blonde who'd always been popular at school could find no familiar faces. Distraught, she hurried to see her former art teacher in order to let her know that she was still alive. 'My teacher had loved me so much that she'd painted a picture of me. I told my family, "She'll be so pleased to see me! I'm going to tell her what happened to us." But she opened the door and said, "You mean you're still alive?" Then she said, "I don't have anything for you." She didn't even ask what happened. She just shut the door. It was such a slap in the face.'

About a month after they arrived home, the sisters received a letter via an uncle in New York who had contacted the Polish authorities. He'd been informed that their brother Berek was in a hospital in Sweden, having been sent there by the Red Cross to recover from the loss of an eye and other injuries sustained in the camps. Thrilled, the sisters contacted Berek, who sent them a photograph of himself with his head heavily bandaged. 'He didn't mention Daddy and we knew then that Daddy didn't make it,' said Sala.

There was no mention either of their teenage brother Moniek, who'd so bravely volunteered to help with the smaller children when the Pabianice ghetto was liquidated. They were told about Chełmno. Nor was there any word of their mother Fajga or the perished innocents – siblings Dora and her twin brother Heniek, fourteen, plus the adored 'baby' of the family, Maniusia, who would have been twelve. Knowing what they knew by then about

Auschwitz, the sisters had to accept that the laughing voices of their mother, brother and sisters had been silenced for ever. They could only hope that their little family had remained together at the end and hadn't suffered too much. Sala said, 'They were young and beautiful and life should have been that way.'

Faced with the loss of their parents and three of their siblings, Bala, to whom Berek had always been closest, suddenly announced that she would travel to Sweden to take care of him. 'He needs me,' she said. And – somehow – she made it and took care of him there for many years. It was from Bala that the sisters learned that Berek's eye had been lost after he was beaten to the ground by a guard when he tried to save their father's life in Bergen-Belsen. 'He had managed to protect his father for all that time even though he was too old and weak to do any work, but then Berek was ordered not to help him with some task. He tried to anyway and the guard kicked him in the face and he lost an eye.' Their father Shaiah was shot dead three days before the camp was liberated.

There was still no word from Monik. Rachel wondered if her husband might be waiting for her in Łódź while he was getting the factory back into shape. With the greatest difficulty, in a country with virtually no transportation system or infrastructure, she travelled there with some male friends for protection only to discover that the factory, too, had been seized. The Jewish population of Łódź, which had numbered more than 200,000 before the war, had dwindled to less than 40,000, most of whom were to move away or emigrate. The family had lost everyone and everything.

'We knew then that we didn't want to stay in Poland,' Sala said. 'There was nothing for us there.' In the tumult of post-war Europe, the sisters went to Munich in the American zone, because they were assured that from there they'd be able to relocate to wherever they wanted to go. They arrived in the bomb-ravaged city with only the clothes on their backs and just a suitcase or two of belongings between them. As word spread that survivors from their district of Poland were settling in Munich, more friends and neighbours drifted there and they soon set up a new community to support each other. Rachel continued to ask anyone who came back if they knew anything of her husband's whereabouts, half-expecting grim news, but there was no reliable information and he never appeared.

After several months, she came to accept that Monik must have died, although she never found out the exact details or had any idea where his remains were. For a long time she believed that he'd probably been sent to Auschwitz and gassed, but someone from Łódź who knew her brother Berek assured him that Monik had managed to avoid the last transport out of the ghetto and tried to stay in the area. He was eventually shot dead by a 'German with a revolver' on the streets of Łódź. However he perished, he never knew that his loyal young wife had survived and given birth to a son. He would forever lie in an imaginary grave on which she could never lay stones, to which she could never take their son.

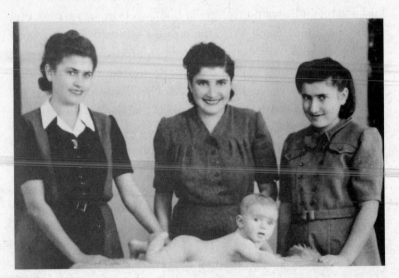

Baby Mark with Sala, Rachel and Bala 1946

Inured to grief, and determined to get on with her life and create a better future for her child, Rachel remained in Munich for four more years. Her son Mark went to school and his first language became German. His mother and aunts spoke Polish only when they didn't want him to understand. On 19 March 1946, Rachel married again. Sol Orviesky (later shortened to Olsky) was a talented Jewish jeweller she'd known since before the war. He would, she knew, be a good father to her son although for years, she felt guilty at remarrying so soon and sometimes wondered what would happen if Monik suddenly appeared on her doorstep. 'I married again because it was very hard for a woman and a child who needs a father,' she said.

Rachel and Mark 1949

Sol, who was forty and from a strict Orthodox family in Pabianice, had been married with a son before the war. A German soldier wrenched his baby from his arms during a round-up and for the rest of his life he blamed himself for not putting up more resistance. Apart from a nephew Henrike, and two brothers who'd fled to America, he lost every member of his family, including his wife and child, and spent the war in a labour camp processing the belongings of the dead. He weighed less than seventy pounds at liberation, lost all his teeth in his forties, and suffered from serious health problems as a consequence.

It was Sol who helped keep the Abramaczyk sisters and his own family solvent after the war. Working with a German chemist who developed a process for converting European gold bullion into the lower American standard of karat purity, he won a contract to process gold being transferred abroad from German banks. Rachel and her sisters helped run the business, and the Americans seemed happier to do business with Holocaust survivors than with the Germans. They always paid in dollars, as Deutschmarks were virtually worthless, so there was a reasonable living to be made as the city was painstakingly rebuilt around them. They even took in and helped survivors from Pabianice.

Three years after Rachel and Sol were married and as soon as it became legal for them to move to the newly created state of Israel, Rachel – who'd been a Zionist since she was a teenager – persuaded her new husband that they should live there. The family caught the first ship out of Marseille, France, and settled in Petach Tivka near Tel Aviv, where they remained for ten years. Unable to make a living there as a jeweller and gold trader, Sol gave up his trade and worked as a manual labourer in a steel factory.

During the war, Rachel had lost all the photographs of her wedding and of her dead husband Monik. But in Israel she came across an ex-girlfriend of his who had one small picture of him from his student days, and she persuaded the woman to part with it. The photograph remained in her possession all her life and was eventually passed on to her son.

Having vowed to protect Mark until her dying day, Rachel refused to have a second child with Sol in case he favoured it over her miracle baby. Then, although they didn't speak any English, she moved the family to live in America in 1958 to avoid Mark being conscripted into the Israeli Army. Sol went back into the jewellery and watchmaking business but suffered a series of heart attacks and died in 1967, aged sixty-one. Rachel worked 'like a dog' to keep their business going and ensure that her son wanted for nothing.

In Munich, her little sister Ester had married Abe Freeman, a man from Pabianice who'd been friends with their brother Berek. Abe had spent almost four years in Auschwitz and bore a tattoo. The couple moved to Nashville, Tennessee, after a Jewish aid organisation at a trade fair in Munich assured them that it 'wasn't far at all' from New York. When they arrived there they discovered that Nashville was 'off the map', but they were happy and successful there and remained in the country of her liberators for the rest of their lives. They had two daughters, Shirley and Faye, and five grandchildren. Ester died in 2003.

Sala had first met her future husband Henrike (Henry) when they were living in the Pabianice ghetto. He was the nephew of Sol Olsky, Rachel's second husband. Sala and Henry were also together in Łódź, but from Auschwitz he had been sent to Mauthausen and on to the tunnels of its satellite camp Ebensee, which had one of the highest death rates of any concentration camp. After the war, she looked for him everywhere. 'I always knew we would be together ... He came back and after eight few weeks he said, "Will you marry me?" and I said, "Yes," and we had sixty-four wonderful years.' Henry, who had also nearly died of typhus, had an uncle in America who promised to vouch for them, so the couple went to night school in Munich to learn English before moving to New York and then on to Chicago. Later, they relocated to Nashville to be near Ester and Abe. Sala changed her name to the more American Sally; she and Henry had two daughters, Ruth and Deborah, who had three children of their own.

Bala remained in Sweden, married a Polish Jew named Jakob Feder and had two sons, David and Mikael, who between them had four children. She died of breast cancer in 1986 and never spoke of her wartime experiences to her sons, who emigrated to Israel after her death.

Berek left Sweden in 1956 and moved to the United States, where he worked in catering in San Francisco, remaining in the city until his death. He married Holocaust survivor Pola Nirenberg and had two children, Leif and Steven, the latter of whom is a neuro-surgeon in Nashville and has four children. Berek first met Rachel's 'miracle' baby when Mark was sixteen and the two became best friends. Between them, the children of the Abramcyzk family who survived the war had nine children and twenty grandchildren. It was, they said, their 'happy ending'.

As with so many other survivors, the siblings tried to blot out all memories of their barbarous history and rarely spoke about them, because it was 'too hard'. In the days when talking therapies were relatively new, some of those who lived through the Holocaust suf-fered from tremendous guilt that they had survived when so many had died. Others sought oblivion through work or alcohol, family or suicide. As survivor Esther Bauer put it, 'The first twenty years we couldn't talk about it. For the next twenty years no one wanted to hear about it. Only in the next twenty years did people start asking questions.'

Instead, each dealt privately with the experiences seared into the memory. They coped as best they could with the unwelcome flash-backs brought on by the triggers that were constantly lying in wait. It might be a jackhammer or a car backfiring; a high stone wall or a passing freight train; someone speaking German or the smell of singed hair; a random pile of clothes or the sound of dogs barking. One survivor broke down when his hairdresser produced electric clippers to trim his hair. Others developed paranoia about insects and blowflies. Some had panic attacks in crowded subway trains. All sense of proportion had shifted as the survivors tried to acclimatise themselves to a life without fear.

And yet, somehow they kept going – just as they had in the camps. Sala said, 'It was enough that we each knew, and it was something we left behind us.' It took a little persuading, but in August 2010 she accompanied her nephew Mark and other members of their family to Louisville, Kentucky, for the final reunion of the remaining members of the 11th Armored Division Association, the 'Thunderbolts', whose men had liberated Mauthausen and who were now disbanding. Of the more than four hundred attendees there were eighty-one veterans, and a few survivors. After a moving ceremony at the Patton Museum, with young soldiers from Fort Knox on hand to pay tribute, a dinner dance was held at which Forties big-band music was played. Mark said it was all very emotional and that his aunt, who'd never previously attended any memorial event, was 'deeply moved'. Having met a few of the veterans, Sally said afterwards, 'The chance of living through that hell was just luck. We were the lucky ones. We made it back. There is nothing more to say.'

Her sister Rachel agreed. 'It was like winning or losing a lottery,' she once told her son. 'We were at the mercy of people who could be kind one minute and unspeakably cruel the next. Some of those who survived prided themselves that they were smarter or stronger and that is how they made it, but there were plenty who died who were even smarter and stronger than they were. The only difference was luck.'

Rachel (left) with siblings Sala, Berek, Ester, and Bala in Israel, 1980s

In spite of her protestations that she had put their experiences behind her, Rachel's hair turned white in her thirties and she lost almost all of her teeth. Her dentist told her that her growing foetus had commandeered all the calcium in her body and had then taken what was left in her breast milk. The passage of years never extinguished her memories and Rachel was an insomniac for most of her life, as was Sol. Mark would hear them crying out or walking around the house on what were, for them, dark nights of the soul.

He knew where he'd been born from 'the time I started speaking', but – surrounded as he was in Israel by the children of other Holocaust survivors – his entry into the world seemed relatively normal. His parents refused to own anything German or drive a German car. Perhaps unsurprisingly, whenever people asked him what he wanted to do when he grew up Mark would reply: 'Kill as many Germans as I can!' Rachel would scold him and say, 'We lost everything and everyone. If we lose our humanity then we will lose the one thing we didn't have to lose.' Only in the final years of her life did she admit that the generation responsible for what had happened in Europe was no longer alive.

Whenever Mark asked her about her experiences she would say, 'There is nothing to learn. It was horrible. The main thing to learn is to protect yourself. If it looks like it's time to leave, then leave.' Then she would get upset and tell him, 'You cannot possibly imagine how bad it was, so it is pointless to try.' A few weeks later, she'd berate him, 'Why do you never ask me about what happened in the war?' She never went back to visit any of the ghettos and camps, or KZ Freiberg, never watched any movies or read books about the Holocaust – apart from *Schindler's List*, which she declared 'wasn't bad'.

Mark, who suffers from multiple allergies including asthma and hay fever, didn't know that Sol wasn't his real father until he came across his birth certificate when he was fourteen years old, but his mother and he never really discussed it. 'Something kicked in with my mother when I was born, she was going to protect me no matter what . . . I just assumed my father had died in the war.' Although his mother became 'driven', an 'unrelenting workaholic' who pushed him to get an education and make something of himself, he said Sol was 'a fantastic father', and both were very proud when he became a respected emergency doctor. Mark and his wife Mary, a Gentile, married in 1969. They have four children and four grandchildren and divide their time in Wisconsin and Arizona.

Like Anka and a lot of women of their generation, Rachel was a great fan of *Gone with the Wind* (a book she'd loved in Poland), and after the war she often quoted Scarlett O'Hara's cry, *As God is my witness, they're not going to lick me. I'm going to live through this and when it's all over, I'll never be hungry again.* She was determined that she would never again be put in a position where she wasn't

Rachel (seated right) in 2002 with (L–R) her grandson
David, daughter-in-law Mary, son Mark, grandson
Charlie and granddaughter Margaret

in control or couldn't feed her family. She especially made sure that the two men in her life never went hungry and insisted on doing all the cooking and chores even after she had finished a fourteen-hour shift, because that was her 'prerogative'.

When she watched the film of *Gone with the Wind* with her grandson Charlie, particularly the scenes depicting how the characters suffered during the American Civil War, she told him, 'They think that's bad?' Later in life, she also took Charlie and some of her other grandchildren to the Yad Vashem Museum in Jerusalem, where she answered more of their questions than she had ever answered of her son's.

Towards the end of her life, Rachel suffered from a series of medical problems including diabetes, high blood pressure and heart issues. She also had nerve damage in her legs, became deaf, and her bones softened with osteoporosis, causing multiple spinal fractures. She would say of her lack of mobility, 'I tell my legs where to go and they don't listen!' Mark said that, in her eighties, his mother was 'weak and tired after years of being strong and healthy ... She found it hard to enjoy life and hoped for the end.' Still, she celebrated her eighty-fourth birthday with family on New Year's Eve 2002, having only just given up being a volunteer at a local hospital. Two months later, she had routine surgery on her bladder, insisting that the operation be timed for when her sisters Ester and Sala were on a trip to Hawaii so that they 'wouldn't fuss'.

Mark flew to Nashville from his home in Wisconsin to be with his mother and was at her side when she suffered catastrophic heart failure immediately after the operation. 'She opened her eyes briefly and looked my way,' said her baby who was born in a coal wagon. Rachel Olsky died on 19 February 2003.

At fifty-seven years of age, and after a lifetime of trying to live up to the legacy of his extraordinary birth, Mark had become an orphan. His indomitable mother, who had so very nearly died sixty years earlier and had endured so much in her lifetime – including the death of two husbands – always played down what she and

Mark had gone through. 'You're making a big story out of such a simple thing!' she would have told her son.

Rachel is buried in a peaceful corner of a Jewish cemetery in Nashville, Tennessee, surrounded by beautiful dogwood trees.

Rachel's grave in Nashville, Tennessee, USA

## Anka

After three weeks of rest and recuperation in the infirmary at Mauthausen, Anka and Eva were finally ready to go home. As she braced herself to be repatriated to Prague, she and her daughter were inundated with baby clothes and gifts from soldiers and well-wishers until Eva was 'very well-equipped'.

With Eva's all-important birth certificate and Anka's brand-new identity papers no longer stamped with a 'J', mother and child boarded buses to České Budějovice and eventually the flower-decked Czechoslovakia-bound train on or about 20 May 1945, and bade a fond farewell to those who'd saved them.

Like those of the other mothers, Anka's journey was tortuous and peppered with long delays. Most railway stations were devoid of staff but crowded with people desperate to get home and who tried to climb aboard, even riding on the roof. The sorry-looking Czech prisoners from Mauthausen eventually reached their destination late one dismal night at Prague's Wilson Station. It was a place Anka knew only too well from the days when she would travel from Třebechovice to visit her aunt and from where she'd alighted after moving to the city to study law. That all seemed like such a long time ago.

Arriving in a post-war, post-revolution Prague, though, was one of the most depressing moments of Anka's war. 'All those years you had to keep going and keep fighting and try not to worry or to think,' she said. 'It never occurred to me until then that there would be no one left to meet me ... my parents and my sisters ... there was nobody there and nothing to come home to.' It was, she added, a 'dreadful realisation ... the worst moment of the entire war for me'.

Aside from the damage done during the revolution, parts of the city had accidentally been carpet-bombed by American pilots who'd mistaken it for Dresden in the February raids, leaving its power and transport systems in chaos. Huge areas of it were still blacked out. Emotionally and physically fragile, Anka had no money and her only plan was that at daybreak she would make her way to her cousin Olga's apartment. Contrary to all logic, she felt sure that Olga would have survived because she was married to a Gentile. In the meantime, Anka and her friends had to wait in the dark until officials from the Red Cross arrived and arranged to put them up in the Hotel Graaf near the station.

The following morning, she slipped away with Eva and found her way to the tram station. As one of the first survivors to return to

Prague after the war, her appearance made her something of a curiosity. Even though horrific images of the liberated camps and their survivors had appeared in cinema newsreels and newspapers around the globe, people were still shocked to see the stick-thin mother with uneven hair wearing the shabby second-hand clothes she'd been given in Mauthausen. Many felt sorry for her and offered her far too many Czech crowns.

'I just need the tram fare,' she insisted, and took only what she required. In daylight the city was surprisingly unaltered, but to a disorientated Anka it seemed changed beyond all recognition. Making her way to the second-floor apartment at Schnirchova Street, near the city's Art Nouveau Exhibition Grounds, she climbed the stairs and was stunned to find bread and salt – the basics of life – waiting outside the door in traditional Czech welcome. Knocking on the door just after 10 a.m., she came face to face with her cousin Olga Šroňková, her husband Olda, and two children, who'd heard she was alive and had been waiting for her to return. 'We haven't got lice!' Anka said, before falling into familiar arms and crying for the first time in years. In fact she and Eva were riddled with lice, but nobody cared, so relieved were they to see them.

'Please can we stay a few days to recover?' Anka asked. They would stay for three and a half years as Olga and her family welcomed them warmly and gave them a new start in life. 'They were angelic. In that small apartment with teenagers they still took us in – and for all that time.'

In the first few days after her arrival, Anka mainly slept and ate. She couldn't get over the idea of having enough to eat and would secretly get up in the night to help herself to as much water as she liked, or raid the store cupboard. She seemed unable to stop eating bread, and would even bake fresh supplies with Olga in the middle of the night if the power was on.

When it became apparent that she and Eva had brought lice home with them, and that both were also suffering from scabies –

caused by parasitic mites – they were admitted to hospital for several days to be treated with insecticide lotions and antibiotics. Olga, who was twenty years older than Anka, visited her often and was extremely patient with her. Gently, she began to answer her questions and recount what had happened in Prague in her absence. Olga and her sister Hana – who'd also married a Gentile – had escaped arrest until the last six months of the war, when they'd been imprisoned in Terezín. Their husbands were sent to a separate camp in Czechoslovakia for non-Jews. All had survived.

She was also able to tell Anka that no other members of their family had yet made contact. There was no word of Anka's proud parents Stanislav and Ida, of sorrowful Ruzena and her pretty blond son Peter, or of her fun sister Zdena and her husband Herbert. Olga showed Anka the postcard that Zdena had been forced to write from Birkenau, containing the codeword *lechem* for bread – her last valiant attempt to let them know they were starving. Zdena, the vibrant, beautiful woman who had so loved her husband and her life, had been snuffed out like a candle.

Olga had heard nothing about her parents, whom Anka had last seen leaving Terezín. Nor was there any word of Bernd. The family had registered all the names of their missing relatives with the relevant authorities. As the days turned to weeks without further news, it seemed increasingly likely that they were the sole survivors from their large extended family.

To add to her woes, Anka's plentiful supply of breast milk dried up virtually the moment they arrived in Prague. 'It was as if her body said, "Enough!" once it decided she could get formula milk or other food for me,' Eva said. 'The irony was that Peter's father sent a whole load of Ostermilk powder from England but when my mother took me to a paediatrician to check me over he told her it was rubbish and she should throw it away, so she did.'

Thereafter, every attempt Anka made to feed baby Eva ended with her weeping in pain and frustration. She had no more milk to offer and her breasts were extremely tender. When a child specialist told her that Eva needed to 'eat and eat and eat', Anka felt she had no choice but to force-feed her. Eva, poorly and unable to do anything but suckle, was tipped upside down on the sofa and fed soup with a spoon until she either choked or swallowed. It was a traumatic experience for everyone.

Anka and Eva, Prague 1945

Anka had other worries too. Stripped of Czech citizenship by virtue of her marriage to a German and her country's expulsion of all Germans, she was worried that she might be in danger, even though she was Jewish. Every day she took Eva in a pram to the various government offices to fill in forms and speak to officials in an effort to recover her citizenship.

Still there was no news of Bernd or her relatives, despite enquiries with everyone Anka met who might have been with them. Refusing even then to relinquish hope, she told herself that he was on his way home to her. Then, gradually, through people who knew her family, she learned the fate of her immediate relatives. Her parents and sisters, as well as Peter and her brother-in-law, had all been placed in the Czech family camp in Birkenau designed to appease the Red Cross. Anka's once proud father Stanislav – whose glasses and spirit had been broken in Terezín – had died of pneumonia within weeks. Smiling Zdena and her handsome husband Herbert were gassed along with Ruzena once the family camp was emptied. Anka's nephew Peter, just eight years old, had been sexually abused by the guards before he too was gassed. Anka's mother Ida, the jovial, buxom matriarch who'd manned the till at the leather factory and entertained the female customers, had lost her mind when her family had all gone and was almost certainly sent to the gas chamber. 'The man who told me about my mother [losing her mind] may have been sorry for me and I don't know if it was true but it would have been a blessing if it were.'

Just as she was trying to take all that information in, Anka bumped into someone in the street. 'I met him by chance in a very smart road which is called Na Příkopech . . . I can't even remember what I was doing there. And there he was. I knew him from before the war and I never realised that he was in the same camp as Bernd . . . And he saw me and he was very pleased to see me and he asked, "Did you know? – Don't wait for your husband. He was killed just before liberation. I was there when he was shot." I will be eternally grateful that he didn't make a song and dance and that he told me straight. He didn't make me wait.'

Anka found out eventually that soon after Bernd had arrived in Auschwitz II-Birkenau in September 1944, he'd been selected to work in the mill and munitions factory of a satellite camp named Bismarckhütte, in Chorzów Batory in Silesia. Located near the Bismarck steel mill run by the Berghütte company, the camp held approximately two hundred Jewish prisoners who were forced to do manual labour or make parts for weapons. He survived the severe winter but on 18 January 1945, all the prisoners were evacuated thirty kilometres to Gliwice on a 'death march' through deep snow. Bernd may even have joined the column of hapless souls among whom was Priska's husband Tibor, but it will never be known if the men ever met.

Anyone on that march who lagged behind or fell to the ground was shot in the back of the head and abandoned by the roadside to freeze solid. Such had been Tibor's fate. Those who remained – they could barely be called 'living' – were then loaded into cattle trucks to be sent by rail to the Nordhausen-Dora or Buchenwald camps. It was on that final leg of the journey that Bernd was shot in front of the train by an SS guard. Months later, nobody could tell his grieving widow what had happened to his body, which was presumably lying abandoned somewhere in the middle of the frozen landscape. She had no idea if he was later buried, and there was nowhere she could ever go to pay her respects.

Nor was she able to find out why Bernd had been killed so close to the end of the war, although – after their five years in the camps – she appreciated that there was almost certainly no reason. Within days of his murder, the Red Army had arrived in the area around Gliwice, an event that would have liberated Bernd and reunited him with his pregnant wife.

The news that he was never coming home almost broke Anka, even if she could barely take it in after all she had been through. Her heart felt like stone but she refused to give in to despair. She had so many others to grieve for and so much else to consider, Eva most important of all. Somehow, she managed to pull herself together, put one foot in front of the other and get on with her life. 'I didn't have time to mourn. Somebody asked me, "How are you coping?" and I said, "I haven't got time to cope. I have to do what's necessary for everyday life," which was more than enough because I didn't know where my next penny would be coming from.'

She had more upsetting news. The maid to whom she'd entrusted her most precious belongings came to see her rather sheepishly to return Bernd's clock and other items. But she confessed that she had sold the green silk curtains and burned all of Anka's sacred photographs because she feared they might incriminate her if ever they were found. 'I could have killed her! Of all the things I wanted back, it was those.' Having lost so much, material goods meant little or nothing to those who returned from the camps; but what did matter most terribly was memory. Personal mementos of their loved ones suddenly meant the world to them, Anka included, and her maid was telling her that all was lost. But she persisted and she went to the studio of the photographer – a fellow Jew – who'd taken their wedding photos. Although he had perished, the negatives were still in his files so she was able to have new ones printed.

Her priority, as always, was Eva. 'I had her to think about and that's what kept me going ... She is the only thing which is mine really, always has been. We all love our daughters, but I feel this umbilical cord hasn't been cut ... I had to be here for her if I wanted her to live. I had to provide for what she needed, mentally and physically.'

When Olga and her family went on holiday that first summer after the war ended, Anka decided to go to Třebechovice pod Orebem and see what was left of her family home and business. All she knew was that it had been requisitioned. Accompanied only by her baby daughter, she went to Wilson Station and caught the train back to the place of her happiest childhood memories. 'I had no money and I couldn't work because Eva needed me so much. I decided that as I was the only heir of the whole family and there was the factory that was still working – even though it was now Communist property – I would tell them I had a little child and I would ask for something.'

When she reached the factory she was flooded with poignant memories of childhood summers, eating on the patio with her family or lying in a corner of the garden with a pillow reading a book. The tall brick chimney that she'd always been afraid might topple and kill them now reminded her of other more sinister chimneys; she could barely walk in its shadow.

She spoke to the Communist directors of the company and, to

her amazement, they agreed to pay her a small monthly stipend. 'It was hardly anything but it was better than nothing.' Her sister's Bauhaus villa had also been requisitioned and was being used as living quarters for one of the workers – a staunch Communist – so she and Eva were allocated the corner of one small room, without access to the kitchen or bathroom and with hardly any furniture. 'They treated me like a bitch.'

Although at first she relished the long-forgotten luxury of not being surrounded by hundreds of people and the joy of fresh untainted air, Anka was quickly overcome by loneliness. The voices of her voiceless family crowded in around her. Her dream of returning home to a place of laughter, warmth and beauty, and of being greeted with loving arms, had turned to a nightmare from which there would never be escape. The past was gone and she was in a new kind of camp almost as cruel as anything she had experienced.

Trapped in her tiny prison, she wasn't even allowed to pluck a tomato from the enormous garden she'd frolicked in so merrily as a child. Worse still, one day when she took Eva out in a stroller someone had donated to her, a Czech grandmother she knew stopped and said cruelly, 'It must be a Nazi baby!' Her comment cut Anka to the quick, and she burst into tears and fled. 'The Czechs treated me very badly and that hurt. These were people I grew up with. I didn't expect anything else from the Germans, but the Czechs and the Communist rabble made me feel that I should have perished as well. It was awful.'

There were unexpected acts of kindness, though. When a few of her parents' friends heard that Anka had survived they came, one by one, to pay their respects. She had no idea that Stanislav and Ida had entrusted their best silver and porcelain, rugs and jewellery to these people, who had bravely hidden them during the war. Anka was immensely touched to have these precious things returned to her and she thanked their friends for their honesty. 'I got practically everything back.' Even with those small acts of decency, though, being 'home' no longer felt the same. When her cousin Olga found

out how and where she was living, she insisted that she and Eva
return to Prague. Soon afterwards, they were visited by a friend of
her brother-in-law Tom Mautner, who arrived with food and clothes
from England. His name was Karel Bergman, a Jewish maker of
wigs and hairnets whose father had owned a factory; Anka had
known Karel before the war, but he like Tom had fled to England,
where he worked as an interpreter for Fighter Command.

With no place of her own and only a little money to live on, Anka
was in an untenable situation. She couldn't stay with Olga for ever
and knew she would have to make her own way. When Karel began
to show some interest, she was relieved, but it still took her three
years to persuade him to marry her. 'I knew that he was the man, not
just for me – that wasn't so important – but as a father for Eva. And
if I ever was right, I was right in that.' The couple eventually became
engaged, but they couldn't get married right away because she was
still waiting for her Czech nationality to be reinstated.

Almost every day, Anka took Eva to the government offices to
plead her case. She would park Eva's pram outside while she went
in to speak to the civil servants and return to find a crowd of adults
cooing over her beautiful baby. Anka soon discovered, however, that
it suited the authorities to obstruct her application, because if she
wasn't officially Czech then they would never have to give her the
factory back or compensate her for its loss. One official she had
been dealing with almost every day for three years asked her finally,
'Do you even speak Czech?' even though they had conversed in her
mother tongue throughout.

As soon as she had finally persuaded the authorities that she was
legitimately Czech again, on 20 February 1948, at the age of thirty,
she became Mrs Karel Bergmanová. Her new husband was fifteen
years older than her at forty-five. In 1939, he had fled the Protectorate and made his way to Britain to join the RAF, but he was too
old to be a pilot so he had become an interpreter instead. Their
wedding took place the same day as the Communist *putsch* that
established a new political order in Czechoslovakia.

Anka's wedding to Karel Bergman 1948

As soon as the newlyweds could legally leave the country, they packed up Eva and their few belongings and caught a train across Germany to Holland, planning to join other Czech refugees in Montreal, Canada. But once in Holland (where they were briefly reunited with Bernd's blind father Louis, who'd survived the war), they were diverted to Wales by a temporary job offer for Karel to supervise a glove factory there. Within five years he ended up buying the factory and the couple never left. From their earliest days living in a small furnished flat on the first floor of a building in Cathedral Road, Cardiff, Anka loved her home and her new life in a country where she felt free and safe. 'It was a very ordinary flat and we shared a bathroom with another refugee family, but I have never been so happy. I didn't have a penny. How I managed, I don't know. I thought mostly of my mother who would be pleased it turned out right.'

One thing she especially loved was rekindling her love of the cinema. Whenever Eva was in nursery or at school, she went to the cinema on her own – almost every single day. 'It doesn't matter what's on,' she'd say. 'It's just that I can.'

Small, undernourished and poorly, Eva appeared to be rather slow physically and at twenty-two months old she still couldn't walk. Anka rushed her from one paediatrician to another, fearing that there might be some lasting damage. She was especially tormented by the progress of a friend's daughter, who was at least six months ahead. Her tough little daughter gradually gained her strength, though, and soon 'caught up admirably'. She went to a school where she didn't understand a word of the language but at five she was fluent and started winning awards. Health-wise, she seemed otherwise unscathed and developed a normal appetite, especially enjoying the Czech dishes her mother made so well – many of which she had learned how to cook with imaginary ingredients in the barracks.

The chief legacy of Anka's time in the camps was that Eva would become hysterical if ever she heard a pneumatic drill. Anka would have to ask workmen to stop, or cover her daughter's ears in order to calm her down. She eventually figured out that Eva must have heard the pneumatic riveting machines at KZ Freiberg while she was in the womb.

Eva was told of her family history from an early age but she didn't discover that Karel wasn't her real father until she was four years old. Hanging on the back of the kitchen door was a shopping bag that someone had made for her mother in Prague, which bore the letters AN: Anka Nathanová.

Her mother explained, 'We were in the kitchen and she said, "Mummy, what does A.N. stand for, because shouldn't it be A.B.?" I thought that this was the moment I would tell her so I said, "You've heard about the war?" And she nodded, so I said, "Well, your father was killed in that war and his surname was Nathan . . . Afterwards I married Daddy and since then I have been called Bergman, so you have two Daddies!" Eva went downstairs to play with the other children and within a minute I heard her say, "I have two Daddies and you only have one!" And from then on I knew that nobody could hurt her.'

Anka and Eva in Cardiff 1952

Later, once Eva found out more, she often told people she was born in a concentration camp, though without realising the true significance of the statement. It was only when she read Anne Frank's *Diary of a Young Girl* as a teenager that she began to understand the full horror of what she was saying. Occasionally, she fantasised that her first Daddy had secretly survived the war and would come back into their lives, but she loved her second Daddy so dearly that such fantasies were rare.

Anka had offered to have a baby with her new husband but he

turned her down and offered instead to adopt Eva, whom he always thought of as his own. 'All my mother wanted was to create a loving home for me,' said Eva. 'So Karel adopted me and he was the only father I ever knew.'

Karel, who had lost his mother, his twin sister and her son along with the rest of his family during the war, rarely, if ever, spoke of his losses. Anka, however, became almost obsessed and saw nearly every film and documentary about the Holocaust. She watched *Schindler's List* when it was first released and described the camp scenes as 'more or less perfect'. One episode especially moved her. It was the moment when the Jews were crowded into the cattle trucks with the doors bolted. Nazis stood laughing as prisoners' hands poked through the cracks pleading for water, at which point Schindler grabbed a hosepipe and sprayed the carriages as if it was another act of cruelty, when in fact he had appreciated their thirst.

She had shelves of books on the Holocaust, several featuring photographs of Josef Mengele, who – like Rachel and Priska – she immediately recognised as the unusually polite, smiling doctor with the gauntlets and the gap between his teeth who had carried out selections in Auschwitz during those few key weeks in the latter half of 1944. There were numerous biographies of other senior Nazis in her bookcase too, a fact which often surprised people. Whenever she was asked why she had them she said, 'Because I'm still trying to find out why.' She also studied the lists of those killed at Terezín and Auschwitz, running her finger down the pages to see how and when those she'd known had lived and died.

After the end of Communist rule in 1989, Anka was finally handed back ownership of the family factory in Třebechovice. 'I sold it immediately – and very badly – because I didn't know the first thing about running a factory, and I didn't want to have anything to do with it somehow.' She couldn't help but feel guilty and think what her father would say – 'First the Germans took it, then the Communists. Now, you sell it of your own free will? How *could* you?' It was a decision she fretted over for the rest of her life.

Anka never went back to Auschwitz and wanted nothing to do with Germans. Like Rachel, she would have nothing German in the house; she was vehemently against the building of the Channel Tunnel because, she claimed, 'The Germans could come!' Years after the war, when new machinery was installed in her husband's factory, an engineer was sent to show the staff how to use it. Karel invited the engineer, a German, to dinner. Anka served the meal, but when her husband asked where the man came from and he replied, 'Freiberg, in Saxony,' she walked out of the room and never spoke another word to him.

Whenever Anka took Eva to London on the train from Cardiff, they had to pass a huge steel works at Newport with tall industrial chimneys that belched smoke and flame. Every time, Anka had to turn her head away. In later life, Anka suffered from an inner ear condition called Ménière's disease. A specialist told her this was most commonly seen in steelworkers, coalminers and pop stars – people who are subjected to incredibly high levels of noise. He couldn't imagine where she had developed it until she enlightened him.

In 1968, aged twenty-two, Eva married Malcolm Clarke, a Gentile who would become a professor of law at Cambridge University. The couple had two sons, Tim and Nick, and three grandchildren – Matilda, Imogen and Theo. Anka knew and loved them all. 'It was marvellous for my mother,' said Eva. 'She couldn't believe that she had survived or that I had survived and then we had two children and they gave her great-grandchildren. It was a miracle.'

When Anka first met Eva's father-in-law, Kenneth Clarke, she discovered that he had been an RAF navigator in Bomber Command during the war. He showed her his logbook, which recorded that on 13 February 1945, at 17.40 hours – as she and the rest of the prisoners were locked in the Freiberg factory – he'd flown overhead and helped bomb Dresden in a Lancaster bomber, before returning to his British base at 10.10. He was in tears as he told her, 'I could have killed you both!' Anka reassured him with a smile and said, 'But, Kenneth, you didn't!'

Anka with Eva, her grandsons Tim and Nick, and great
grandchildren Matilda, Imogen and Theo, England

When Eva was living in Singapore with her husband in the late six-
ties, she wrote and asked her mother to put her story down in
writing for posterity. Anka agreed. Reading through the account
by chance was the first time her husband Karel learned about
all that had happened to her during the war, and it moved him
deeply.

In later years, Anka went on an emotional journey back to
Terezín with Eva as she showed her daughter where she had lived
and almost died. When Eva returned alone to the ghetto years afterwards, she was especially touched to find her brother Dan's name
had since been inscribed on a memorial wall there – the only physical trace of the baby whose death had guaranteed Eva's life.

Anka's cousin Hana, who had probably only survived the war
because she'd married a Gentile, later edited a book of children's
poems and drawings from Terezín called . . . *I never saw another*

*butterfly* ..., quoting the poem by young Pavel Friedman, one of those who'd perished. Hana also became curator of the Jewish Museum in Prague and played a part in arranging for the names of the lost – including those of Bernd and all fifteen members of Anka's family – to be inscribed on the wall of the Pinkas synagogue.

Having worked behind the scenes in education all her adult life, Eva eventually retired and decided to tell her mother's story, primarily in schools, travelling all over the country with the Holocaust Educational Trust. Her work inspired a ballet called *Anka's Story* by a Cambridge dance group, which has been performed at the Edinburgh Fringe. Eva has been to Auschwitz several times with groups of students and teachers and each time she is near the *Sauna* building in Birkenau, her eyes cannot help but scan the ground for her mother's wedding band and amethyst engagement ring, which were never found.

She took her two sons and Malcolm to Mauthausen for her fortieth birthday in 1985. The former camp is now a beautifully preserved memorial site where visitors from around the world are allowed in at no charge. In 1985, only survivors were allowed in for free and when Eva tried to explain to the man at the gate that she qualified, he laughed in her face and made her cry, refusing to believe her because of her age.

A committed non-believer, Anka's religious views never changed. 'Nobody can answer the question – where was He?' she said. 'Nobody has solved this, or why we were sought out for this treatment.' Ever the optimist, she added, 'If this whole experience had to happen to me, then it was the right age physically and mentally because I was young and strong ... As I told my daughter about it at a very early age so I could let go, sort of ... I seem to have survived it reasonably well and my child is healthy and her mind is all right, and so for me personally (but only for me, not for my family), it turned out as well as it could have ... Eva was my affirmation of life. She took me forward and she helped keep me sane.'

Anka's husband Karel died of a heart attack in 1983 aged eighty-one. At his cremation, she saw black smoke coming out of the chimney, shuddered and cried, 'Why did I have to look?' His ashes were scattered in the Jewish cemetery near his hometown in the rural Czech Republic. It is not far from an impressive stone memorial, erected to him and to other local people who either left the country to fight the Nazis from abroad or perished in the camps. After Anka had scattered her husband's ashes, she suggested that Eva cremate her too when the time came, even though that was not in the Jewish tradition. 'Well, it's how the rest of my family ended up!' she joked.

Anka lived with Eva and her husband in Cambridge for the last three years of her life. At ninety-six, she was lucid to the end and always wanted to look her best. Even in her final days, the woman who'd curled her eyelashes en route to see her husband in a ghetto put on make-up to greet her eldest grandson. Immensely proud of her daughter's work in speaking to students about the Holocaust, she would have been delighted to be remembered in a book. 'The more people who know about what happened, the less likely it is to happen again, I hope,' she said. 'This is a story which should teach people that it *mustn't* happen again.'

Anka on her 95th birthday with her great-
granddaughter Matilda, 2013

Eva agreed. 'It is very important to remember all those millions of people who were killed. And especially all those who have never had one single person remember them because all of their families and their communities were destroyed. It is our duty to tell that story and to try to prevent such atrocities from happening again and again.'

Anka Nathan-Bergman died at home with Eva by her side on 17 July 2013. In accordance with her wishes, her ashes were scattered at the same site as those of her second husband Karel in the serene Jewish graveyard in the middle of a wood near Drevikov in the Czech Republic.

After sixty-five years in Britain, a country she came to adore but where she had always felt to be an outsider and a refugee, Anka had finally returned to the country she so loved.

Anka's grave, Czech Republic

# 10

# Reunion

The babies reunited with their liberators, the Thunderbolts

'The Thunderbolts liberated us and the Thunderbolts reunited us,'
Hana Berger Moran insisted from her home in the country of her
liberators. She should know. It was Priska's daughter who, in the
summer of 2003, decided to search for the doctors who'd saved her
life in Mauthausen fifty-eight years earlier.

'My mother was still alive and living in Bratislava and I wanted to find out if Pete was still around too so that we could meet and thank him.' Searching online, she came across the website of the 11th Armored Division Association of US veterans and discovered that they were about to hold a convention in Illinois. She sent them a letter which appeared on their website and in their quarterly magazine *Thunderbolt*.

After explaining the circumstances of her birth, she wrote:

When the liberation of Mauthausen happened, I was a barely three-week-old baby. As my dear mother loved to say, the tanks had white stars on them and she was absolutely amazed how young all the soldiers were. She remembered the song 'Roll Out the Barrel' being played ... The surgeons who operated on me did not believe I would survive if I did not get the proper treatment and begged my mother to return with them to the US. She refused to follow their advice, reasoning that she must return home to Bratislava to wait for her husband, my father ... I would very much like to find out the names of the surgeons or surgeon and how to contact any person who helped the prisoners following the liberation ... I would like to express my deep gratitude to all liberators of the concentration camp Mauthausen.

Hana, who described herself as an 'underweight little worm' when she was born, claimed that she was never the heroine of the story. 'It was my mother who was incredible.' It took a while, but in early 2005 she received a message from a man who had been nineteen when he was liberated from the Ebensee sub-camp of Mauthausen, and who had since become the US representative of the International Mauthausen Committee. Max Rodrigues Garcia, who lived not far from Hana in San Francisco, had seen her letter and invited her to travel to Mauthausen for the sixtieth anniversary of the liberation, which he hoped that eighty-two-year-old Pete Petersohn might also be able to attend.

In May 2005, Hana and her husband Mark flew to Austria from San Francisco, and Pete and his son Brian flew in from Chicago. At the Hotel Wolfinger in the grand main square of Linz, liberators and their families plus a few survivors were gathering to share stories with men they hadn't seen in years. Hana was in the crowded dining room when a group in yellow and white Thunderbolt baseball caps walked in, one of whom looked to be older and visibly tired. She had a sudden clear sense that this was Pete. After he'd settled at a corner table she sat down quietly next to him in the middle of an animated conversation, and waited. A sudden silence fell over the room and Max Garcia, sitting near by, was so excited that he had to put a hand over his mouth to stop himself from crying out.

A few minutes later, Pete somehow sensed Hana's presence. He stopped talking, turned to the stranger at his side and, with tears in his eyes, said quietly, 'Hana.'

The two embraced for several minutes, neither able to speak.

'I thought she was going to kill me, she hugged me so tight!' Pete said.

It had been sixty years since they had last met and Hana couldn't have remembered a thing about it, but clasping the hand of the medic who'd persuaded his superior officer to try to save her life in that place where so many others were in equally urgent need of their attention proved to be one of the most moving experiences of both their lives. Her face wet with tears, Hana told him that she loved him and she thanked him for keeping her alive. She showed him some of the scars on her arms and chest from the surgery she'd undergone at the field hospital.

Pete, too, felt the emotion of their reunion deeply. Within weeks of the liberation of Mauthausen, he'd sat down at a typewriter and begun writing up his experiences, augmenting them with scores of photographs that he had taken. Even at such a young age, he had appreciated the importance of eyewitness testimony.

Hana meets US medic who saved her in Mauthausen, 2005

The process had taken its toll. In an interview he gave to historian Michael Hirsch in 2008, Pete said, 'I had a breakdown [in Mauthausen] ... I had put in long hours and ... I needed some rest ... I bled from the nose, I bled from the inner ears, and I just couldn't sleep ... I had two days that my officer ordered me to rest. I am still fighting today ... because I have a mental condition that needs to be taken care of ... when I go to bed at night. I think I'm going to get a good night's sleep and then the bodies start to appear ... the piles of dead bodies and the rats eating them ... I'm seeing ... psychiatrists but I don't know what else they can do for me ... Over the years it has grown worse ... I guess I'll just carry it to my grave.'

Hana asked for any news about Major Stacy but discovered that, sadly, he'd passed away. Further enquiries with the major's family disclosed that, like so many servicemen, he had never spoken of his wartime experiences. Nor did he mention the baby he'd helped to save.

As Pete and Hana talked some more, he was finally able to give her an explanation as to why her mother kept asking in her confusion, 'Will you forgive me?' He believed it might have been related to the fact that Priska had 'given up' her baby twice, first to the *Kapo* when she arrived at the camp and then to the doctors – each time not knowing what the outcome would be. 'Pete told me that my mother was so "gracious" and knew that they were trying to help but he added, "I was amazed what she did – she just handed you over to me. She didn't know she would ever see you again. She trusted me to save you and bring you back." I think that is what she felt guilty about.'

Hana affectionately dubbed Pete 'Dad' or 'Daddy Pete', and the two kept in touch via email and telephone for the next few years. In one email to her not long after their reunion in 2005, he wrote of his trip to Europe:

> Overall, it was great and the very best was when you and I got to meet each other for the second time after sixty years and the happy moments that came back to me, and finding the answer to the question I often asked myself – did things work out? – and prayed that everything was a success for your sake. The duties I had performed in the field had come to an end. I prayed that all those I had taken care of survived and that I had guessed right in treatment. Then there was the baby at Mauthausen, there was much to wonder about and try to put behind me, but I must confess the baby entered my mind many, many times.

Sadly, Priska was too unwell to meet Pete and thank him herself. She died a year later. Hana remained in contact, however, and visited him at his home just before his death aged eighty-eight in 2010, not long after she'd been made an honorary lifetime member of the 11th Armored Division Association. Pete left four sons, thirteen grandchildren and ten great-grandchildren. Even though he'd had a difficult time after the war, LeRoy Petersohn always said that the fact that he'd saved a baby was the most positive experience of it all.

As one door closed for Hana, so another one opened. In 2008, Eva Clarke, the sixty-three-year-old daughter of Anka (who was still alive aged ninety), happened across the 11th Armored Division website herself and decided to reach out. In an email dated Tuesday 20 May, she wrote and thanked the US soldiers for liberating her and her mother. She added:

> I was born in Mauthausen on 29th of April 1945. My mother, Anka Bergman, says that hundreds of photographs were taken of us by US soldiers but we have never found any. We would be most grateful to hear of the existence of any mother and baby photos. Our story features in the Thunderbolt.

On the other side of the Atlantic, Hana spotted the article and could hardly believe what she was reading. Another baby? Born in Mauthausen? Before they were liberated? Since the publication of a German book cataloguing the records that were left of KZ Freiberg, she'd been aware that – incredibly – there had been other pregnant women in Freiberg and on the train, including a Polish *Kapo*, but it was her understanding that none of the babies and not all of the mothers had survived. (Years later she found out about one baby born in Mauthausen after liberation and named Robert after the Belgrade obstetrician who'd delivered him. The child lived for only a few weeks and his mother, Gerty Kompert, the cousin of survivor Lisa Miková, was also dead.)

Via the Thunderbolts' website, Hana responded to Eva's post and the two 'babies' – who lived more than 6,000 kilometres apart – were finally connected. Eva, too, was shocked to think that there was somebody else out there in the world whose mother had gone through the same ordeal. She found Hana's original letter in an old edition of *Thunderbolt* and couldn't get over the similarities between their mothers' experiences. Priska and Anka had been just two prisoners among thousands who never met or were even aware of one another, and yet they had each miraculously given birth to babies who – even more remarkably – survived.

After a series of emails between the two of them and the Austrian authorities who'd turned KZ Mauthausen into an impressive memorial site in the 1960s (partly at the urging of the Thunderbolts), Hana and Eva both agreed to attend the sixty-fifth anniversary of the liberation of the camp on 8 May 2010. It was to be the last time that the surviving American veterans made an official visit because of their diminishing numbers and the age and infirmity of those who were left. The numbers of those who'd been liberated were also dwindling, so officials at the Austrian Ministry of the Interior in Vienna were planning a huge event attended by several heads of state. When the veterans' website announced the details, plus the exciting news that both Eva and Hana would be attending, another door was opened.

Across the country, a young man in New York who'd been trawling through the site to find out more about the men who liberated his father spotted the bulletin. Charlie Olsky, thirty-two, was Mark and Mary's youngest son. Head of publicity at a Manhattan film distribution company, Charlie was the family's unofficial historian and the one who'd been able to get more information from his grandmother Rachel than almost anyone else. It was Charlie who'd walked through the rooms of the Yad Vashem with her as a boy, and it was he who decided to organise a birthday surprise for his father.

'Charlie told me, "I'm going to Mauthausen for your sixty-fifth birthday and you're coming with me,"' said Mark. 'I had never been back there since 1945 even though I'd been within thirty miles of it when I visited Dachau. I'd asked Mom a couple of times if she'd like to go back but she always said it was the last thing in the world she wanted. She told me, "That was an evil, horrible, ugly camp. Yet even more depressing than the place itself was that just outside was one of the most beautiful spots in the world."'

Unbeknown to Mark, Charlie had planned their whole trip, as well as the 'reunion' with Hana and Eva, down to the last detail. Then, a few days before they left (and on the advice of his mother Mary, who was concerned at Mark's reaction to such a surprise), he let his father in on the secret.

'He said, "I have something to tell you," and then he told me about the two other "babies" born in the camps and said he'd been communicating with them and that I would be able to meet them in Mauthausen. I was stunned. Although my mother had heard there were babies in the camp, she never saw them and didn't know if she believed it. As a doctor, I hadn't even thought about the possibility that other children could have survived that transport as I did. I really didn't have a chance to absorb the information before we were on the plane.'

It was on the flight from New York to Europe with Charlie that Mark had time to consider the forthcoming encounter and wonder what the two other 'babies' might be like. 'My first thought was that they were two random individuals who had nothing in common with me apart from our age and where and how we were born. I told myself not to build up too many expectations. I talked myself down and said it will be nice, but they're probably not people you'd want to live next door to.'

The officials and organisers at Mauthausen warmly welcomed the 'babies' when they arrived and arranged for them to be put up in hotels in Linz before the daylong commemoration services began the following morning. Within hours of settling in, the three of them arranged to meet at a café on the historic main square for which Hitler had once had such grand plans; each of them felt surprisingly nervous.

Eva and her husband Malcolm arrived early, took their seats at a table and waited. Hana walked in first with her husband and then Mark and Charlie arrived.

'We said hello and suddenly we were laughing and crying all at the same time,' said Eva. 'It was amazing. When we found one another and all met there for the first time it was an incredible reunion. It felt completely natural and we formed a real emotional bond.'

The three survivors stayed in the café talking all afternoon while Charlie filmed the whole thing. Diplomatically, Hana and Eva's husbands slipped away so that the children of Priska, Rachel and Anka could each talk about their mothers and what they had been told of their births. They parted only reluctantly and a few hours later met again for dinner at a local restaurant, where they carried on chatting like old friends.

Eva, Mark, and Hana meet in Mauthausen 2010

Mark said, 'We met and they were both nice and sweet and pretty and pleasant and cute. Then we got talking and I thought, "Hey, these are really interesting, wonderful people! This isn't just a coincidence. They have interesting lives and, yes, they feel like family!" They were the sort of people I would love to have as my friends. I can't explain it but I felt reunited – instantly we had a really nice warm friendship. It was like meeting my family. The sad part was that because of dispersion of everyone after the war, we were never to meet until then.'

Having each been raised as an only child, all three survivors felt the same unexpected sense of fellowship and knew, straight away, that they'd always remain close. Mark said, 'It's amazing to have people who share the same story. There are so many who didn't make it or who were killed or tortured. We made it. I feel like one of those people who has been abducted from my original family and suddenly we've been reunited!'

Hana said, 'We've been brought together by chance but we now have a permanent bond and feel such a sense of togetherness. I am absolutely delighted to call them my sister and brother.' She likes to joke with her new 'siblings' that – as the eldest (born on 12 April 1945) – she should be offered the most respect. Mark (born on 20 April) counters that, as the only boy, he warrants their highest esteem. Eva (born on 29 April) is the baby, and enjoys reminding her siblings how much younger she is. 'Our mothers were all very strong women and we are very grateful for that,' she adds.

The following day they travelled together to the Mauthausen Memorial, where they each felt the weight of history on them. Although she was the only one to have visited the camp before, Eva still felt especially emotional staring up at the forbidding entrance in the shadow of whose gates she'd been born. The barracks down the hill into which sickly Hana and Mark had been thrown with their mothers and left to die no longer existed, but the views across the Austrian hills to the Alps were just as their late mothers had described.

The bodies of all those buried in the boneyard under the football pitch had been moved and reinterred within a serene walled grave-yard in the centre of the camp. And where row upon row of prisoner barracks had once lined the terraces, now stood a well-tended garden dominated by a series of hugely impressive and emotive stone and metal monuments to the dead of every *Häftlinge* nation in the camp.

The Czechoslovak memorial and gates where Eva was born

The 'babies' walked together down the few steps to the door of the gas chamber with its white-tiled walls and sinister black pipes and could barely speak. Under Nazi ideology, all three of them should have gasped their last in that stifling space, cradled by their half-dead mothers. But Fate had other plans for them all. Brought home from the war, never to meet their fathers, each child had grown up believing that the desperate circumstances of their birth and the miracle of their survival meant that they'd been the only one born into that living hell who could have lived. They were wrong.

One year after their visit to Mauthausen the three 'siblings of the heart' met again, this time in England. They travelled to Eva's hometown of Cambridge in January 2011 to take part in a special commemoration service for Holocaust Memorial Day at the Guildhall. There, Hana and Mark met Anka for the first time. Aged ninety-three, physically frail but with a lively mind, Eva's mother was visibly moved to meet the other babies who'd also survived and she embraced them warmly. Hana said, 'To meet Anka was so very emotional. I only wish she could have met my mother. She told me, "You are my daughter too," and I really felt like I was.'

Mark agreed. 'It felt so special. She was such a wonderful lady – so happy and bright and articulate, with a great sense of humour and her memory completely intact.'

It wasn't long before the 'babies' met again, back in Mauthausen on 8 May 2013, where they opened a new exhibition, part of which features the remarkably accurate replica of Hana's baby smock and bonnet made from the originals loaned to them by the United States Holocaust Memorial Museum in Washington, DC. Anka, who had just celebrated her ninety-sixth birthday, wasn't well enough to travel to Austria with them and passed away two months later. Her funeral in Cambridge was broadcast over the internet so that her grandson and his family in Australia could feel a part of the service of celebration. Hana and Mark – Anka's surrogate children – watched it online too and were able to say their own quiet farewell to the last surviving mother.

Of blessed memory, those remarkable women had not only found the will to carry on and survive the unsurvivable during the war years, but their fortitude and determination ensured that their infants survived too. Their babies went on to have babies of their own and create a second and then a third generation, all of whom continue to live their lives to the full in defiance of Hitler's plan to erase them from history and from memory.

The ghosts of their mothers and of the millions of others who died during the war demand that their stories are told and retold, never to be forgotten. As Hana said, 'We all try to live our lives as best we can and to fill those shoes that are so empty. In memory of their memories, each new day is a promise.'

Never far from each other's thoughts, the miraculous children of Priska, Rachel and Anka – all of them born survivors – were sadly unable to attend the town of Freiberg's 2015 commemoration project. Entitled 'We Are Still Here', it involved three generations of townspeople and relatives of KZ survivors in a cultural festival featuring Holocaust literature, music, poetry and art, working with local schoolchildren and with exchange students from Freiberg's twin city of Ness Ziona in Israel.

Three hundred miles south of Freiberg, the 'babies' returned instead to the breathtakingly beautiful hilltop site of the Mauthausen Memorial in May 2015 to commemorate the seventieth anniversary of the liberation.

In the place that was meant to have been their graveyard even as Nazi tyranny was in its death throes, the seventy-year-old orphans tightly gripped each other's hands and walked together through the gates of the camp in the footsteps of three women who not only survived unimaginable horrors, but who defied death to give them life.

Mark, Eva and Hana take part in the
memorial parade at Mauthausen

# Roll Call

The three women whose story is at the heart of this book lost more than twenty members of their immediate families to Hitler and his accomplices. Beyond the circles of these once close-knit families the death toll rippled onwards and outwards to encompass grandparents, aunts and uncles, cousins and in-laws as entire generations and communities were wiped off the face of the earth.

The names and faces of these cherished family members represent a tiny fraction of the millions of the disappeared who perished at the hands of those who presided over life and death.

Many of their names may never be known.

None of these loved ones lie in consecrated ground or have tombstones.

There is no final resting place to mark the brutal manner of their passing.

There is nowhere to go to remember their once-hopeful faces.

There is only here ...

*Husbands and fathers*

Tibor Löwenbein (1914–1945)
Monik Friedman (1916–1945)
Bernd Nathan (1904–1945)

## Parents

Emanuel Rona (1884–1944)
Paula Ronová (1889–1944)
Shaiah Abramczyk (1870–1944)
Fajga Abramczyk (1898–1944)
Stanislav Kauder (1870–1944)
Ida Kauderová (1882–1944)
Selma Nathanová (1880–1944)
Ita Friedmann (1899–1944)

## Siblings

Boežka Ronová (1910–1944)
Moniek Abramczyk (1923–1943)
Heniek Abramczyk (1931–1944)
Dorcka Abramczyk (1931–1944)
David Friedman (dates unknown)
Avner Friedman (dates unknown)
Anička 'Maniusia' Abramczyk (1933–1944)
Zdena Isidorová (1904–1944)
Herbert Isidor (1916–1944)
Ruzena Mautnerová (1906–1944)

## Children

Peter Mautner (1935–1944)
Dan Nathan (February–April 1944)

*'No day shall erase you from the memory of Time.'*
Virgil

# Bibliography and Sources

*Author research and previously unpublished sources:*

Author interviews with Holocaust survivors Hana Berger Moran, Mark Olsky, Eva Clarke, Sally Wolkoff, Gerty Meltzer, Esther Bauer, Lisa Miková, Esther Bauer, Werner Reich, Max R. Garcia, and Bronia Snow.

Author interviews with survivors' families Charlie Olsky, Shirley Speyer, Jana Zimmer, Brian K. Petersohn, Jean Gore, Larry Kosiek, Stephanie Sullivan, Julie K. Rosenberg, David Feder, Miki Feder, and John Tygier.

Author research visits to Krakow, Auschwitz I and II, Łódź, Pabianice, Chełmno, Prague, Terezín, Horní Bříza, Trebechovice pod Orebem, Zlaty Moravce, Hradec Králové, Drevikov, Bratislava, Sered', Freiberg, Linz, Most, Plzeň, České Budějovice, and KZ Mauthausen.

Documents and photographs from historian Dr Michael Düsing, and author interviews with him and with Cornelia Hünert of Freiberg's City Cultural Department, Germany.

Author interviews with Pascal Cziborra of the Faculty of History, Philosophy and Theology at the University of Bielefeld, Germany.

Author interviews with the Horní Bříza Deputy Mayor Zdeněk Procházka, his daughter Michaela, the late historian Mrs

Bozena Royová, and locals Jaroslav Lang and Vaclav Stepanek, Czech Republic.

Author interview with Dita Valentová in Třebechovice pod Orebem, Czech Republic.

Author interview with Martin Winstone of the UK National Holocaust Centre and Museum, Nottinghamshire, UK.

Author interview with midwife Abby Davidson, Bsc (Hons), London.

Unpublished personal account of Anka Bergman's experiences written for her daughter Eva Clarke, 2009.

Unpublished personal account of Klara Löffová's experiences written for her daughter Jana Zimmer, 2000.

Unpublished letter detailing her experiences from Priska Lomová to the Union of Anti-Fascist Fighters, 1990.

Unpublished letters between Tibor Löwenbein and his wife Priska, 1941.

Interviews with Anka Bergman by Frances Rapport, Professor of Qualitative Health Research Interview, Swansea University, Wales, 2007.

Unpublished survivors' letters, railway and official documents, and photographs with permission from the Museum of Horní Bříza, Czech Republic.

Documents and photographs with permission from the Auschwitz Memorial Museum, Poland and author interviews with Wojciech Płosa, Ph.D., Head of the Archives, Dr Piotr Setkiewicz, Ph.D., Head of the Research Department, and memorial guide Anna Ren.

Documents and photographs with permission from the Jewish Museum of Prague, Czech Republic, and author interviews with archivists Julie Jenšovská and Radana Rutová.

*Archive witness statements:*

Lomová, Priska, Interview 15134. Web 2014. *Visual History Archive.* USC Shoah Foundation (sfi.usc.edu)

Olsky, Rachel, Interview 15161. Web 2014. *Visual History Archive*. USC Shoah Foundation (sfi.usc.edu)

Bergman, Anna, Interview 28239. Web 2013 *Visual History Archive*. USC Shoah Foundation (sfi.usc.edu)

Wolkoff, Sally, Interview 12886. Web 2014. *Visual History Archive*. USC Shoah Foundation (sfi.usc.edu)

Meltzer, Gerty, Interview 1686. Web 2014. *Visual History Archive*. USC Shoah Foundation (sfi.usc.edu)

Freeman, Abraham, Interview 16384. Web 2014. *Visual History Archive*. USC Shoah Foundation (sfi.usc.edu)

Filmed interview with Anka Bergman by Jean Laurent Grey and Solomon J. Salat for the Mauthausen Memorial

*The Baby Born in a Concentration Camp*, BBC documentary, producer Emily Davis, 2011

*Defiant Requiem: Voices of Resistance*, PBS documentary director Doug Schultz, 2012

*Nazi Propaganda Film About Theresienstadt/Terezin*. Film ID 2310, Steven Spielberg Film & Video Archive

*Liberation of Mauthausen* (and KZ Gusen I, II & III) by Former Staff Sgt. Albert J. Kosiek. Published in: *Thunderbolt*, the 11th Armored Division Association, Vol. 8, No. 7, May–June 1955, with permission of his son Larry Kosiek

Interview with Priska Lomová by editor Eva Richterová in *Bojovník* newspaper, part of the Sväz Protifašistických Bojovníkov, 1980

Interview with Anka Bergman by Helga Amesberger for the Mauthausen Survivors Documentation Project, 2003.


*Bibliography:*

*A Time to Speak*, Helen Lewis, The Blackstaff Press, 1992

*After the Holocaust*, Marek Jan Chodakiewiczs, Columbia University Press, 2003

*Against All Hope: Resistance in the Nazi Concentration Camps 1938–1945*, Hermann Langbein

*All Hell Let Loose, The World at War 1939–45*, Max Hastings, Harper Press, 2011

*Anus Mundi, 1500 Days in Auschwitz/Birkenau*, Wieslaw Kielar, Times Books, 1972

*Beyond Violence: Jewish Survivors in Poland and Slovakia, 1944-48*, Prof Anna Cichopek-Gajraj, Cambridge University Press, 2014

*Bomber Command*, Max Hastings, Pan, 1979

*Defying Hitler*, Sebastian Haffner, Weidenfeld & Nicholson, 2002

*Doctor 117641, A Holocaust Memoir*, Louis J. Michels MD, Yale University, 1989

*Dresden*, Frederick Taylor, Bloomsbury, 2004

*Five Chimneys*, Olga Lengyel, Academy Chicago, 1947

*Forgotten Voices of the Holocaust*, Lyn Smith, Avebury Press, 2005

*Fragments, Transcribing the Holocaust*, Francis Rapport with Anka Bergman, Terry Farago and Edith Salter, Hafan Books, 2013

*Helga's Diary*, Helga Weiss, Penguin, 2013

*Holocaust Poetry*, Hilda Schiff, St. Martin's Griffin, 1995

*Holocaust, The Nazi persecution and murder of the Jews*, Peter Longerich, Oxford University Press, 2010

*I Escaped from Auschwitz*, Rudolf Vrba, Robson Books Ltd, 2006

*I Never Saw Another Butterfly*, Shocken Books, 1993

*In the Shadow of Death: Living Outside the Gates of Mauthausen*, Gordon J. Horwitz, The Free Press, 1990

*Jews are Coming Back*, David Bankier, Berghahn Books, 2005

*KZ Freiberg*, Pascal Cziborra, Lorbeer Verlag, 2008

*Kunst und Kultur im Konzentrationslager Mauthausen 1938–1945*, Die Austeller, 2013

*Landscapes of Memory*, Ruth Kluger, Bloomsbury, 2003

*Landscapes of the Metropolis of Death*, Otto Dov Kulka, Penguin, 2014

*L'homme barbelé*, Beatrice Fontanel, Grasset & Fasquelle, 2009

*Łódź Ghetto Album*, by Thomas Weber, Martin Parr, Timothy Prus, Chris Boot, 2005

*Mauthausen, The History of a Death Camp*, Evelyn Le Chêne, Methuen, 1971

*Mengele*, Gerald L. Posner & John Ware, First Cooper Square Press, 2000

*Never Again, A History of the Holocaust*, Martin Gilbert, Harper Collins, 2000

*On the Edge of Destruction: Jews of Poland between the Two World Wars*, Celia S. Heller, Wayne State University Press, 1993

*Pearls of Childhood*, Vera Gissing, Pan Books, 1988

*People in Auschwitz*, Hermann Langbein, The University of North Carolina Press, 2004

*Poetry of the Second World War, An International Anthology*, edited by Desmond Graham, Pimlico, 1998

*Prague in Danger: The Years of German Occupation, 1939–45*, Peter Demetz, Farrar, Straus and Giroux, 2009

*Railways and the Holocaust: The Trains that Shamed the World*, Robin Jones, Mortons Media, 2013

*Shoah*, Claude Lanzmann, Da Capo Press, 1995

*Singing for Survival: Songs of the Łódź Ghetto, 1940–45*, Gila Flam 1992

*St. Georgen-Gusen-Mauthausen. Concentration Camp Mauthausen Reconsidered*, BoD, 2008

*Survival, Holocaust Survivors Tell Their Story*, Quill, 2003

*Survival*, produced by the Holocaust Centre

*Survival in Auschwitz*, Primo Levi, Touchstone, 1996

*The Cap or the Price of a Life*, Roman Frister, Weidenfeld & Nicholson, 1999

*The Chronicle of the Łódź Ghetto, 1941–44*, edited by Lucjan Dobroszycki, Yale University Press, 1987

*The Concentration Camp Mauthausen 1938–1945*, New Academic Press, 2013

*The Diary of Dawid Sierakowiak: Five Notebooks from the Łódź Ghetto*, edited by Alan Adelson, Bloomsbury, 1997

*The Emperor of Lies*, Steve Sem-Sandberg, Farrar, Straus and Giroux, 2011

*The German Trauma, Experiences and Reflections 1938–2000*, Gitta Sereny, Penguin, 2000

*The Holocaust: A History of the Jews of Europe During the Second World War*, Martin Gilbert, Holt Paperbacks, 1987

*The Holocaust Sites of Europe: An Historical Guide*, Martin Winstone, I.B. Tauris, 2014

*The Last Album: Eyes from the Ashes of Auschwitz-Birkenau*, Ann Weiss, W.W. Norton & Co, 2001

*The Last Goodbye*, Edith Hofman, Memoirs Publishing, 2012

*The Liberators, America's Witnesses to the Holocaust*, Michael Hirsh, Bantam Books 2010

*The Righteous*, Martin Gilbert, Doubleday, 2002

*The Terezín Diary of Gonda Redlich*, edited by Saul. S. Friedman, University Press of Kentucky, 2008

*The Terezín Ghetto*, Ludmilla Chladková, Pamatnik Terezín, 2005

*The Tin Ring*, Zdenka Fantlová, Northumbria Press, 2010

*The Trains of the Holocaust*, Hedi Enghelberg, Engpublishing, 2014

*The Visible Part, Photographs of Mauthausen concentration camp*, Mandelbaum, Vienna, 2005

*To the Bitter End, The Diaries of Victor Klemperer*, Trafalgar Square, 1999

*Triumph of Hope*, Ruth Elias, Wiley & Sons, 1998

*Wir Waren zum Tode Bestimmt*, Michael Düsing, Forum Verlag Leipzig, 2002

*Witnesses to the Holocaust*, Martin Berenbaum, Harper Collins, 1997

*Other archive sources:*

Memorial and Museum Auschwitz-Birkenau – (http://en.auschwitz.org)

*Terezín Memorial* (http://www.pamatnik-terezin.cz)

*KZ-Memorial Flossenbürg* – (www.gedenkstaette-flossenbuerg.de)

*Mauthausen Memorial Museum* – (http://www.mauthausen-memorial.at/)

United States Holocaust Memorial Museum (http://www.ushmm.org)

*Yad Vashem* (http://www.yadvashem.org)

*Jewish Virtual Library* – (www.jewishvirtuallibrary.org)

The Foundation for Commemorating the Victims of Slave Labour in Auschwitz – (www.fcsla.org)

*Janusz Korczak Communication Centre* (www.korczak.com)

The Museum of Jewish Heritage (www.jewishgen.org)

Information Portal to European Sites of Remembrance (www.memorialmuseums.com)

*The 11th Armored Division* (www.11tharmoreddivision.com)

The Jewish Museum in Prague (www.jewishmuseum.cz)

*Holocaust Educational Trust* (www.het.org.uk)

The National Holocaust Centre and Museum (www.holocaustcentre.net)

*The Educational Website Holocaust CZ* (http://www2.holocaust.cz/en/main)

*The Imperial War Museum* (www.iwm.org.uk)

# Acknowledgements

When researching events long past in which few of the participants are still living, we writers owe an enormous debt of gratitude to those who chose to record their own experiences, as well as the ones who thought to chronicle their stories before it was too late. I am no exception, and without the remarkable generosity of both the people who lived through these extraordinary times and the diligent historians who sought them out, then this book would never have been possible.

With humility and gratitude, I specifically acknowledge the courage and tenacity of Priska, Rachel and Anka – the three mothers whose indomitable will to live form the central narrative of this book. Sadly, I was never able to meet them in person, but after spending so long in their company, I feel as if I have. I've been further blessed in having unlimited access to the personal testimonies that they shared with their families, oral and written, and in the numerous filmed, recorded and documented statements they gave to numerous researchers over the years. Throughout them all, their hope shines through.

Much of my research would never have been possible without the generous assistance of their three 'babies' – Hana, Mark and

Eva – who I am proud to say have made me their honorary sister. Their kindness, patience, graciousness and co-operation in filling in the gaps made this book far richer than it might otherwise have been. I only hope I can do justice to their incredible stories. I am also grateful to their immediate families who have extended me the same courtesy, including Mary and Charlie Olsky, Shirley Speyer, Mark Moran, Tommy Bergen, Julie Z. Rosenberg, David and Miki Feder, and Professor Malcolm A. Clarke.

When I came across the story of babies born to the Holocaust by chance in 2013, Eva Clarke was my first point of contact. Back then, I thought that she might have been the only baby who had survived her mother's particular Holocaust journey. The moment she told me of the existence of Hana and Mark and how they'd since become 'siblings of the heart,' I knew that I had to incorporate the stories of all three into one epic volume spanning more than a century. And so *Born Survivors* was conceived.

I have been assisted in its long gestation by numerous individuals and organisations across eight countries, including survivors, family members, fellow authors, government officials, and untold dedicated people who work in historical archives. All of them have been remarkably open and generous with their time and their expertise. My special thanks goes to survivors Sally Wolkoff in Tennessee; Gerty Meltzer (née Taussig) in Arizona; Lisa Miková in Prague; Esther Bauer in Yonkers, Max R. Garcia in San Francisco, Werner Reich in New York, and Bronia Snow in Surrey, all of whom entrusted me with their sacred memories. I am also indebted to Jana Zimmer in California for the invaluable reflections of her late mother Klara Löffová; to Brian K. Petersohn in Chicago for the memories of his father LeRoy 'Pete' Petersohn; to Larry Kosiek in Illinois for recollections of his father Sgt. Albert J. Kosiek, and to Jean Gore for memories of her father Major Harold G. Stacy. Thanks to Stephanie Sullivan for access to the photographs of her father Paul E. Soldner, who was one of the liberators of Mauthausen, and to my friend John Tygier in London for sharing some of the experiences of his family in Łódź, Treblinka and Russia.

The dedicated Mauthausen Memorial team who work under the Austrian Ministry of the Interior in Vienna have been exceptionally helpful and welcoming. I was grateful that the Ministry agreed to the launch of this book at the very site where the mothers and babies were liberated in May 1945 and were thus 'born again'. Under the inspirational direction of Dr Barbara Glück, those who deserve special mention at the Memorial Project include Thomas Zaglmeier, who not only served as my personal guide to the camp on my first visit there but who has continued to keep the memory of the survivors alive with his steady, quiet commitment.

He and the educational team at the site have been ably assisted by Christian Angerer, Peter Egger and and Helga Amesberger of the Mauthausen Survivors Documentation Project, who have both been most generous with their time and material. I would also like to thank Professor Dr Albert Lichtblau of the University of Salzburg for his encouragement and assistance. In the Memorial headquarters in Vienna, I must thank Stephan Matyus, Jochen Wollner, Doris Warlitsch and Renate Paschinger. Robert Vorberg was not only the most helpful of all the historians and archivists I worked with, but was kind enough – with his colleague Christian Dürr – to proof-read and check the facts in the sections of the book relating to Mauthausen. And in Munich, I acknowledge Ulrich Fritz of the Bavarian Memorial Foundation, Project Concentration Camp sub-camps in Bavaria.

In Freiberg, Germany, one man has worked tirelessly to keep the stories of the women prisoners alive. Dr Michael Düsing has tracked down survivors and written a number of books on the subject, as well as engaging local children with memorial projects, and arranging a plaque in honour of those who lived and died there under the Nazi regime. In his determination to ensure that his home town never forgets the slave labour camps situated in its midst, he has been assisted diligently by Cornelia Hünert of Freiberg's City Cultural Department. Both have gone out of their way to help me in my research and were kind enough to give up a weekend and take me on a guided tour.

For research into what happened at Freiberg, Johannes Ibel, the Head of the Historical Department at the Flossenbürg Concentration Camp Memorial, has been more than patient with me. As has author and historian Pascal Cziborra of the Faculty of History, Philosophy and Theology at the University of Bielefeld, who kindly answered my endless lists of questions. Thanks too to Dr Peter Schulze in Hannover for his research on my behalf.

My first tour of Auschwitz was always going to be emotional but my excellent guide Anna Ren was so good at conveying the horrors with composure that it was somehow made bearable. I am also grateful for the time and patience of Wojciech Płosa, Ph.D., Head of the Archives, and Dr Piotr Setkiewicz, Ph.D., Head of the Research Department, who met me at the camp to answer my questions and help me source key photographs and search the database. Alicja Bialecka was also a lifeline. My trip to Poland was facilitated in every way possible by my exceptional driver, translator and guide Łukasz Jaros.

In the Czech Republic, special thanks to Julie Jenšovská and Radana Rutová at the Jewish Museum of Prague. In Terezín I am grateful to Aneta Plzáková of the Terezín Initiative Institute Tomáš Fedorovič, editor of historical artefacts, and Eva Němcová of the documentation department.

The people of Horní Bříza deserve special mention in this book, and the welcome I received in the town from Deputy Mayor Zdeněk Procházka and his daughter Michaela gave me a taste of the great kindness their forebears showed to the prisoners. I am also beholden to local historian Mrs Bozena Royova, and to Jaroslav Lang and Vaclav Stepanek for their moving testimonies, never before shared.

I am indebted to Dita Valentová, the owner of Anka's family's former factory in Třebechovice pod Orebem who kindly showed me where Anka had grown up. In Slovakia, I am grateful to Eva

Richterová for the sensitive interview she conducted with Priska. Professor Frances Rapport generously gave me access to the transcripts of her health interviews with Anka Bergman at Swansea University, Wales. I would also like to thank producer Emily Davis and the BBC team who made the remarkable documentary *The Baby Born in a Concentration Camp*, which allowed me to see Anka in the flesh. The Elevation Youth Dance Company of Cambridge have done a great job in creating their ballet *Anka's Story*, which Eva and I were fortunate enough to see at the Edinburgh Fringe – even though it reduced us both to tears.

I pay homage to the profound work of the USC Shoah Foundation and its archived testimonies, which have given voice to so many stories never before told. And to the courage of all those who recorded their memories in order for us to remember what some would have had us forget. I would especially like to acknowledge the help of curator Crispin Brooks, as well as that of Doug Ballman, Manager of External Relations Online Archive, and Georgiana Gomez, Access Supervisor, at The Institute for Visual History and Education University of Southern California. In the UK, I was helped by the capable Russell Burke, Information Consultant at the Bedford Library, Royal Holloway, University of London, who allowed me access to the Shoah Foundation's files not on public view.

At the excellent National Holocaust Centre and Museum in Nottinghamshire, England, I am grateful to James Cox, Head of Public Affairs, but especially to fellow author Martin Winstone, who kindly read an early draft of the manuscript for me. At Yad Vashem, I would like to thank Maaty Frenkelzon from the Photo Archive for his help. At the Museu d'Història de Catalunya thanks too to Francesca Rosés for sharing information about their photographs.

At the University Press of Kentucky, I am obliged to Fred M. McCormick, Publicity and Rights Manager, for allowing me to use extracts from the diaries of Gonda Redlich. In the US, I am grateful to Dan O'Brien, editor of the 11th Armored Division website, and all the survivors and families of the 'Thunderbolts', many of whom contacted me. Several fellow authors have been especially generous with their time and information, including Michael Hirsh and Ken Breck, who kindly opened up his book of contacts relating to the liberators.

Midwife extraordinaire Abby Davidson, Bsc (Hons), gave me invaluable information about the birth process as well as the medical requirements for malnourished mothers and tiny babies. I owe my friend Michael Bröllochs several beers for his invaluable German translations, and Anne Gray a bottle of Montrachet for the French translations.

I have been blessed with an extraordinary publishing team headed up in London by the brilliant Adam Strange at Little, Brown, whose enthusiasm for this project has never waned from the moment I read him the opening page and almost made him cry. I believe that we have created the legacy book he hoped for. Thanks too to the inimitable Ursula Mackenzie, Chief Executive at Little, Brown, with whom I have always worked so successfully, to desk editor Rhiannon Smith and copy editor Steve Gove. Last but not least, my thanks to publicity, picture research and marketing supremos Victoria Gilder, Kirsteen Astor, Zoe Hood, Linda Silverman and Charlie King for their encouragement and to Sophie Burden for the UK jacket.

The tireless rights department of Andy Hine, Kate Hibbert and Helena Doree held my hand through the delicate international negotiations and bidding processes. Helping me pick my way through the legal minefield of contracts were the unflinching duo of Sarah Burton and Kate Pool at The Society of Authors in London. I would like to thank all the foreign editors who so enthused about this book at the 2014 London Book Fair and since, and to all the international sub-agents and translators, art directors, sales and marketing professionals who have done such a great job in bringing this incredible story to light. I am especially grateful to my Polish publisher Sonia Draga, who met me in Auschwitz. At House of Books in the Netherlands my thanks to Joeska de Wijs; to

Anja Benzenhöfer at RBA Libros, Spain; Claudia Coccia at Edizioni Piemme SpA, Italy; Henrik Karlsson at Massolit Forlagsgruppe AB, Sweden; Kirsten Fasmer at Rosinante & Co., Denmark; Nikolay Naumenko at AST, Russia; Marcus Strecker and Mauro Palermo at Globo Editora; Frédérique Polet at Presses de la Cité, France; Antonín Kočí of Milada Fronta in the Czech Republic; Juhami Korolainen at Minerva, Finland; Gisela Lal Aghighi at Weltbild, Germany; Guilherme Pires at 20/20 Editoria, Portugal.

At Harper Collins US, my thanks to editor Claire Wachtel, herself the daughter of a Holocaust survivor, who has been ably assisted by associate editor Hannah Wood as well as executive director of publicity, Leslie Cohen, senior marketing manager, Penny Matras and US cover designer Milan Bozic. Also in the US, I am grateful to talented literary scout Mary Anne Thompson for getting the buzz going like nobody else can. Lucy Ferguson, my publishing champion and stalwart friend, assured me I was on the right track. Carly Cook is one of a handful of editors whose publishing skills I most admire, and a formidable woman of exceptional insight. I am so grateful that she agreed to cast her professional eye over the manuscript before I let others see it.

The intensity of this project has been kept in perspective throughout by my almost daily contact with my best friend Clare Arron. Her strength, courage and unfailing good humour in the face of adversity continue to inspire me. Together, we made it through another year.

Last but by no means least, I owe heartfelt thanks to Chris, my husband and best mate – the man with the jackpot laugh, big capable hands, and a bigger even more capable heart. As has happened countless times, he lost me for months on end and not only never complained, he immersed himself in the story, escorted and supported me, provided me with endless pots of tea and emergency gin and tonics. Sorry for the nightmares.

*Wendy Holden*

# Picture Credits

# About the Author

WENDY HOLDEN was a journalist for eighteen years, including a decade at the *Daily Telegraph*. She is the author and coauthor of more than thirty books, including several internationally acclaimed wartime biographies, plus the *New York Times* bestsellers *A Lotus Grows in the Mud* (with Goldie Hawn) and *Lady Blue Eyes* (with Frank Sinatra's widow Barbara). She lives in Suffolk, England, with her husband and two dogs, and divides her time between the UK and the US.